Flex 4 Fun

Flex 4 Fun

Chet Haase

artima

ARTIMA PRESS
MOUNTAIN VIEW, CALIFORNIA

Flex 4 Fun
First Edition

Chet Haase was a computer scientist on the Flex SDK team at Adobe Systems, Inc., during the development of the Flex 4 release. He currently works at Google, Inc., on the Android UI toolkit team.

Artima Press is an imprint of Artima, Inc.
P.O. Box 390122, Mountain View, California 94039

First edition published as PrePrint™ eBook 2010
First edition published 2010
Build date of this impression August 9, 2010
Produced in the United States of America

14 13 12 11 10   1 2 3 4 5

ISBN-10: 0-9815316-2-8
ISBN-13: 978-0-9815316-2-5

Library of Congress Control Number: 2010911201

Cover photo of sea dragon by Romain Guy.

To my parents.
For all of the hassle and expense of raising me,
here's a book that you'll never read.

- Chet

Overview

Contents

Contents

Foreword

Working as a software developer in 2010 I sometimes feel blessed by the amazing tools I can use to create applications. Powerful IDEs almost write all the code for me, and extensive frameworks let me implement complex features in no time. Despite the incredible sophistication of the tools of our trade, today's developers must learn and master many platforms, libraries, patterns, techniques, and APIs … more every year. Learning is a very important part of our job and even though the Internet can provide us with countless tutorials and examples, books remain the best way to quickly gain the knowledge we need. Books are also easy to find; any bookstore, online or offline, usually carries at least one book on the topic I need to learn about. They even have sometimes too much choice! Go to the nearest bookstore and try to pick a book about Java, Flash, or CSS. Which one will you choose? I usually go with the one that doesn't have the author's photo on the cover; it's less creepy.

Graphics is one topic, however, for which the choice is very easy: there is no choice. Sure, you can find books that will describe the APIs the same way the SDK does, but you won't find books to teach you how graphics APIs work and how to put them to good use to create a compelling user interface.

Luckily for you, you have this book. Chet cares deeply about graphics and cares as much about *teaching* graphics. I have had, and still have, the chance to work with him on various projects, and I am constantly amazed by his passion for the field of graphics and animation. I am equally amazed by his skills as a teacher. Chet not only knows how to teach other developers how to use graphics and animations libraries, he also knows how to make them understand how everything works under the hood. He's even shockingly entertaining while doing so.

I must warn you though, although you will learn what you need to do your job, you might also discover a new passion for the wonderful world of graphics programming. Do not blame Chet if you later sacrifice your spare time to write your own exciting graphical effects and animations. He's only the teacher.

You are about to embark on a great journey with the best possible companions: the solid Flash engine, the versatile Flex framework and a very good teacher. You will seldom enjoy a programming book as much as you will this one.

Romain Guy
Millbrae, California
July 1, 2010

Acknowledgments

Many people have contributed to this book and to the material it covers. I am grateful to all of them.

First, I'd like to thank Daniel Steinberg, whose editorial work, advice, and friendship helped make the book possible. Although there were some odd hiccups along the way, what journey on life's highways is truly complete without the occasional flat tire, speeding ticket, and seventeen car pileup? Thanks, Daniel.

Second, I'd like to thank Romain Guy, my friend and co-author on the book *Filthy Rich Clients*, whose bright idea it was to write a book about Flex in the first place. I would prefer his name be on the cover with mine, instead of just his photograph of a sea dragon ... because it would mean he would have actually helped write the darn thing he helped start. Nevertheless, I appreciate his time and interest in the project, and hope that he joins me again in the next book adventure. After I recover from this one. And, by the way, besides the picture on the cover, Romain contributed the pictures to many of the demos in the book. Be thankful that you can enjoy his beautiful photography instead of whatever pictures I could have come up with from my family snapshots.

I am also grateful to the entire Flex 4 SDK team, without whose hard work and dedication there would be no *Flex 4 Fun* book, because there would be no Flex 4. The product team included Evtim Georgiev, Jason Szeto, Hans Muller, Gordon Smith, Glenn Ruehle, Ely Greenfield, Deepa Subrmaniam, Ryan Frishberg, Peter Farland, Peter Donovan, Tom Kraikit, Greg Burch, Kevin Lin, Jono Spiro, Chiedo Acholonu, Corey Lucier, Alex Harui, Joan Lafferty, Joann Chuang Anderson, Lauren Park, Matt Finitz, Steven Shongrunden, Jacob Goldstein, Ella Mitelman, Brian O'Laughlin, Rob Vollmar, Peter DeHaan, Jody Zhang, Gaurav Jain, Paul Reilly, Jim Murphy, Darrell Loverin, Carol Frampton, Kari White, Vera Carr, Matt Chotin, Steve Breinberg, Susan Lally, Ed Rowe, and David Wadhwani.

Finally, I'd like to thank the technical reviewers of the book, including Ella Mitelman, Darrell Loverin, Chiedozi Acholonu, Ryan Frishberg, Gaurav Jain, Evtim Georgiev, Peter DeHaan, and Tom Kraikit. I can honestly say that I really enjoy writing, and really hate revising. But it is the reviewing and subsequent suicidally painful revisions that take the book from a big steaming pile of words and code into a book that's ready for the bookshelves of the world.

Flex 4 Fun

Chapter 1

Introduction

Welcome to this book. I'm glad you're here! Over the next many pages we'll have some fun exploring the graphical and animation side of the Flex 4 SDK.

Flex 4 is a powerful and flexible set of libraries that enable rich client applications running on the Flash Platform. That's a mouthful, so here's another attempt at it: Flex helps you write Flash applications. In particular, Flex gives you facilities for writing GUI applications that are otherwise difficult to manage with just the Flash APIs and Flash Pro authoring tool. For example, Flex provides a rich and extensible component library, data binding for easy communication between objects in the application, and the declarative MXML language that enables you to write your GUI logic in a very simple and straightforward way.

But you know all of this: you've written some Flex programs already...

1.1 Flexpectations

This is not a book on how to write Flex applications overall, or even how to write Flex 4 applications in particular. Lots of other books exist out there that cover the basics of the platform: MXML, ActionScript 3, Flex components, data binding, application architectures, *etc.* This book is not attempting to cover that same area, so if that's what you're looking for, I invite you to check out one of the many other books available.

Instead, this book assumes that you have done some Flex programming, enough to know the basics of MXML and ActionScript, so that when you look at the simple examples in this book you are not confused. I'm not expecting you to be an advanced Flex developer, and I don't assume any

3

advanced knowledge for the topics in this book. I'm also not assuming that you are an expert on Flex 4, although some passing familiarity with some of the changes might be helpful to understand some of the code that you'll see. For example, a new `Declarations` block and new namespaces in exist in Flex 4 MXML code, so these might be a surprise if you haven't seen Flex 4 applications before. But you can pick up these nuances on the fly, or check out some of the Flex 4 articles on the devnet site at adobe.com: `http://www.adobe.com/devnet/flex/`.

I also expect that you already have the Flash Builder IDE, or a previous version of the tool, which was formerly known as Flex Builder. If you don't have Flash Builder 4 installed, you probably want to get at least the sixty day trial version, because it will make building and playing with the many sample applications in this book much easier (more on this at the end of this chapter). To download the trial version of Flash Builder 4, follow the links from this book's resources page, `http://booksites.artima.com/flex_4_fun`.

Finally, I expect that you know how to access and use the API documentation for the Flex 4 SDK. Rather than cover all of the relevant classes that I discuss in gory detail down to the last infrequently used property, I leave some of the details of APIs to the docs since they do a pretty good job of explaining things. I would rather spend the pages of this book talking in more detail about the stuff that's not as obvious. So sometimes I may defer to the docs for a particular item. If you want to know more about that particular item that I didn't cover, go find the docs and look it up. You can view or download the documentation at `http://www.adobe.com/devnet/flex/?view=documentation`.

Okay, so if this is the stuff that I'm *not* covering in the book, just what is the book about, anyway?

1.2 Flexciting stuff

Sure, there are other books out there on Flex, Flex 4, and RIA technologies in general—but they usually don't cover the techniques that help you write cooler applications. This book is specifically about the graphical and animation aspects of Flex 4 that enable better user experiences: the "fun" stuff.

Flex sits atop the powerful Flash graphics engine, which provides all kinds of great capabilities for drawing shapes with various fills and strokes and even image-processing filters to alter objects' appearances. The Flex

4 release has a new component model that enables a very flexible way of changing the look of your components. Flex also offers a "states" model that makes it easy to describe what your application and GUI components look like at different stages in their life. And Flex provides a rich library of animation capabilities that makes it possible to animate anything in the GUI, which enables rich experiences for the user as objects in the GUI gradually change from one state to another instead of making sudden, discontinuous changes. These are some of the capabilities that this book will cover in detail, along with many example programs to show how all of it works.

1.3   Flex 4: A very brief introduction

I'll talk about various aspects of the new features in Flex 4 in the pages of this book. But it seems helpful to give an overview of what the Flex 4 release brings to the Flex SDK. Flex 4 was a significant release in which much of Flex was re-architected to make the toolkit even more powerful and flexible. In particular, several areas are worth noting if this is your first view of Flex 4, including the new spark components, the new graphics classes, the new spark layout system, the new state syntax, new elements of MXML files, and the new effects system.

Spark components

As of Flex 3, Flex already made it easy to build good-looking applications. The component set was rich and the standard component skins had a distinctive and designed look. It was also possible to modify the look of the components with CSS and with various properties and styles on the components themselves. But if you wanted a truly custom look to your components, you had a harder time. For example, you could change the fill color of a `Button`, but you could not change its label placement. So you were forced to create custom components by subclassing and probably writing and copying a lot of code to get it right. Meanwhile, the standard Flex components had accumulated a veritable plethora of styles and properties that was starting to make the component APIs unwieldy.

Flex 4 changed all of this. There is now a new set of "spark" components based on a new architecture that separates the component's logic, or how the component does its job, from its visuals, or how the component looks. The logic is handled by ActionScript code in the component's class, such

5

as `Button.as`. The visuals are contained in an MXML file called a "skin," where the visual aspects of the component are described with graphical and sub-component elements.

Now, in order to provide a custom look for a component, a developer or designer may create their own skin file to give a component a truly unique look. This skin file can be substituted for the standard skin file by simply telling the component where the skin file is located. Because the visuals have been separated from the logic in spark components, they are independent and the component can use any skin that follows the simple component/skin contract. You'll see how this all works with skinning examples in Chapter 6.

Graphics

One of the biggest additions in Flex 4, and one of the most exciting to me personally, being the graphics geek that I am, is the ability to create graphics objects directly in Flex. Previously, if you wanted to draw graphics in your application, such as rendering elements of custom component, you needed to drop down to ActionScript code and issue calls to the Flash graphics API. Flex 4 adds higher-level graphics classes directly to the Flex APIs which are both easier to use and able to be created in MXML. You'll read all about how this works in Chapter 2, and you will see how we use this capability to create custom skins for spark components in Chapter 6.

Spark layout

Flex 3 containers use a layout system that is hard-coded for that container. For example, a `Canvas` uses absolute layout, where each child object is positioned and sized with explicit properties like `x`, `y`, `width`, and `height` or constraint properties like `left` and `right` instead of being positioned automatically. And a Flex 3 `TileList` container arranges its children in a grid of rows and columns.

In Flex 4, layout is independent of containers. Now, you can specify a `layout` property for any container, even changing the layout on the fly to get different layouts at runtime. For example, in Flex 4, there is a `TileLayout` class that you can assign to any spark container to manage that container's children in rows and columns. In fact, you can even write your own layout class and use it as the `layout` property of any of the standard spark containers to get your own custom container layout.

6

Some containers in Flex 4 have predetermined layouts, such as HGroup and VGroup, but these classes exist just to simplify common cases and also use the new flexible layout approach internally. For example, HGroup is essentially just a façade over a Group with a HorizontalLayout.

I do not cover layouts in this book explicitly, other than using various containers and layouts in the book's demo applications, but you can read more about spark layout in the article "Spark layouts with Flex 4" on the Flex devnet site here: http://www.adobe.com/devnet/flex/articles/ spark_layouts.html.

New state syntax

"View states" are one of the most interesting and powerful features of Flex GUI programming, allowing you to encode the various states that your application or components are in over the life of an application. For example, some components may exist only in certain states and other components may change size or orientation between states.

However, the syntax of state programming was always rather tricky, both to write and to read. State code was better left to Flash Builder's Design View tool, a graphical GUI builder that could easily output state-specific code that would have been difficult to code by hand. But even so, you would still have state code that was difficult to understand, making the code less maintainable and making states difficult to use effectively in general.

In Flex 4, a new state syntax was introduced that makes it much easier to write and read state code, allowing you to write state-specific information for objects in-line with the object declaration. I'll talk more about this in Chapter 4, with example code to show how to use the new syntax.

MXML changes

MXML has gained some new elements since Flex 3 that you will see in the book's examples. The changes are relatively minor, but they may be a mystery to you if you haven't seen Flex 4 code yet.

A new namespace was introduced for the new spark components in Flex 4: library://ns.adobe.com/flex/spark. You usually refer to this spark namespace at the top of your MXML file with the abbreviation s, as in xmlns:s="library://ns.adobe.com/flex/spark". You can still use the old mx namespace if you want to use Flex 3 objects (some of which have no spark equivalent yet, for example, Canvas and DataGrid), like this: xmlns:mx="library://ns.adobe.com/flex/mx". Additionally, a new fx namespace, xmlns:fx="http://ns.adobe.com/mxml/2009", was added to hold common language elements. Here's what an Application tag, for example, might look like in an MXML application that uses spark, mx, and language elements:

```
<s:Application xmlns:fx="http://ns.adobe.com/mxml/2009"
               xmlns:s="library://ns.adobe.com/flex/spark"
               xmlns:mx="library://ns.adobe.com/flex/mx"
```

The Declarations block is a new addition to support adding non-visual items to the MXML file. Previously, you could add anything to an MXML file, regardless of whether it was a component or data structure or an effect or anything else; as long as the compiler knew how to compile that tag, you could put it in the code. Being able to use any object in MXML was convenient, but it made for sometimes messy code in which elements in the hierarchy of the container being defined by the MXML code were mixed with objects that did not live in that visual hierarchy. The Declarations block was introduced in Flex 4 to enforce a separation between the non-visual items, which go into this block, and the items that are in the visual hierarchy of the object being defined, like components and graphics.

Effective Flex 4

The last new element of Flex 4 that I'll mention in this overview is the new effects system. Effects are what Flex calls animations; they are used to animate changes in the display, such as components moving around or fading in and out. In order to support some of the new capabilities and classes in Flex 4, such as the new graphics objects, Flex effects were rewritten to be more flexible and robust, and several new effects were added to support new capabilities in recent Flash player versions such as 3D and pixel shaders. I'll talk much more about the new Flex effects system in Chapters 9, 10, and 11.

But wait, there s more!

This overview is just meant to give you a taste of what Flex 4 has to offer. Many of the details of the new SDK are discussed in this book as we cover topics like graphics, components, states, and effects. But there is much more to the Flex 4 SDK that I don't discuss in this book because there simply isn't room or time enough. If you want to learn more about the improvements in Flex 4, check out the Flex devnet site at `http://www.adobe.com/devnet/flex/`, which has many articles on the various aspects of Flex 4, including this one on the differences between Flex 3 and Flex 4: `http://www.adobe.com/devnet/flex/articles/flex3and4_differences.html`.

1.4 Flextreme programming

I wanted to add a brief word about coding style and architecting Flex applications. Although it is perfectly legal to have ActionScript (AS) code in an MXML file, typical applications separate that logic from the declarative MXML code by having separate files. AS code goes in `.as` files, MXML code goes in `.mxml` files. Many of the demos in this book sprinkle in small sections of AS code in Script blocks. But note that this is done in the book's examples because (a) these demos are quite small, so the amount of AS code is not too distracting in those MXML files, and (b) the main intent of the demos is to show as simply as possible how the code works. I find it easier to demonstrate this with one single file (when possible). So don't do what I do: separate the logic and the GUI declaration code in your Flex applications.

1.5 Flexamples

One of the highlights of this book is code from nearly seventy applications written exclusively for the book. Much of the code is shown directly in these pages, in snippets that are explained by the surrounding text. These excerpts are usually prefaced by the name of the file they come from, as seen here:

```
(File: components/DrawingCanvas.as)
addEventListener("mouseDown", mouseDownHandler);
```

In this example, the code is from the file `DrawingCanvas.as` in the `components` directory. All of the examples in any chapter are in a Flash Builder project named after the chapter title, with the source code found in the `src` directory. So if you've downloaded and unzipped the code for the book onto your system, as explained later in this section, then you could find

9

this snippet of code in `Graphics/src/components/DrawingCanvas.as`. Sometimes several code snippets come from the same file, broken up by explanatory text between them. In these cases, the file name is only listed with the first such snippet.

All of the code in the book comes from complete applications that you can download, build, and run yourself. This is probably something you should plan to do, at least for those parts of the book you want to thoroughly understand. Also, these applications provide useful code that you can copy from or start from for projects of your own.

You will want to do three things with these applications: run them, download their code, and build them. So I'll cover the details of how to do each of these tasks here.

Running the applications

The easiest way to run the applications is to go to `http://booksites.` `artima.com/flex_4_fun/apps`. This site is set up specifically to allow you to launch any of the applications in the book. The applications are organized by chapter. So in order to run any particular application that you see called out in one of the chapters, go to the site in a browser, select the chapter that the demo is in, and then choose the application from the list at the bottom left for that chapter. The application will load into the page and you can play with it right there.

Of course, the interesting part of most of the demos is not running them, but seeing the code and tinkering with it. So the next step you'll want to take is downloading the code.

Downloading the application code

All of the applications are hosted on the book's site, `http://booksites.` `artima.com/flex_4_fun`. Like the site where you can run the applications, the application source is organized per-chapter. The applications for each chapter are in a single Flash Builder project (see more in the next section about this). All of the chapter projects are in a single zipfile that you can download. To get the code for each chapter, just download the zip file and unzip it somewhere on your local system. Then you can open each project folder, go into its `src` directory and explore the files. Or better yet, load the project into Flash Builder and explore the source code in the IDE.

Of course, once you have the source code, it won't be good enough to just look at it. You'll want to build it and start tinkering with it to produce your own applications. So you'll want to know how to build the applications.

Building the applications

As I said in the previous section, the source code for the applications is organized into projects for each chapter. Once you've downloaded the source code and unzipped it, you'll have a Flash Builder project folder on your local system. You can now run Flash Builder and load that project into the IDE.

To load any of the chapter projects into Flash Builder, you'll need to import it using the following steps:

- In the File menu, select the Import item.

- In the Import sub-menu, select the Other... item. This brings up the "Import" dialog.

- Open the "General" item, select "Existing Projects into Workspace," and click the Next button.

- Click the Browse... button next to the Select root directory item and navigate to and select the chapter project on your hard drive.

- Click the Finish button in the "Import" dialog.

You should now see the project loaded into the Flash Builder package explorer window. The source code for all of the applications in the chapter is in the src/ folder inside the project. To build and run any particular application, double-click on that application in the package explorer window and select Run in the Run menu.

You can also use the command-line compiler that comes with the free open source Flex SDK. So if you really don't want to use the Flash Builder IDE to work with Flex, you can do so; just edit the code in some text-editing application (or other IDE) and use the command-line compiler to build the applications. Because this book is targeted at people that are currently doing Flex development, I expect that most of you already have Flash Builder, or will want to get it soon to help with your Flex 4 development. But even if you don't have the tool, and don't yet want to spend the money now to buy it, you can download and install a free fully-functional trial version for sixty days. So rather than go through the details of building these applications on the command line,[1] I'm going to just assume that you have Flash Builder 4 (or later) installed.

And that's it: using the simple steps above, you can download, build, and run all of the demos in this book. Now get reading. And when you see a demo described in the book, run it your yourself to see it in action. Better yet, download and play with the code and see what else you can do.

Now, let's have some Flex 4 Fun!

---

[1] The details are basically: download the Flex 4 SDK, download the appropriate version of the Sun Java JDK (JDK 1.5 or later), install the appropriate version of the Flash player, set some environment variables, and you're good to go. You can find out more about doing this on the Flex open-source site if this is what you want to do. But really, just download the free trial of Flash Builder and use it instead. It'll save you time and hassle.

Chapter 2

Graphics

Graphics are the heart of GUI applications. Graphical objects are used to describe the visual appearance of components as well as to create custom rendering like gradient backgrounds. The richness of the graphics platform in a GUI toolkit determines how easily you can build rich client applications with that toolkit. Since Flex sits atop the Flash platform, there is a wealth of graphics capabilities available, enabling very rich clients indeed.

You can see the use of graphics objects in every Flex 4 component, like this panel full of controls:

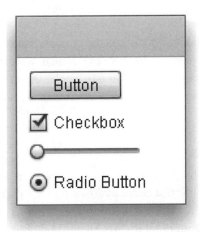

Every one of these components is made up of simple graphics primitives. The panel consists of a couple of rectangles with a darker fill for its header. The button is a rounded rectangle filled with a light gradient and stroked with a darker border color. The checkbox has a filled and stroked rectangle for the box and a path object for the check mark. The slider is composed of a rounded rectangle for the track and a circle for the thumb. And the radio button has one circle for the button and one for the selection indicator.

You use these same graphics primitives to create very custom and dynamic objects on the screen, as seen here:

(Demo: Shapely)

In this drawing application, all of the control panel objects on the left as well as the scribbled face on the drawing canvas were created with graphic elements. We'll see more of the Shapely application later in this chapter as we explore various shapes and drawing attributes available in Flex 4.

2.1 Flex 4 graphics

Once upon a time (as far back as Flex 3), if you wanted custom graphics, you had to dive into ActionScript code, override a method or two, create and use Flash display objects, and issue calls into their Graphics objects. It was the only way to draw custom graphics from your Flex application. For example, here's how you might draw a circle in Flex 3:

(File: ThreeCircles.mxml)

```
var component:UIComponent = new UIComponent();
var sprite:Sprite = new Sprite();
sprite.graphics.beginFill(0xff0000);
sprite.graphics.drawEllipse(0, 0, 100, 100);
sprite.graphics.endFill();
component.addChild(sprite);
addElement(component);
```

Flex 4 provides a new graphics API that allows you to easily create objects that describe visual elements. The Flex library internally handles the details of telling Flash how to create and render these objects. For example, here's a simple circle using the new graphics classes of Flex 4:

```
var circle:Ellipse = new Ellipse();
circle.width = 100;
circle.height = 100;
circle.fill = new SolidColor(0x0000ff);
circle.x = 100;
addElement(circle);
```

And here's a even better example of the Flex 4 approach, using some of the new MXML tags:

```
<s:Ellipse x="200" y="0" width="100" height="100">
    <s:fill>
        <s:SolidColor color="green"/>
    </s:fill>
</s:Ellipse>
```

You will notice some important differences between the old way of creating graphics and the new way of doing it in Flex 4:

Declarative The approach of creating graphics in Flex 4, like much of the rest of Flex, is object-oriented and declarative. You create the graphics primitive you need, set the properties of that object to tell it how to draw itself, and add it to the appropriate container in your application. The old way of drawing in Flex 3 was, by contrast, very manual. You got a reference to Flash Graphics object and called drawing functions on that object to tell the object how to render itself.

MXML Because the new graphic elements are declarative, you can use MXML markup to describe your visuals. You can now use MXML to describe the visual aspects of your program, and only dive into ActionScript for the more programmatic functionality of your application, like the business logic. This is particularly important when customizing the look of Flex 4 components through their *skins*. These component skins, which are written in MXML files, hold the graphical elements that describe the component's appearance. We will see more about component skinning in Chapter 6.

Flex-friendly You'll notice, in the Flex 3 code in the previous example where we draw into a sprite graphics object, an indirect approach of adding our sprite to a `UIComponent`, which is then added to our Flex application. This is because Flex 3 applications only understand components, not raw Flash display objects like our `Sprite` above. So whenever we want custom graphics in a Flex 3 application, they need to be drawn into a custom component, or added into a UIComponent, or by some other means added indirectly to the Flex display list. The Flex 4 approach is much more tightly integrated with Flex overall. We create `GraphicElement` objects, like the `Ellipse` in the Flex 4 code in the example, and add them directly to Flex containers.

For the rest of the chapter, we'll see the different kinds of graphics objects that we can create.

2.2   Shapely: a simple drawing tool

As you read through this chapter, learning about strokes and fills and the various graphic elements that you can use in Flex 4, you will see these objects in use in the Shapely drawing application seen earlier on page 14. But in order to understand how the various objects fit into that application, we'll first need to understand how the application works in general. Let's go over its basic architecture and mechanisms.

The Shapely application is a simple drawing application that allows the user to select between a small set of shapes (lines, rectangles, ellipses, and paths) along with different stroke and fill modes for the shapes. The user can then draw these shapes on the canvas with the mouse. In order to keep the application simple, both in terms of the UI and the code that we need to digest, the application does not expose the full spectrum of graphic primitives and fill/stroke options that we cover in this chapter. But the application is a good place from which to start if you want to further enhance it with that additional functionality yourself.

Some of the code that you will see in the application uses techniques or functionality in Flex 4 that we have not yet covered. For example, some of the code in the ControlPanel class uses the new states syntax (which I talk about in Chapter 4) to change the look of the drawing primitive icons when the icons are selected. Don't worry too much about these bits of the code. The real point in this chapter is to understand how the application UI is drawn, using the graphics primitives and fills/strokes that we discuss here, and how the shapes are created by the user when dragging the mouse around. So let's get into the code.

First of all, take a look at the application GUI. As you can see in the screenshot on page 14, a control panel at the left contains buttons that the user selects to choose the current shape and the drawing options for that shape. The rest of the window contains a drawing canvas, where the user drags the mouse to draw shapes. The following sections will cover how the main application, the control panel, and the drawing canvas work.

The Shapely application class

The top-level application is very simple; it just instantiates and positions the custom components for the control panel and the drawing canvas:

```
(File: Shapely.mxml)
<components:ControlPanel id="controlPanel"
    width="52" height="100%"
    currentStateChange="drawingModeChange()"
    drawingStateChange="drawingStateChange(event)"/>
<components:DrawingCanvas id="canvas"
    left="52" right="0"
    top="0" bottom="0"/>
```

Some additional logic is in script code to handle setting the drawing state for the application. The drawing state is determined by actions in the control panel. A change in the shape to be drawn results, through the event mechanism, in a call to the drawingModeChange() function:

```
private function drawingModeChange():void
{
    switch (controlPanel.currentState)
    {
        case "lineMode":
            canvas.drawingMode = DrawingCanvas.LINE;
            break;
        case "rectMode":
            canvas.drawingMode = DrawingCanvas.RECT;
            break;
        case "ellipseMode":
            canvas.drawingMode = DrawingCanvas.ELLIPSE;
            break;
        case "pathMode":
            canvas.drawingMode = DrawingCanvas.PATH;
            break;
    }
}
```

A change in the stroke or fill controls sends a drawingStateChange event and results in a call to the drawingStateChange() function:

```
private function drawingStateChange(
    event:DrawingStateChangeEvent):void
{
    canvas.stroke = event.stroke;
    canvas.fill = event.fill;
}
```

When the application receives these events, it sets the appropriate state in the drawing canvas to be used in future drawing operations. These events are received when the user interacts with the control panel.

The Shapely control panel

Now let's take a look at the control panel, from the file ControlPanel.as. This component is a subclass of Group, the simplest Flex 4 container and the base class for other container classes. ControlPanel is just a basic container for the various icons that control drawing state.

Each of the drawing primitive icons (the line, rectangle, ellipse, and path) have the same structure: a Group contains the icon graphics and listens for click events to signal that the user wants to switch to this drawing mode. For example, here is the group container for the line drawing icon:

(File: components/ControlPanel.mxml)
```
<s:Group id="line" width="40" height="40"
    click="setMode(event)">
    <!-- group contents -->
</s:Group>
```

You can see in the previous code that a mouse click results in a call to the setMode() function. This function sets the drawing mode by setting the currentState of the component:

```
private function setMode(event:MouseEvent):void
{
    switch (event.currentTarget)
    {
        case line:
            currentState = "lineMode";
            break;
        case rect:
            currentState = "rectMode";
            break;
        case ellipse:
            currentState = "ellipseMode";
            break;
        case path:
            currentState = "pathMode";
            break;
    }
}
```

When any icon is clicked, it dispatches an event to this function, which sets the currentState property according to the button that was clicked. That change to currentState causes Flex to dispatch a currentStateChanged event, which is received by the drawingModeChange() function in Shapely that we saw earlier. This function sets the drawing mode for the canvas (which we will see later).

19

Finally, components at the bottom of the control panel determine the stroke and fill used when drawing:

Two checkboxes determine whether the object will be stroked and/or filled. In between the checkboxes are `ColorPicker` components for the stroke and the fill gradient (choose both fill colors to be the same to get a solid color). A preview rectangle between the stroke and fill sections shows the user what shapes will look like with the current stroke and fill settings. When any of these settings are changed, the `setDrawingState()` function is called. This function will be discussed later, after sections on the stroke and fill mechanisms for graphics primitives.

That's it for the control panel; onto the canvas, where the work is done for creating and drawing the shapes.

The `Shapely` drawing canvas

The main job of the `DrawingCanvas` class is handling mouse events and turning them into shapes on the canvas. It does this by listening first for `mouseDown` events, then to further `mouseMove` and `mouseUp` events to track mouse dragging actions by the user. The `mouseDown` listener is added to the canvas object in its constructor:

(File: components/DrawingCanvas.as)
```
addEventListener("mouseDown", mouseDownHandler);
```

When the user drags the mouse around the canvas, the code creates and manipulates different shapes according to the drawing mode that the user selected in the control panel. The following constants and variables are used to track the shape that is created on `mouseDown`:

```
public static const LINE:int = 0;
public static const RECT:int = 1;
public static const ELLIPSE:int = 2;
public static const PATH:int = 3;

public var drawingMode:int = LINE;
```

The drawingMode property is set by the application code in Shapely in its drawingModeChange() function, as we saw earlier. This property is used when we handle mouseDown events in our mouseDownHandler() function.

A mouseDown event on the canvas results in an event which causes a call to the mouseDownHandler() function. This function creates a new shape (which we'll see later, when we discuss shapes) and adds listeners for both mouseMove and mouseUp events:

```
addEventListener(MouseEvent.MOUSE_MOVE, mouseMoveHandler);
addEventListener(MouseEvent.MOUSE_UP, mouseUpHandler);
```

Note that the application only bothers listening for mouseMove and mouseUp events after receiving an initial mouseDown event. If the user is simply moving the mouse around without pressing it first, then it does not matter because they are not drawing a shape. But as soon as the user presses the mouse button, a shape is created and mouse movement is tracked to allow editing the shape with drag operations.

A mouse drag causes a call into the mouseMoveHandler() function:

```
private function mouseMoveHandler(event:MouseEvent):void
{
    dragTo(event.localX, event.localY);
}
```

This function calls the dragTo() function to change the shape currently being drawn, according to the current location to which the user has dragged the mouse. When the user releases the mouse button, there is a call to the mouseUpHandler() function:

```
private function mouseUpHandler(event:MouseEvent):void
{
    dragTo(event.localX, event.localY);
    removeEventListener(MouseEvent.MOUSE_MOVE,
        mouseMoveHandler);
```

21

```
removeEventListener(MouseEvent.MOUSE_UP,
    mouseUpHandler);
}
```

As in the mouseMoveHandler() function, we call dragTo() to change the shape according to this final mouse location. We then remove our move/up listeners because we no longer care about these events until the next time the user presses the mouse button down.

That's it for the main application functionality of Shapely. The rest of the application code is about the shapes that are created and the drawing attributes that those shapes have. We'll see how all of these work as we cover these topics in the rest of this chapter.

2.3   Graphics primitives: getting into shape

Your first reaction to learning about the graphic elements in Flex might have been: "What can I draw?" You may think, given that all of the Flex components are drawn with these shapes, there would be a myriad of different shapes to choose from. But in fact, there is just a small set: Line, Rect, Ellipse, and Path. With just these four shapes, and with the stroke and fill options that we'll discuss later, you can draw all kinds of things, from simple graphics for components, like lines, circles, and rounded rectangles, to very custom artwork.

In this section, we'll see how each of these shapes are created and used in the Shapely application.

The Line class

Lines are the simplest graphics primitive; they are just single-segment connectors between endpoints. You can change what the lines look like using the stroke properties that we'll see in Section 2.4, but the basic geometry of lines is very simple: they start at one point and end at another.

The Line class defines simple endpoint properties for a single line segment. These two endpoints are described by the (xFrom, yFrom) and (xTo, yTo) properties. Here are two sample lines created in MXML code:

```
(File: SimpleObjects.mxml)
<s:Line xFrom="20" yFrom="20" xTo="100" yTo="100">
```

22

```
    <s:stroke>
        <s:SolidColorStroke color="black"/>
    </s:stroke>
</s:Line>
<s:Line xFrom="30" yFrom="20" xTo="110" yTo="100">
    <s:stroke>
        <s:SolidColorStroke color="gray" alpha=".8"
            weight="5"/>
    </s:stroke>
</s:Line>
```

This MXML code results in the following graphics on the screen:

(Demo: SimpleObjects)

Don't worry about the stroke objects in the code yet; we'll read more about strokes in Section 2.4.

Now let's see how we create Line objects in the Shapely application. When the user presses the mouse key down on the drawing canvas, the function mouseDownHandler() is called and the appropriate shape is created. When lines are selected, the following code in that function is executed:

(File: components/DrawingCanvas.as)

```
if (drawingMode == LINE)
{
    shape = new Line();
    var line:Line = Line(shape);
    line.xFrom = event.localX;
    line.yFrom = event.localY;
    line.xTo = event.localX;
    line.yTo = event.localY;
}
```

This code creates the line object and sets its x and y from/to properties, just like in the previous MXML code example. In this case, we're setting the from/to points to the same point because the user has not yet dragged the mouse, so the start and end points of the line are both set to the location of that initial mouse event.

The line object is then assigned the current `stroke` attribute, which we'll talk about later, and is added to the drawing canvas, which makes it visible in the application window:

```
shape.stroke = stroke;
addElement(shape);
```

A mouse drag caused a call to the `mouseMoveHandler()` function, which then calls `dragTo()`, as we saw earlier. The shape is then changed appropriately. In the case of lines, we simply change the (xTo, yTo) endpoint:

```
case LINE:
    Line(shape).xTo = dragX;
    Line(shape).yTo = dragY;
    break;
```

When the user releases the mouse button, the `mouseUpHandler()` function is called, which again calls the `dragTo()` function to set a final (xTo, yTo) endpoint for the line.

That's it for lines. They are very simple objects with just two endpoints. The way that the line between those points is drawn depends on the `stroke` property, which we will discuss in Section 2.4.

The Rect class

Many GUI controls use rectangular graphics. Rectangles are useful for defining the boundaries of objects, like the edges of buttons, or the box of checkboxes, or the borders of panels and windows. Rectangles are also useful for defining the backgrounds of containers, such as a gradient background in an application window. Unlike lines, which have only a `stroke` object to define the line characteristics, rectangles have both outline graphics, defined by a `stroke`, and interior graphics, defined by a `fill`.

The Rect object draws a rectangle with optional rounded corners. The dimensions of the shape are determined by its `width` and `height` properties. The dimensions of the rounded corners, if any, are determined by the radiusX and radiusY properties, which apply to all corners of the rectangle. Some situations call for different rounding on each corner, so there are also overriding properties, such as bottomLeftRadiusX and similar properties for the other corners.

Here is an example of creating a simple black square in MXML:

```
(File: SimpleObjects.mxml)
<s:Rect x="150" y="20" width="80" height="80">
    <s:fill>
        <s:SolidColor color="0"/>
    </s:fill>
</s:Rect>
```

In the Shapely application, rectangles are created as the user drags the cursor when the rectangle drawing mode is selected. In the mouseDownHandler() function, we switch on drawingMode to create the appropriate shape:

```
(File: components/DrawingCanvas.as)
switch (drawingMode)
{
    case RECT:
        shape = new Rect();
        shape.x = event.localX;
        shape.y = event.localY;
        break;
```

Only the location of the object is set; its width and height have the default value of 0, because the user has not yet dragged out the shape to give it dimension. The shape is then filled with the current fill object, which we'll discuss later:

```
FilledElement(shape).fill = fill;
```

Then the object's stroke is set and it is added to the scene, as we saw in the earlier Line section.

As the user drags the mouse around and then releases the mouse button, the dragTo() function is called. This function sets the rectangle's dimensions according to the new mouse position:

```
case RECT:
    shape.width = dragX - shape.x;
    shape.height = dragY - shape.y;
    break;
```

The Ellipse class

Ellipses are less common in UI controls, although circles (ellipses with equal width and height values) are useful for components like radio buttons. Circular controls are also used in custom UIs, where you may not want your buttons to look like standard rectangular buttons. Ellipse is similar to Rect; it is positioned with x and y and sized with width and height.

This code creates a gray circle with a black outline in MXML:

```
(File: SimpleObjects.mxml)
<s:Ellipse x="20" y="220" width="80" height="80">
    <s:fill>
        <s:SolidColor color="gray"/>
    </s:fill>
    <s:stroke>
        <s:SolidColorStroke color="black"/>
    </s:stroke>
</s:Ellipse>
```

And this is what it looks like:

(Demo: SimpleObjects)

The code for ellipses in Shapely is very similar to that for rectangles, because both shapes are positioned and sized in the same way. First, the shape is created based on the value of the drawingMode variable in the mouseDownHandler() function:

(File: components/DrawingCanvas.as)

```
case ELLIPSE:
    shape = new Ellipse();
    shape.x = event.localX;
    shape.y = event.localY;
    break;
```

On mouse move and up events, the shape is resized according to the new mouse location in the dragTo() function:

```
case ELLIPSE:
    shape.width = dragX - shape.x;
    shape.height = dragY - shape.y;
    break;
```

The Path class

Lines, rectangles, and ellipses are great for creating simple shapes and lines. But if you want an irregular shape, curved lines, or custom artwork from design tools, you're going to need to draw Paths. The Path object constructs a path, filled or empty, from a set of line and curve segments. You specify the segment information for a path in the data property, which is a String specifying the various move/line/curve pieces that construct the path. An optional winding property can be used to specify which side of the path should be filled (if the fill property is not null).

Several different commands can be used in a Path's data string. Each one is abbreviated with a single letter, followed by applicable numerical values.[1] A capital letter indicates the values are absolute coordinates, whereas a lower case letter indicates a position relative to the current position:

move (example: data="m 10 20") move the pen to the specified location

line (example: data="l 10 20") draw a line to the specified location

horizontal line (example: data="h 10") draw a horizontal line to the specified x location (a simplification of the line command)

---

[1] The syntax and abbreviations used for the string match those of the Path element of SVG (Scalable Vector Graphics), a W3C standard vector API.

vertical line (example: `data="v 20"`) draw a vertical line to the specified y location (a simplification of the line command)

quadratic Bézier (example: `data="q 0 0 10 20"`) draw a curve[2] with one control point whose x and y are specified first, followed by the x and y location the curve will draw to.

cubic Bézier (example: `data="c 0 0 5 10 10 20"`) draw a curve with two control points whose x and y are specified first, followed by the x and y location the curve will draw to.

close path (example: `data="... z"`) close off the path by drawing a line to the starting point of the path. This item is optional; if it is not supplied, the path will end at the last data point.

It is important to note that each drawing operation, whether move, line, or curve, starts from the current pen position and ends with the pen in the position specified in the command. So you only need to move the pen explicitly if you wish to start a segment from a different location than its current one. For example, if you want to draw a path that goes from (0, 0) over to (100, 0) and then down to (100, 100), you could simply type `data="H 100 V 100"`. Here's a simple path constructed in MXML:

(File: SimpleObjects.mxml)

```
<s:Path x="20" y="320" data="L 80 80 V 0 L 0 80 V 0">
    <s:stroke>
        <s:SolidColorStroke color="black"/>
    </s:stroke>
    <s:fill>
        <s:SolidColor color="gray"/>
    </s:fill>
</s:Path>
```

---

[2] A Bézier curve is specified by *anchor points*, the endpoints of the curve, and *control points*, which specify the path the curve follows between the anchor points. A quadratic Bézier curve starts at one anchor point going in the direction of a single control point and ends at the other anchor point coming from the direction of that control point. A cubic Bézier curve leaves the starting anchor point in a direction of a first control point and arrives at the endpoint in a direction from a second control point. These curves generally do not pass through the control points unless those points lie in a straight line between the anchor points. In the Path data string, the first anchor point is implicitly specified by the current location of the pen; the curve operations need only specify the control point(s) and ending anchor point.

Path to confusion

It may not seem like hand-coding paths with complex curves would be simple at first glance. But upon using the `Path` API for a while ... it's still not simple. Instead, paths can be easy to code for simple primitives, but more complex paths will probably come from tools instead. For example, Adobe Illustrator and Adobe Fireworks can export drawings into a format called FXG, which is a simplified form of exactly the graphics primitives detailed in this chapter. Vector paths are used extensively in Illustrator, and these shapes output as `Path` primitives in the FXG files. So you might want to consider the `Path` primitive as something that you may encounter in code that is generated by tools, but you probably won't be using it much in your hand-coded graphics.

And this is what that path looks like:

(Demo: SimpleObjects)

Now we'll create `Path` objects in `Shapely`. As with the other shapes, paths are created in the `mouseDownHandler()` function. But we do not yet add data to the path since the user has only told us where it will be located, not where it will draw to next. Instead, we create the `pathPoints Vector` to hold the points of the `Path`:

(File: components/DrawingCanvas.as)

```
case PATH:
    shape = new Path();
    pathPoints =
        new <Point>[new Point(event.localX, event.localY)];
    break;
```

29

When the user moves the mouse or releases the button, the dragTo() function is called, where the new point is added to pathPoints and the function constructPath() is called:

```
case PATH:
    pathPoints[pathPoints.length] = new Point(dragX, dragY);
    constructPath();
    break;
```

The constructPath() function turns the set of points in pathPoints into a data string for the path:

```
private function constructPath():void
{
    var dataString:String = "M " +
        pathPoints[0].x + " " + pathPoints[1].y;
    for (var i:int = 1; i < pathPoints.length; ++i)
    {
        var pt:Point = pathPoints[i];
        dataString += " L " + pt.x + " " + pt.y;
    }
    Path(shape).data = dataString;
}
```

This function walks through pathPoints, turning the first point into a *move* operation and subsequent points into *line* operations in the data string. This process causes a multi-segment line to be created, starting at the point where the user first pressed the mouse (the first point in pathPoints) and continuing through every other point we recorded. Because mouse motion is handled very quickly, this line-segment approach results in a reasonable approximation to freehand scribbling because each straight line segment will only be as long as the distance covered between each mouseMove event.

The reason for the extra layer of indirection with pathPoints is that we cannot simply edit the existing Path shape's points, like we do with the Line, Rect, and Ellipse shapes that we saw earlier. Instead, the only way to change a Path is to supply a new data string. So we record the path's points in a separate data structure and re-create the data string every time we add a new point.

30

Now that we've seen the different shapes that are possible to create, it's time to talk about the attributes with which the shapes are drawn. Let's learn about `stroke` and `fill`.

2.4 Strokes of genius: lines and outlines

You may want to draw lines in your UI to achieve a particular effect, like borders on filled areas, outlines on empty areas, or separator lines between different elements in the interface. These may be straight or curved lines, or bounding lines around larger, filled areas. These lines can be drawn in different ways, with different colors, widths, and joins at the corners. These line properties are defined as *strokes* on the objects.

All of the graphics objects in Flex 4 except for `BitmapImage`, which we'll see later, have an optional `stroke` property that defines the characteristics of the object's lines, like their color and width. For the one-dimensional Line object, the `stroke` is all there is. The object's `stroke` is all that you see of the object. For the rest of the objects, `Path`, `Rect`, and `Ellipse`, the stroke is the border line around the object's filled area.

Strokes come in three varieties: `SolidColorStroke`, which has a single color, and two strokes that use gradients, `LinearGradientStroke` and `RadialGradientStroke`. You'll see more about gradients later when I discuss `fill` objects. For now, we'll talk about solid color strokes, which is the common case for lines.[3]

A `stroke` has a few properties that are necessary for specific situations, but for which the defaults are generally sufficient. For example, the `joints` and `miterLimit` properties are useful for controlling how the intersections look with multi-segment stroked objects like `Path` and `Rect`. And the `scaleMode` property controls how scaling on the object affects the width of the stroke. Here we'll focus on just the more common stroke properties used to achieve particular effects on the stroke.

weight determines the width of the stroke in pixels. A value of 0 is equal to a one-pixel-wide line, but the line stays at that thickness even when scaled. This behavior is in contrast to that when `weight` equals 1, which also results in a one-pixel-wide line on an unscaled object. But

---

[3] You can see cases of gradients used in strokes in some of the standard Flex 4 component skins like `ButtonSkin`. These skins have very subtle effects that call for rich graphic elements like gradient strokes and fills. But more typical lines and borders are drawn with single colors.

31

a line with `weight` equal to 1 will scale with the object so an object with a scale factor of 2 will have lines twice as wide as that object with a scale factor of 1.

`color` an unsigned integer value that describes the red, green, and blue (RGB) values that contribute to the final color value. This is a standard RGB representation in an integer, where the bottom-most (least significant) byte represent the blue value, the next byte holds the green value, and the next byte holds the red value. You can picture the color in hex form as the number 0xRRGGBB. The left-most (most significant) byte of the 32-bit value is unused.

For convenience, the MXML compiler will turn standard color names into the appropriate integer values. You can also use the numeric form of a color in either hex, integer, or HTML-color formats. For example, a value of "blue" is equivalent to "0xff", "255", and "#FF".

`alpha` the amount of translucency that the object's stroke has. A value of 1 causes the stroke to be completely opaque (nothing behind the object's stroke can be seen through it). A value of 0 causes the stroke to be completely transparent (the stroke is not seen at all, and objects behind it are fully visible). Any value between 0 and 1 causes the stroke to be translucent, allowing both the stroke and the objects behind it to be partially visible, with greater values of alpha making the stroke more opaque. The opacity of the overall object you create is typically controlled with the object's `alpha` property, not the object's stroke's alpha, but if you want separate control over the stroke's opacity, use the stroke's `alpha` property.

Here is an example of two lines drawn with different strokes:

```
<s:Line xFrom="20" yFrom="20" xTo="100" yTo="100">
    <s:stroke>
        <s:SolidColorStroke color="black"/>
    </s:stroke>
</s:Line>
<s:Line xFrom="100" yFrom="20" xTo="20" yTo="100">
    <s:stroke>
        <s:SolidColorStroke color="gray"
                alpha=".6" weight="10"/>
```

```
    </s:stroke>
  </s:Line>
```

The first object is a black line with the default `weight` (0) and `alpha` (1). The second object is a wide gray that is translucent (note that you can see the black line through the wide gray line), as seen here:

(Demo: SimpleObjects)

The `StrokeTest` application helps visualize how the various stroke parameters affect the look of our stroked primitives. This code draws a `Rect` object with a stroke:

(File: StrokeTest.mxml)
```
<s:Rect x="20" y="170" width="30" height="30"
        scaleX="{Number(scaleXInput.text)}"
        scaleY="{Number(scaleYInput.text)}">
    <s:stroke>
        <s:SolidColorStroke color="black"
                weight="{Number(weightInput.text)}"
                miterLimit="{Number(miterLimitInput.text)}"
                joints="{jointsInput.selectedItem}"
                scaleMode="{scaleModeInput.selectedItem}"/>
    </s:stroke>
</s:Rect>
```

The `Rect` object takes its scale factors from the text input fields so that you can see how scaling in either direction affects the results. The `stroke` object is an instance of `SolidColorStroke` with a color of `black`. The `stroke` object has other properties that are bound to the values of the various controls in the GUI. You can see the results from a nonzero line weight and rounded joints in this screenshot:

33

(Demo: StrokeTest)

The application is pretty simple as Flex applications go. The interesting part is in how the properties affect the look of the graphic primitive. Be sure to play with it to get a feel for how the properties interact.

2.5 Fills: it's what's on the inside that counts

All of the Flex shapes except Line can have a fill as well as a stroke. The fill specifies what happens on the interior of the object. So, for example, a rectangle's stroke is drawn on the outside of the area and its fill is the interior of that area. As with stroke, the fill property is optional, so any of these objects can have a stroke or a fill or both or neither (although having neither one makes for a pretty useless shape).

Three types of fills are possible. As with stroke, you can fill with a solid color or a gradient. Additionally, you can fill the area with a bitmap image. We'll discuss all of these options next.

Solid color fills

The simplest way to fill an area is with a single solid color. For example, the drawing canvas of Shapely is filled with a solid white color. Just like the solid color stroke discussed in Section 2.4, the solid color fill has the properties color and alpha. These properties are exactly the same for both strokes and fills; see Section 2.4 for more information on them.

Here is an example of two filled rectangles:

34

(File: SimpleObjects.mxml)

```
<s:Rect x="150" y="20" width="80" height="80">
    <s:fill>
        <s:SolidColor color="0"/>
    </s:fill>
</s:Rect>
<s:Rect x="250" y="20" width="80" height="80">
    <s:fill>
        <s:SolidColor color="black" alpha=".5"/>
    </s:fill>
    <s:stroke>
        <s:SolidColorStroke color="black" weight="5"/>
    </s:stroke>
</s:Rect>
```

The first object is a black-filled rectangle with the default `weight` (0) and `alpha` (1). The second object is filled with translucent black (`alpha=".5"`), making the result gray since the rectangle is drawn over a white background. This second rectangle also has a black, wide `stroke` object. Note that the opacity of the `stroke` object is independent of the `fill`'s opacity.

(Demo: SimpleObjects)

Bitmap fills

Sometimes, you want to fill an area with an image. If you simply want a rectangular image in the scene, it's probably easier to use the `Image` or `BitmapImage` class (which we will see more of later in this chapter). But you can fill any arbitrary shape, like a path, rounded rectangle, or circle, with an image using a `BitmapFill`.

Several properties exist on `BitmapFill` to define the image resource that the fill uses and the way the image is displayed in the filled area:

`source` defines the bitmap that is displayed in the fill. This parameter is flexible and can be used to specify an embedded image file, an instance of a `Bitmap` or `BitmapData` object, or the class name or instance of a display object. Typically, you use an embedded image file, like this: `source="@Embed('tree.jpg')")`.[4]

`smooth` defines whether the image is "smoothed" when it is scaled to a different size than the original bitmap image. By default, `smooth` is false, which results in using the "nearest neighbor" approach, where pixels are chosen from the original image based on which one is closest to the current pixel being drawn. This approach is the fastest option when the image is scaled to fit into the fill area, since it requires no calculations. But scaling without smoothing can result in rendering artifacts. If `smooth` is set to true, scaled images will use a simple bilinear smoothing algorithm, where the pixels to the left, right, top, and bottom of the destination pixel are combined to create a blended pixel value. This property only comes into play when an image is scaled; an image that is displayed in its original resolution will simply use the original pixel values with no smoothing applied.

`fillMode` tells the graphic object how to fill the shape area if the source bitmap is smaller than the shape in either dimension. Three possible values are available, all of which are specified in the `BitmapFillMode` class (or you can choose to use the equivalent strings, like "scale" instead of `BitmapFillMode.SCALE`):

> SCALE the default value, which causes the bitmap to be scaled (either down or up) to fit the dimensions of the shape that it fills.

---

[4] The @Embed directive tells the compiler to bundle the specified resource with the application (here an image, but Embed can be applied to other assets as well). With `BitmapFill`, as well as with the `BitmapImage` object you'll see later in this chapter, any image resource must be embedded. If you use the `Image` control from Flex 3, you can also refer to an image by relative or absolute URL, without embedding the file. If you do not use Embed, the image will be loaded when the `Image` component is created, and may not be shown immediately if there is a loading delay. When Embed is used, the resource is bundled with the application and is loaded synchronously when the component is created. The Embed approach trades off faster image loading time with larger application footprint size, since embedded image assets are packaged into the downloaded application's SWF file.

CLIP causes the bitmap to be drawn in its original size, either being clipped by the size of the region (if the bitmap is larger than the dimensions of the BitmapImage) or leaving empty space (if the bitmap is smaller).

REPEAT causes the bitmap image to repeat or tile itself inside the region, filling the dimensions of the shape.

alpha represents the amount of translucency that the bitmap fill has. This property acts just like the same property on the solid color fill that we discussed earlier.

BitmapFill also has properties for positioning and transforming the bitmap within the filled area. But those parameters are less commonly used and self-explanatory, so I'll defer to the SDK documentation.

Here is a simple example of using a BitmapFill on a rectangle object:

```
(File: SimpleObjects.mxml)
<s:Rect x="350" y="20" width="80" height="80">
    <s:fill>
        <s:BitmapFill
            source="@Embed('images/SanFrancisco.jpg')"/>
    </s:fill>
    <s:stroke>
        <s:SolidColorStroke color="gray" weight="5"/>
    </s:stroke>
</s:Rect>
```

The rectangle has a fill with just one parameter specified: the source. Note that the bitmap, by default, scales to fit the area of the object, so little else is needed unless you want to change the way the image maps into the area.

(Demo: SimpleObjects)

37

Gradient fills

Gradients are so useful in creating rich UIs that it is worth taking a moment to talk more generally about them before diving into the details of the API of the gradient-based fill classes.

Gradients are used to fill an area with a series of colors. Two types of gradients are supported in Flex: linear and radial. Linear gradients have a color change along one dimension (left to right, top to bottom, or along arbitrary degree of rotation). Radial gradients change colors from some center point out to some perimeter of a circle. Both gradients can be defined with several colors along the way, so that they can change either from one start color to a single end color, or they can change from the start color through a series of other colors (called *gradient entries*, or sometimes, *gradient stops*) along the way before finally reaching the end color.

 Gradients provide a simple way to liven up a GUI, from rich backdrops to 3D effects to interesting reflection techniques.

Gradients can be used to liven up a GUI in very simple ways, from providing a rich backdrop to giving components a 3D look, with highlight and shadow effects that really make 2D objects pop out of the screen. Gradients can also be used for some special effects like reflections, where the gradient operates on a translucency value to fade out a reflection for a more realistic look (we'll see this effect in Chapter 3). It's definitely worth learning about the gradient classes so that you can start applying them to your objects and components. And better yet, gradients are much easier to use with the new graphic elements defined in Flex 4, so there's every reason to start using gradients in your rich client applications.

Both types of gradients, linear and radial, use the same method of specifying the set of colors that the gradient transitions between: GradientEntry.

The GradientEntry class

This class is a simple data structure that holds the information for a particular gradient stop in a linear or radial gradient. For each entry, we need to know the color, alpha, and ratio, which is the point in the overall gradient where the entry's color is sampled at 100%. In other words, the ratio is the point in the overall gradient where the transition from the color in the previous entry to the color in this entry ends and the transition to the next entry's color begins. This information is represented in the following properties:

alpha The translucency of the color for this gradient entry. This value acts just like the alpha property that we saw earlier for solid color strokes and fills, except that it holds just for this single object in the set of gradient entries instead of for the entire fill.

color The color at this point in the gradient, represented as an unsigned integer. This property is just like the color property in the solid color stroke and fill discussed earlier, except that this color is true just for this entry and not for the whole fill.

ratio The point in the gradient where this entry is applied. This is a percentage value, with 0 representing the start of the gradient and 1 representing the end of the gradient.

A gradient (either linear or radial) consists of a set of GradientEntry objects which define how the color and translucency of the gradient changes over the course of the object it fills.

For example, this set of entries defines a gradient that changes smoothly from black to white to gray:

```
<s:GradientEntry color="black"/>
<s:GradientEntry color="white"/>
<s:GradientEntry color="gray"/>
```

Note that this code does not set a ratio value for any of the entries. By default, the entries spread themselves equally over the available area. Not defining ratios for these three entries is equivalent to specifying a ratio of 0 for the black entry, .5 for the white entry, and 1 for the final gray entry.

Linear and radial gradient shared properties

Most of the functionality of linear and radial gradients is shared in the common superclass, GradientBase. These are the more commonly used shared properties of that class:

entries This property defines an Array of GradientEntry objects, as we saw in the previous section.

rotation This property defines the angle of rotation, in degrees, along which the gradient proceeds. By default, gradients move from left to right, horizontally. For example, the black/white/gray gradient entries example in the previous section would, by default, show up with black at the left, white in the middle, and gray at the right. A gradient moving in a different direction is defined using the rotation property. For example, a vertical gradient is defined by setting rotation to 90. Vertical gradients are more common in UI elements because gradients are often used to give a pseudo 3D lighting effect, where the virtual light source is somewhere above the scene.

spreadMethod This property defines what happens outside of the defined gradient area. If the area covered by a gradient does not completely cover its target object, then it needs to know how to color the remaining pixels in the object's area. This property has three possible values, from the SpreadMethod class: CAP, REPEAT, and REFLECT. CAP causes the color values at the end of the gradients to extend to the boundaries of the filled area. REPEAT causes the gradient to repeat itself over and over to fill the target area. REFLECT is like REPEAT, except each time it repeats it reverses itself.

There are also properties for positioning the starting point of the gradient within the filled area (x and y), a property for changing the method of color interpolation (interpolationMethod), and a property for performing more complex transformations of the gradient fill (matrix). I'll just refer you to the Flex SDK documentation for these less commonly-used properties.

That's it for the shared properties. Now let's see how all of this gets put together in the linear and radial gradient objects, along with some examples of the visual results.

The LinearGradient class

Linear gradient fills transition through their colors along a straight line. This type of gradient is useful for backgrounds that are much richer than solid colors. Linear gradients are also useful for some 3D effects, such as making UI components look convex or concave, because they are good at mimicking shadows and highlight drop-off.

The LinearGradient class provides a single property in addition to those inherited from GradientBase: scaleX. This property is responsible for defining the scale factor of the gradient, which is an easy way to define the area covered by the gradient. By default, the gradient fills the area of the target object, but this scale factor can be used to define the gradient pattern over a larger or smaller area. Note that the scale factor is only in the x direction; no scaling in the y direction exists since the gradient only operates in one dimension. So if you want the gradient to be half the size of a 100-pixel wide shape that it fills, you set `scaleX = 50`.[5]

Here are some simple examples that show different linear gradient fills inside `Rect` objects:

(File: SimpleObjects.mxml)

```
<s:Rect x="20" y="120" width="80" height="80">
    <s:fill>
        <s:LinearGradient>
            <s:GradientEntry color="black"/>
            <s:GradientEntry color="white"/>
            <s:GradientEntry color="gray"/>
        </s:LinearGradient>
    </s:fill>
</s:Rect>
<s:Rect x="120" y="120" width="80" height="80">
    <s:fill>
        <s:LinearGradient rotation="90">
            <s:GradientEntry color="0xb0b0b0"/>
            <s:GradientEntry color="0x404040"/>
        </s:LinearGradient>
```

---

[5] This use of scaleX seemed non-intuitive to me when I first saw it. I'm used to the scaleX and scaleY properties, which are on Flash display objects and Flex components, representing a proportion of an object's pixel size. So if an object has a width of 100 and I want it to be 50 pixels wide on the screen, I expect to set a scaleX value of .5. But with gradient fills, it doesn't work that way. If a gradient fills an area 100 pixels wide, but I want it to stop at 50 pixels, I set scaleX to 50. What's up with that?

It turns out that scaleX for gradient fills means exactly the same thing that it does for display objects; it is a proportion of that object's current size. But the key to understanding scaleX with gradient fills is that a gradient fill has a natural size of *one* pixel. So by specifying a scaleX value of 50, we're actually saying that the gradient should fill 50 times its natural size, or 50 pixels. One of the confusing things here is that if you don't specify any value for scaleX, it fills its object completely. But this is not because the gradient fill has a scale value of 1 (as do typical objects in Flex and Flash). Instead, the scaleX property has a default value of NaN, which tells the gradient to fill whatever area it occupies, regardless of size.

41

```
        </s:fill>
    </s:Rect>
    <s:Rect x="220" y="120" width="80" height="80">
        <s:fill>
            <s:LinearGradient rotation="90">
                <s:GradientEntry color="0x808080"/>
                <s:GradientEntry color="0xa0a0a0" ratio=".25"/>
                <s:GradientEntry color="0x202020"/>
            </s:LinearGradient>
        </s:fill>
    </s:Rect>
    <s:Rect x="320" y="120" width="80" height="80">
        <s:fill>
            <s:LinearGradient rotation="90">
                <s:GradientEntry color="0x808080"/>
                <s:GradientEntry color="0x202020" ratio=".1"/>
                <s:GradientEntry color="0x404040" ratio=".75"/>
                <s:GradientEntry color="0xa0a0a0"/>
            </s:LinearGradient>
        </s:fill>
    </s:Rect>
```

This code results in the following:

(Demo: SimpleObjects)

The first of these rectangles is the result from the same black/white/gray gradient entries that we saw earlier. This example uses the default rotation, so the linear gradient proceeds from left to right. The second example shows a subtle vertical gradient between two shades of gray, caused by using a rotation value of 90. This gradient is appropriate for some application window and container backgrounds.

42

The third and fourth examples show the pseudo-3D effects that linear gradients are sometimes used for. The third object simulates a convex object lit from above, where the light shows most at the top of the object. The rounded effect is achieved by having the gradient proceed from one color to a lighter color at a `ratio` of .25, then down to a darker color at the bottom. The final object shows more of a concave effect, with the light showing most at the bottom of the object.

To see a slightly more involved example, take a look at the example `LinearGradientProperties`. The application uses several GUI controls to allow the user to change the gradient colors, the `rotation`, and other properties of the gradient. The gradient is specified with data bindings to those input values, such as the gradient's `rotation` property being set by the `rotationInput` text control, and fills a `Rect` object as follows:

```
(File: LinearGradientProperties.mxml)
<s:Rect id="rect" width="180" height="180">
    <s:stroke>
        <s:SolidColorStroke color="black"/>
    </s:stroke>
    <s:fill>
        <s:LinearGradient
            rotation="{Number(rotationInput.text)}"
            x="{Number(xInput.text)}"
            y="{Number(yInput.text)}"
            scaleX="{Number(scaleXInput.text)}"
            spreadMethod="{spreadMethodInput.selectedItem}">
            <s:GradientEntry
                color="{startColor.selectedColor}"/>
            <s:GradientEntry
                color="{endColor.selectedColor}"/>
        </s:LinearGradient>
    </s:fill>
</s:Rect>
```

The `stroke` on the `Rect` is defined just to give the shape a visual boundary. When you run the application, you can play with various properties of the gradient to see how they affect the visual result, as seen here:

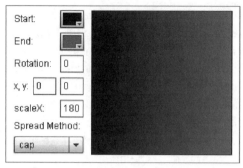

(Demo: LinearGradientProperties)

The RadialGradient class

Radial gradients are useful for some special effects like specular highlights and spotlights. They help give graphical objects a 3D look by mimicking circular shadows and highlight drop-off. They are also good for emphasizing areas of focus through spotlight effects.

Radial gradients in Flex are handled with the RadialGradient class, which sets up a gradient to start at some center point and radiate outwards to end at the perimeter of the filled area. This class has three properties, beyond the shared ones in GradientBase, that help define the way that the gradient fills the area. The scaleX and scaleY properties act like the scaleX property in LinearGradient, but since this is a two-dimensional fill, scales happen in two directions. Like the linear gradient's scaleX property, these properties default to a value of NaN, which causes the gradient to fill the entire area of the object that it is assigned to. So if you don't need to change that behavior, you won't need to set these properties.

The other property of RadialGradient is focalPointRatio, which is used in conjunction with the rotation property to set the location of the center point from which the gradient radiates. The gradient radiates outward toward the boundaries of the gradient area, starting from some point inside. That point is determined by the rotation parameter, which tells the gradient the degrees to rotate, and the focalPointRatio, which tells the gradient where on that rotation axis to place the center. The focalPointRatio is a value from -1 to 1, with -1 placing the point on the left edge of the gradient area and 1 placing it on the right edge. A value of 0, the default for this property, places the value in the middle of the gradient area. Meanwhile, the rotation property determines the angle of the center line, with the default value of 0 being no rotation, so the center line simply extends from left to right through the middle of the gradient area. For example, a `rotation` of 45 and a `focalPointRatio` of .5 will place the center of the gradient at the lower right corner of the gradient area.

You can play with the relationship of `rotation` and `focalPointRatio` in the `RadialGradientProperties` demo. Besides showing how these properties affect the look of the gradient, the application has optional guides to display the current `rotation` (the line through the middle of the circle) and `focalPointRatio` (the small circle on top of the line). For example, this screen shot shows a gradient with a `rotation` of 45 degrees and a `focalPointRatio` of .5:

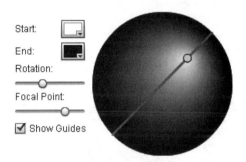

(Demo: RadialGradientProperties)

You can see some simple examples of radial gradients in the following code from `SimpleObjects`:

(File: SimpleObjects.mxml)
```
<s:Ellipse x="120" y="220" width="80" height="80">
    <s:fill>
        <s:RadialGradient>
            <s:GradientEntry color="black"/>
            <s:GradientEntry color="white"/>
            <s:GradientEntry color="gray"/>
        </s:RadialGradient>
    </s:fill>
</s:Ellipse>
<s:Ellipse x="220" y="220" width="80" height="80">
    <s:fill>
        <s:RadialGradient>
```

```
                <s:GradientEntry color="0xf0f0f0"/>
                <s:GradientEntry color="0x404040"/>
            </s:RadialGradient>
        </s:fill>
    </s:Ellipse>
    <s:Ellipse x="320" y="220" width="80" height="80">
        <s:fill>
            <s:RadialGradient rotation="-45"
                    focalPointRatio=".5">
                <s:GradientEntry color="0xf0f0f0"/>
                <s:GradientEntry color="0x404040"/>
            </s:RadialGradient>
        </s:fill>
    </s:Ellipse>
```

This code results in the following:

(Demo: SimpleObjects)

The first circle uses the gradient entries used in previous examples, where the gradient starts at black, in the center of the circle, transitions through white halfway through, and ends at gray at the perimeter of the circle. It's not a very effective use of this gradient; I just used it for comparison purposes to the earlier examples. The other two circles are more representative of the power of radial gradients.

The second circle transitions from a light gray color in the center to a darker gray at the edge. This simple, two-color gradient effect really pops the circle out of the page, giving it a 3D look that belies its simple composition. The reason that it works so well is that that lighter color in the middle acts just like a *specular highlight*. A specular highlight is the reflection of a light source on an object. On a 3D object with a matte surface, the specular highlight of most light sources, like the sun, show up as bright spots that gradually fade toward their edges to the normal object color. The radial gradient mimics a specular highlight because it is lighter in the center and falls off smoothly toward a darker color at the edges.

The third example takes the circle a step closer toward mimicking reality. The second example works, but only if you don't actually think about the light source. If you stop and think about it, it doesn't make much sense; the light seems to be coming from the viewer. Unless the viewer is wearing a miner's helmet with a light shining directly out from their forehead,[6] it's not very realistic.

A typical light source is usually one that shines from above, like the sun or the lights in a room. And a typical light source also isn't usually so symmetrically located on the vertical plane between the viewer and the object being lit. The third circle addresses these problems by offsetting the gradient center, and therefore the virtual light source, to the upper-right of the object. It's a subtle change from the second example, but I like it because it gives a more real-world feel to the object.

 Radial gradients that are offset from dead center of the object look more natural; the real world rarely lights objects from the direction of the viewer.

2.6 Setting strokes and fills in Shapely

Now that we've talked about stroking and filling objects, we're finally able to discuss how the Shapely application sets the drawing state that is used when creating graphics shapes.

The components at the bottom of Shapely's control panel determine the stroke and fill attributes that are used when drawing. The checkbox at the top controls whether a stroke is used and the checkbox at the bottom controls whether a fill is used. In between these components are ColorPickers for the stroke and the fill gradient. And a sample rectangle between the stroke and fill sections shows the user a preview of what shapes look like with the current stroke and fill settings:

---

[6]This is probably not a demographic that is worth targeting in general, although such users could be interesting for data-mining applications.

(Demo: Shapely)

These objects are created by the following code:

(File: components/ControlPanel.mxml)

```
<s:CheckBox fontSize="9" label="Stroke" id="strokeCB"
        selected="true" change="setDrawingState()"/>
<mx:ColorPicker id="strokeColor" change="setDrawingState()"
                width="100%" selectedColor="0xff0000"/>
<s:Rect id="sampleRect" x="10" width="100%" height="20"/>
<s:HGroup enabled="{fillCB.selected}">
    <mx:ColorPicker id="fillColor"
                change="setDrawingState()"
                selectedColor="0xffffff"/>
    <mx:ColorPicker id="fillGradientColor"
                change="setDrawingState()"
                selectedColor="0x0"/>
</s:HGroup>
<s:CheckBox id="fillCB" label="Fill" fontSize="9"
                change="setDrawingState()"/>
```

When any of these stroke and fill settings change, the setDrawingState()
event handler function is called:

```
private function setDrawingState():void
{
    var newStroke:IStroke;
    var newFill:IFill;
    if (fillCB.selected)
    {
```

```
if (fillColor.selectedColor ==
        fillGradientColor.selectedColor)
    newFill = new SolidColor(
            fillColor.selectedColor);
else
{
    newFill = new LinearGradient();
    LinearGradient(newFill).entries = [
        new GradientEntry(
            fillColor.selectedColor),
        new GradientEntry(
            fillGradientColor.selectedColor)
    ];
}
}
if (strokeCB.selected)
    newStroke = new SolidColorStroke(
        strokeColor.selectedColor);
sampleRect.stroke = newStroke;
sampleRect.fill = newFill;
var drawingChangeEvent:DrawingStateChangeEvent =
    new DrawingStateChangeEvent("drawingStateChange",
    newStroke, newFill);
dispatchEvent(drawingChangeEvent);
}
```

The setDrawingState() function sets up the new stroke and fill objects to be used by both the sampleRect visible in the control panel and future shapes that are drawn to the canvas. If the stroke checkbox strokeCB is not selected, the newStroke object will be null and both sampleRect and future shapes will not be drawn with a stroke. The same thing is true for fills and the newFill object, based on whether fillCB is selected.

If a stroke is selected, it is set to a simple SolidColorStroke based on the color selected in the strokeColor ColorPicker control. Fills are a bit more complicated. To simplify the UI and the explanation of how Shapely works, the fill color is always specified in terms of a gradient, with a separate ColorPicker for each color. If both gradient colors are the same, then a SolidColor fill is created with that color. Otherwise, a LinearGradient

49

fill is created. Note that this gradient is always left-to-right; no option exists to change the gradient direction. Also, the user cannot choose more than two entries in the gradient and the gradient is always a LinearGradient, never a RadialGradient. These were conscious decisions made to limit the complexity of the UI and the code. Changing any or all of these options is hereby left as an exercise for the reader.[7] It shouldn't be difficult to add these features using what we learned in this chapter.

Once we've set values for the newStroke and newFill objects, we create a DrawingStateChangeEvent, which is a simple Event subclass that contains the new fill and stroke objects to be sent to the event's listeners. We dispatch this event, which is received by the drawingStateChange() function in Shapely:

(File: Shapely.mxml)

```
private function drawingStateChange(
        event:DrawingStateChangeEvent):void
{
    canvas.stroke = event.stroke;
    canvas.fill = event.fill;
}
```

2.7   Image is everything

One graphic area that we haven't covered yet, but which is no less important than the vector-based shapes we discussed earlier, is images. Images can be useful in many different places in rich client applications, from the icons in buttons to photographs in media applications. Images can also be useful in ways that aren't obvious, such as capturing GUI objects as bitmap images and manipulating those objects in visually interesting ways (a technique that we will see applied later when we discuss Pixel Bender shader-based animation effects in Chapter 10).

---

[7]I've always wanted to say "left as an exercise for the reader." Too many years of math classes with infuriatingly non-obvious proofs in the textbooks marked with that catch phrase engendered a sense of vengeance which is only overcome through propagating the same phrase through my books. But hopefully my use is a bit less devious; I do think that the details here are obvious and doable. It's just that they just require more work and code than is worth delving into in the pages of this book, especially for the goal we're trying to achieve here, which is knowledge of how the graphics classes work.

Here's a simple application that displays an image, along with controls that let the user change the way the image is rendered:

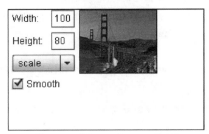

(Demo: BitmapImageTest)

The image control in the application is a `BitmapImage` object, with its properties determined by the values in the UI controls:

(File: BitmapImageTest.mxml)

```
<s:BitmapImage source="@Embed(source='images/Bridge.jpg')"
        smooth="{smoothInput.selected}"
        fillMode="{fillModeInput.selectedItem}"
        width="{Number(widthInput.text)}"
        height="{Number(heightInput.text)}"/>
```

The `Image` and `BitmapImage` controls display images in a GUI. We focus on `BitmapImage` in this chapter, but you may also want to look at the `Image` class for your applications. An important limitation exists for `BitmapImage`; it can only handle embedded assets (where the bitmap supplied to the object is loaded at compile time and stored as an asset with the application). If you want to dynamically load image assets (such as from a network location), then you'll want to look into using `Image` instead. Most of the demos in this book use embedded assets, so the simpler `BitmapImage` class does the trick.

A `BitmapImage` object displays a specified bitmap in a given position (x and y) and size (width and height). `BitmapImage` also has the same three properties `source`, `smooth`, and `fillMode` that are on `BitmapFill`, so you might want to refer to the section on `BitmapFill` earlier in this chapter for information on these properties.

We can see the results of the different fill modes in the demo application, `BitmapImageTest`. When the user selects different `width` and `height` values, the size of the `BitmapImage` object changes to the new dimensions.

51

To make it more obvious what's going on in the window, a bounding rectangle is drawn at the selected size. Setting the `left`, `top`, `right`, and `bottom` values all to 0 pins the rectangle to the boundaries of its containing group, which is sized according to the dimensions of the `BitmapImage` object, so the rectangle assumes that same size:

```
<s:Rect left="0" top="0" right="0" bottom="0">
    <s:stroke>
        <s:SolidColorStroke color="black"/>
    </s:stroke>
</s:Rect>
```

When the size is doubled, the image scales to fill the new size:

When the `fillMode` is changed to `clip`, the bitmap stays at its original size, even though the space it occupies (which we can see from the border rectangle) is much larger:

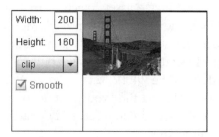

When `repeat` is chosen as the `fillMode`, the bitmap is repeated across the size of the `BitmapImage` space:

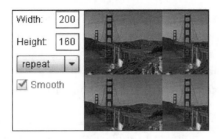

You can also play around with the Smooth checkbox to see the pixelization artifacts that result from not smoothing during scaling operations. The impact of these artifacts varies based on the original image, the size of that image, and the scaling factor.

 Reflections, like gradient fills, are one way to make a 2D interface more rich and 3D-like, by giving the user the impression that the objects interact like they would in the real world.

As one final view of how you might use bitmaps and graphics in different ways in an application (and as a subtle teaser for techniques that we will elaborate on in the next chapter), let's see how to create a simple reflection effect. First, we need a rich background for our application which we'll get with a gradient fill:

(File: Reflexion.mxml)

```
<s:Rect width="100%" height="100%">
    <s:fill>
        <s:LinearGradient rotation="90">
            <s:GradientEntry color="0x404040"/>
            <s:GradientEntry color="0xf0f0f0"/>
        </s:LinearGradient>
    </s:fill>
</s:Rect>
```

Next, we want to display an image with a reflection of itself. This is done with a VGroup, which automatically stacks the two objects (the image and its reflection) vertically. The reflection is exactly the same image, but reflected vertically, so it is scaled it in the y direction:

53

```
<s:VGroup id="reflectionContainer" x="50" y="50" gap="0">
    <s:BitmapImage id="image" source="{Harbor}"
          x="50" y="50" width="400" height="200"/>
    <s:BitmapImage source="{Harbor}" scaleY="-1" alpha=".4"
          width="{image.width}" height="{image.height}"/>
</s:VGroup>
```

You should note a couple of things about this code. First, the gap in the VGroup is set to 0 because the reflection should start exactly where the image stops (unless we are trying to mimic the object floating above the reflected surface). Second, the way that the reflection is achieved is by scaling the image by -1 in y. This scaling operation effectively inverts the image vertically, which is exactly what we want. Third, a fractional alpha value is set on the reflection to make it translucent. This is necessary because true reflections are never perfect, unless the reflecting surface is a mirror. We want to mimic an imperfect reflecting surface, so we dim the reflected image by giving its alpha property a translucent value. The effect is easy to achieve, and provides a reasonable, if simple, approximation of a reflected image:

(Demo: Reflexion)

54

Reflections in the real world are never perfect; the more we can mimic real-world reflection effects, the more natural they will seem to the user.

We can improve on this effect, however. The translucent reflection in this effect, while better than a fully opaque version, just isn't real enough. There are other things that we can do to make the reflection much more realistic. But these techniques require knowledge of Flex filters, which is both an interesting topic and excellent segue to the next chapter.

Conclusion

In this chapter, we saw how Flex 4 allows you to create shapes with different stroke and fill properties to create custom graphics for you application, in either MXML or ActionScript code. You can use these drawing primitives to create anything from drawing applications to image viewers. These graphics shapes and attributes are also useful for creating custom component skins, as we will see in Chapter 6.

In the next chapter, we will see how to use Flex filters to add rich graphical effects to your applications.

Chapter 3

Filters: Easy Image Processing

One of the most important techniques in creating rich user interfaces is image processing, which allows us to alter the appearance of visual objects. In fact, just a simple blur can be useful in a wide variety of different visual effects.

For example, take a look at the UponFurtherReflection application, which builds on the Reflexion application in the previous chapter:

(Demo: UponFurtherReflection)

The reflection of the image is more realistic than it was in the earlier example, by using a blurring technique.

Although it is interesting to understand some of the fundamentals under-lying the image processing techniques, one of the greatest things about Flex and the Flash platform is that we get many image processing-based effects for free, under the name of "filters." The filter classes, and the ability to apply them to any Flash display object, make it easy to apply these techniques individually to our GUI objects, or to combine them in various ways to make a truly rich user experience.

Since the filter classes are built into the platform, we can just use them without worrying too much about the details of how they work. But the more we understand about the underlying concepts and technologies, the more effectively we can use the built-in classes. Besides, isn't understanding how things work part of the fun of being a software developer?

To understand image processing techniques, and how they are used by the built-in classes in Flex, we'll discuss Flex filters.

3.1   Flex filters

Flex filters are operations that work on an original source image (or, more correctly, on the pixels of a component or graphical object) and result in a new visual representation of that image. For example, you may attach a filter to a `Button` to alter its appearance. The filter takes all of the pixel values in that `Button` (the way the `Button` would normally look on the screen) as input and produces a new version of the `Button` as output after applying the operations specified in the filter. The resulting pixels displayed on the screen are the filtered output.

One of the handy things with filters is that you, the developer, don't have to worry about the fact that the filters are operating on pixel values as input and producing pixel values as output. Instead, you simply assign one or more filters to a graphical object, and these filters automatically change the appearance of that object and the filtered object is displayed in place of the original object.

Let's look at a simple example. In `SimpleBlur`, we apply a blur filter (which we'll read more about in Section 3.2) to our `Button` when it is clicked. Clicking the button successive times toggles the blur on and off. The blur filter is created like this:

(File: SimpleBlur.mxml)
```
<s:BlurFilter id="blur"/>
```

58

The `BlurFilter` class has various properties, but the only one we must set here is the `id`, so that the button can reference it:

```
<s:Button id="b" label="Blur Me" x="50" y="50"
  click="b.filters = b.filters.length==0 ? [blur] : []"/>
```

Clicking on the button toggles its filter off and on based on whether any filters are currently attached to the button. No filters are active if the `filters` property is an empty array (the default). If the array is not empty, it must be the case that the blur filter is currently set on the button, so we remove it by setting `filters` to an empty array. Note that the `filters` property is an array of filter objects, so that more than one filter can be applied at the same time. To attach a filter to an object, you add it to the object's array of `filters`. Conversely, to remove a filter from an object, you remove it from the `filters` array. So to attach our blur filter to the button, we write: `filters = [blur]`, and to remove it, we set `filters` to an empty array, like this: `filters = []`.

The most important thing to notice about this example is how simple it is to get this interesting visual effect. We applied a blur to our object in one step (`button.filters = [blur]`) without thinking about image processing, box blurs, Gaussian convolution kernels, performance optimizing blur techniques, or anything else. This is the magic of Flex filters; they take standard image processing techniques and wrap them up into filters which are easy to create and apply, allowing you to get many interesting and powerful graphical effects without much effort or code.

All of the Flex filters work this way. The desired filter class is instantiated and applied to the target object by adding it to the `filters` property of that object. The Flex filters work on any object of type `UIComponent` or `GraphicElement`, which comprise all of the components and graphics objects in Flex UIs.[1]

Of course, the default parameters for the `BlurFilter` used in the previous example may not always suit your purposes. So let's discuss this filter and other related filters in more detail.

---

[1] It is also possible to display raw Flash `DisplayObjects` in a Flex application, which are neither Flex components nor graphic elements. Filtering these objects is possible, using the Flash filter classes that underlie the Flex filter classes, and then setting the `filters` property on those display objects. See the sidebar on page 60 for more information on the difference between Flex and Flash filters.

Flex filters vs. Flash filters

Flex 3 has no filter classes. Or, rather, Flex 3 programmers use the Flash filter classes directly. When properties are changed on these filters, as happens when filters are animated, the application must re-apply the `filters` property on the target object. Flex 4, on the other hand, offers parallel filter classes that wrap these Flash filter classes. The main piece of additional functionality that the Flex filters provide over the Flash filters is that they automatically re-apply a changed filter to the objects that use it. This may not seem like much, but it removes one of the gotchas with the previous approach to using filters, since it was all too easy to forget to re-apply filters whenever they changed.

3.2 Blur-based filters

Three Flex filters—`BlurFilter`, `GlowFilter`, and `DropShadowFilter`—are all based on the underlying technique of blurring an image. In the case of `BlurFilter`, the end result is exactly that technique: the filter blurs an object. For `GlowFilter`, the end effect is a glow around the original object, where the glow is blurred to achieve the right look. For `DropShadowFilter`, the desired effect is a shadow behind the object, where the shadow itself is blurred to get a more realistic soft shadow. You can see all of these effects in this screenshot:

(Demo: BlurGlowShadow)

Each of the buttons has a single filter applied. The first, blurry, button has a `BlurFilter`, the second, glowing, button a `GlowFilter`, and the third, shadowed, button has a `DropShadowFilter`, as you can see in the code:

(File: BlurGlowShadow.mxml)

```
<fx:Declarations>
    <s:BlurFilter id="blur"/>
    <s:GlowFilter id="glow"/>
    <s:DropShadowFilter id="shadow"/>
```

```
</fx:Declarations>
<s:HGroup verticalCenter="0" horizontalCenter="0">
    <s:Button label="Blur" filters="{[blur]}"/>
    <s:Button label="Glow" filters="{[glow]}"/>
    <s:Button label="Shadow" filters="{[shadow]}"/>
</s:HGroup>
```

In order to understand how these filters work, let's first talk about the blurring technique in general. Then we'll talk more about these three blur-based filters in particular.

The blurring technique

A blur effect is useful in many different situations, from de-emphasizing items of less importance to motion blur in animations to combinations with other filters for more complex effects. In fact, blurring is probably one of the most useful filtering techniques because it is used in combination with so many others to achieve a wide variety of effects.

 Blurring is a fundamental image-processing technique that is useful on its own, but also in conjunction with other techniques like drop shadows and glows.

At the most basic level, a blur is simply a way of combining several pixel values to calculate the final color value of each pixel in an image. In particular, each pixel in the resulting image is a combination of its original pixel value plus the values of its neighboring pixels in some proportion. It is the details behind "neighboring pixels" and "some proportion" that affect the result, the quality, and the performance of a blur operation.

One of the simplest blur techniques combines all of the pixels in a rectangular region (called a *convolution kernel*) around a given pixel, averaging their color values to produce the final pixel value. This approach is called a *box blur* because of the rectangular box shape of the area of pixels that are averaged together. For example, a 3 3 box blur around each pixel combines nine pixels total, using one ninth of each source pixel's color value to calculate the final blurred pixel value.

We can apply a box blur filter to an image to get a gentle blur effect. We can then increase the size of the box to average in more pixel values for each final pixel value, giving a blurrier result. Here is an example showing a button with no blur, with a mild 3×3 box blur, and with a more pronounced 5×5 box blur:

(Demo: BlurSize)

This blur technique is sufficient in many cases, but you may sometimes notice artifacts of the box filter. In particular, source images with horizontal and vertical elements will end up with strong horizontal/vertical artifacts in the resulting image, where the original areas are not blended with their surroundings. For example, we can see some artifacts from the simple 3×3 blur of the button above. Zooming in on the button shows how the horizontal and vertical aspects of the original Button are emphasized, creating boxy artifacts in the result:

To fix these problems, a more involved calculation called a *Gaussian blur* is sometimes used, where the surrounding pixels are combined in unequal proportions, weighting the pixels toward the center more than those at the edge. The convolution kernel for a true Gaussian blur is not necessarily a square. Instead, pixels are included in the calculation according to their distance from the final pixel location. In theory, every pixel in an image could be part of the convolution kernel. In practice, simplifying assumptions are made for performance reasons to limit the size of the kernel to a tighter circle around the final pixel location.

Although the Gaussian blur algorithm is not too complicated to understand, it is considerably more performance-intensive than the box blur. A simple way to achieve faster near-Gaussian results is to use a multi-pass approach, in which the box blur is applied several times in succession. This approach gives the blur a higher quality, reducing the boxy artifacts and resulting in a smoother final result. In the figure below, we see the same three buttons as before in the top row. In the next row, the blurs on the second and third buttons have been applied twice, resulting in a smoother blur. In the final row, the blurring operation is applied three times, making the buttons even more smoothly blurred:

Here is a closeup view of the 3×3 blur with two passes:

You can see that the horizontal and vertical artifacts are lessened with this multi-pass approach. Note how all of the pixels inside the bounds of the text are some shade of gray. Compare this result with that of the previous single-pass approach which showed some white pixel regions because of box-blur artifacts. Because of its nice tradeoff of speed and quality, the multi-pass box blur approach is the one used by the Flex BlurFilter.

3.3 The BlurFilter class

BlurFilter blurs the visual objects to which it is attached. Two ways in which we can change the result of a BlurFilter are as described in the previous discussion of the general blur technique: which neighboring pixels we take into account and how these pixel values are combined. For `BlurFilter`, these aspects are manipulated by use of the `blurX`, `blurY`, and `quality` properties.

`blurX, blurY` These properties tell the filter how many pixels in the horizontal and vertical directions to use when calculating each final pixel value. The larger the values of `blurX` and `blurY`, the larger the area that will be used to calculate the final pixel values and the more blurry the final image will be.

`quality` Rather than forcing every developer to ponder convolution kernels and multi-pass techniques, the Flex filters expose a simple `quality` property that determines the quality of the result. This property sets the number of times that the blurring calculation happens successively on the image. A higher `quality` value takes longer to complete the operation since it causes more passes and therefore more calculations. The need for higher quality depends heavily on the situation, so you should make the right tradeoff decision for your application.

The value of `quality` is an integer, although it is typical to use the constant values in `BitmapFilterQuality`: `LOW` (which equals 1, so a single pass will occur in the blurring operation), `MEDIUM` (which equals 2), and `HIGH` (which equals 3). The default is `LOW`. You can actually use integer values all the way up to 15, but with the increased performance cost of each additional calculation, you might want to use a maximum value of 3, or `HIGH`, for most quality-sensitive situations. Or better yet, stick with the default of `LOW` if that result is good enough; there is no sense spending CPU cycles needlessly.

Always consider performance implications of UI decisions you make; if your visual result doesn't benefit from a higher `quality` setting, leave it at the default value and let your CPU do work where it's needed instead.

It's far easier to understand how these properties affect the results by seeing them in action. Run the application `FilterProperties`, which initially looks like this:

64

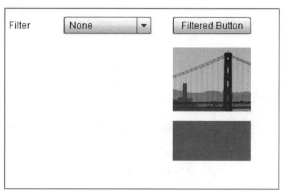

(Demo: FilterProperties)

By selecting different filters from the drop-down list, you can see the effects that those filters have on the button, the image, and the gray rectangle on the right side of the window. For example, here's what the default blur filter looks like:

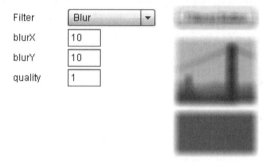

You can change the values of the filter properties in the UI to see what impact they have on the results. For example, here's what the button looks like with the default quality setting of 1 (scaled up so to show the details):

65

And here's what that same button looks like when the quality value is increased to 2:

Notice how the whole button is much more blurry and that many of the sharp-edge artifacts that a simple box blur causes have gone away in this higher-quality version. So put the book down and go play with the application. Get a sense of how the size and quality of the blur filter affect the results in different types of GUI objects.

Now that we've seen the basics of how blurring works and how to use Flex filters, and the BlurFilter class in particular, to achieve a blur, let's look at two other filters that build on the blur technique to provide other related effects: GlowFilter and DropShadowFilter.

3.4   The GlowFilter class

The GlowFilter class allows you to easily achieve a glow effect on any visual object by surrounding the object with a colored area that is the same shape as the object. This effect can be used to draw attention to a particular object in the UI, because the glow distinguishes its appearance from the other objects in the UI. This attention-drawing effect is even more pronounced when the glow is animated to produce a pulsation effect. The colored area is basically a translucent, blurry shape, so the GlowFilter class builds on the capabilities and properties of BlurFilter.

blurX, blurY Like the same properties in BlurFilter, these values specify the size of the area taken into account for blurring any pixels in the
glow shape. These properties effectively set the size of the glow, since
the size of the blurred area determines how far beyond the boundaries
of the shape the glow will extend. A value of 1 creates a glow the same
size as the object that it is filtering. The default is 4.

quality As with the BlurFilter class, the quality property sets the number of times that the blur on the glow is applied. Higher values result in a smoother glow, but the default value of LOW is generally sufficient. When BlurFilter is applied to arbitrary images or components, blurring artifacts may sometimes be obvious. But since glows have a single color and are usually less pronounced and significant than foreground images or graphical UI objects, blurring artifacts on the glow are less noticeable, so a higher quality setting is generally not as important with GlowFilter as it is with BlurFilter.

GlowFilter has several properties of its own, in addition to the blur-related properties, which allow you to parameterize various aspects of the glow:

alpha This property, like the alpha property on components and graphic primitives, determines the level of translucency. In this case, it affects the translucency of the glow itself. And while the value varies from 0 to 1, like other alpha values, 1 will not give you a fully opaque glow. The glow still has some translucency and it gets more transparent towards its edges. A value of 0 means completely transparent, which makes the glow invisible. While an invisible glow is not useful in general, animating to and from a value of 0 makes sense for techniques like a pulsating glow. A value of 1 represents the full opacity of the glow (not fully opaque, as noted, but as opaque as it's going to get).

color This unsigned integer value is the base color of the glow. For example, a value of 0xff0000 results in a red glow.

inner By default, the glow surrounds the target object. In actuality, it is under the object as well, although we don't see it when the glow is applied to opaque objects. But if you put a glow on a translucent object (such as a standard Flex button, which is slightly translucent), you will see the glow both surrounding the object and, dimmed by the object itself, under it. The inner property reverses the effect at the borders of the object, so that the glow is only on the inside of the object, fading out as it approaches the center.

knockout This property can be set to true to cause the filtered object to be completely transparent. You will still see the glow, but the object itself will be invisible. The default value is false.

67

Once again, it is easier to play with this filter's properties to see the visual impact that they have. Selecting the glow filter in the FilterProperties application exposes several glow-specific properties and causes a soft glow around the target objects to appear:

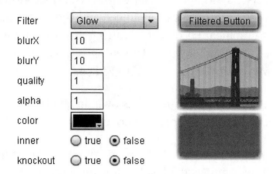

Setting the inner property causes the objects to look like this:

And setting the knockout property causes this result:

Once again, put the book down and go play with the `FilterProperties` application to understand how `GlowFilter`'s properties affect UI objects.

3.5   The DropShadowFilter class

A drop shadow is a handy effect to have around, giving you an instant way to make objects stand out from the GUI by having them cast a fake shadow. This technique is used frequently in user interfaces, giving UI components a richer feel by making them more substantial and 3D-like. We're used to seeing objects in the real world cast shadows, so seeing UI objects cast shadows makes those objects seem more real. Flex uses a drop shadow for some components by default, such as the `Panel` container. Flex also makes it easy for you to use drop shadows on your UI objects by providing the `DropShadowFilter` class.

 Drop shadows provide an easy way to make some objects in your UI stand out by giving them a substantial, 3D-like appearance.

A `DropShadowFilter` is essentially a `GlowFilter` that is offset by some distance and angle, changing the glow into more of a shadow. The class exposes all of the same properties that we saw on `GlowFilter`:

blurX, blurY Just as they do on the `BlurFilter` and `GlowFilter` classes, these properties specify the size of the area taken into account for blurring any pixels in the shadow area. These properties help determine the overall size of the shadow and how gradually it fades out around its edges. The size of shadow can imply the sharpness of the light source casting the shadow. A very tight, crisp shadow is cast by a single light source like a spotlight, whereas a muted, larger shadow is cast by multiple or larger light sources. So in order to get a tighter shadow, use smaller values for `blurX` and `blurY`, or to get a larger shadow use larger blur sizes.

quality This property acts like it does on the `BlurFilter` and `GlowFilter` classes. The value assigned to `quality` is the number of times the blur algorithm is run on the drop shadow, where more passes results in a smoother effect. This is not as important for drop shadows as it is for blurring foreground UI objects, since drop shadows by nature have less detail which would make blurring artifacts more obvious. But if you need to eliminate any horizontal or vertical artifacts from your shadows, you can experiment with this property. The default is 1.

alpha This property determines the level of translucency of the shadow, just as it does for the glow in GlowFilter. Along with the color, strength, and blurX/blurY properties, the alpha property helps determine the color and contrast of the shadow. The default value is 1.

color This unsigned integer value is the color of the shadow. Shadows are normally gray, but the color of a drop shadow can be changed to imply different colored lighting, or just to achieve a color or effect that blends well with other elements in the UI. The default value is black, although this ends up creating a gray shadow because of the combination of the color, the alpha, and the strength properties.

inner As with GlowFilter, this property causes the drop shadow to be cast inside the object instead of outside of it. By default, the shadow is behind and outside the target object. The inner property reverses the effect at the borders of the object, so that the shadow is only on the inside of the object, fading out as it approaches its center.

knockout This property can be set to true to cause the filtered object to be completely transparent. You still see the shadow cast by the object, but the object itself is invisible. The default value is false.

DropShadow also has some unique properties specific to the shadow effect:

distance This property sets the distance, in pixels, of the object's shadow from the object itself. A shadow is normally offset by some distance from the object which casts it (an offset of 0 results in no shadow, since the shadow is directly behind the object). The distance of this offset can be used to show that shadowed objects are closer to or further from the surface on which their shadow is cast. The default value is 4.

angle This property sets the direction in which the shadow is offset by the distance property. The angle implies the direction of the virtual light source that is causing the shadow. For example, a shadow that is cast to the lower right of an object implies a light source to the upper left. The default value is 45, or down and to the right of the object.

strength This property, along with the blurX and blurY properties, helps determine the crispness of the shadow, and therefore the type of virtual lighting. strength determines the contrast between the shadow color and the colors around it. A higher value causes more contrast and a stronger shadow. Values range from 0 to 255, with the default being 1. Fractional values below 1 are also sensible, and values above 1 have decreasing impact on the results.

hideObject Like knockout, this property makes the shadow-casting object transparent, while the shadow remains visible.

DropShadowFilter is the final filter to play with in FilterProperties. Selecting this filter puts a shadow behind the UI elements, causing them to stand out more from the application:

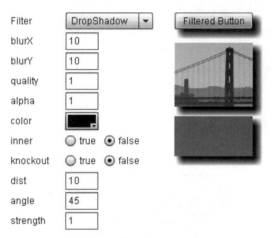

(Demo: FilterProperties)

As an example of how the properties affect the look and feel of shadows, I increased the blurX and blurY properties to 15, changed the color to a light gray, and increased the distance to 20. These changes to the shadow give the objects a feeling of standing further out from the window; a larger, lighter, and fuzzier shadow results from objects being further away from the surface on which their shadows are cast:

71

(Demo: FilterProperties)

One last time, put down the book and go play with `FilterProperties`. I mean it. The interesting part is not in the code itself, but rather in how the various properties of these filters affect the look of the filters and, more importantly, the feel of the objects being filtered. Just don't forget to come back afterwards and pick the book up again. It won't read itself.

As a fun way to get a feel for how shadow properties affect the look and feel of shadowed objects, take a look at the `ShiftingShadows` demo. In this application, the mouse acts as a virtual light source for the buttons, causing the shadows to shift depending on the location of the mouse. For example, when the mouse is in the upper-left corner of the window, shadows are cast down and to the right:

(Demo: ShiftingShadows)

As the mouse gets closer to the center of the window, the shadows get shorter and become centered around the objects, as they would in the real world with a light source directly in front of shadowed objects:

72

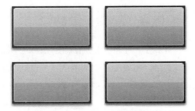

These shadow effects are implemented by dynamically modifying the angle and distance properties of the shadow filters.

The DropShadowFilter is declared like this:

(File: ShiftingShadows.mxml)
```
<s:DropShadowFilter id="shadow" strength=".5"/>
```

The filter has an id because we refer to it later when changing its properties. The strength is set to a non-default value to soften the shadows.

Each of the buttons is declared in the same way:

```
<s:Button width="100" height="50" filters="{[shadow]}"
          opaqueBackground="true"/>
```

Each button uses the same shadow filter to create its own shadow. Each button also has its opaqueBackground property set to true. This property is not normally set on buttons, but drop shadows tend to look better on opaque objects. Otherwise, you see a lighter version of the shadow behind the object and the effect is not as nice, especially with the moving shadows in this particular application. So for the purposes of this demo application, the buttons are made opaque.

The shadow shifting happens in a mouse movement listener on the application. Every time the mouse moves in the window, the updateShadow() handler function is called:

```
mouseMove="updateShadow(event)"
```

The updateShadow() function computes the new shadow properties every time the mouse moves. We take the new mouse position, calculate the angle of the mouse relative to the center of the window, and translate that into a shadow angle. We also calculate how far the mouse is from the center of the window (with 1 being the right edge of the window and 0 being the center) and multiply that factor times a maximum distance value for the shadow:

73

```
private function updateShadow(event:MouseEvent):void
{
    // Compute the angle the light source (mouse position)
    var tempX:Number = event.stageX - (width / 2);
    var tempY:Number = event.stageY - (height / 2);
    var angle:Number;
    if (tempX != 0)
        angle = 180 * Math.atan(tempY / tempX) / Math.PI;
    else
        angle = (tempY < 0) ? -90 : 90;
    if (tempX < 0)
        angle += 180;
    // Now set the shadow angle to be opposite
    // the light source angle
    shadow.angle = angle + 180;

    // Calculate the distance from the center
    var dist:Number =
        Math.sqrt(tempX * tempX + tempY * tempY);
    var maxDist:Number =
        Math.sqrt(width * width + height * height) / 2;
    shadow.distance = 15 * (dist / maxDist);
}
```

As the mouse moves around the window we calculate its angle relative to the center of the window. We then calculate the shadow's angle (which is simply the inverse of the other angle, since the mouse represents the sun and we want to position the shadow), and the distance to offset the shadow. This gives the shadows a different feel depending on where the mouse is and gives the user a different impression of where and how far away the virtual light source is.

The ShiftingShadows application is not intended to provide code that you copy for your application. I don't think that many users would appreciate you changing your application's virtual light source around as they move the mouse on the screen. Instead, the demo application is meant to show two things: how to use the DropShadowFilter class in general, and how different angles and distances affect the look and feel of drop shadows. Notice that as the mouse gets further from the window center the shadows get more pronounced, as if the objects are positioned further out from the win-

Making light of the situation

Note that the "light source" in this example is infinite (like the sun[a]). That is, the angle between any of the buttons and the light source is the same for any particular mouse position.

A local light source casts shadows at different angles depending on the angle between it and each object. For example, a light source in the center of the window might cast no shadow on the button directly below it (as in this demo), but it would cast a shadow to the right on the buttons at the right edge of the window and a shadow to the left for buttons on the left edge. In fact, a light source very close to the objects would cast a shadow shape more complex than the simple shape-of-the-shadowed-object approach that DropShadowFilter provides. Imagine a light source sitting right at the top edge of a button. The resulting shadow would expand to the left and below the left corner and to the right and below the right corner. But such situations are way beyond the simple effects we're going for here. It's sufficient for our current purposes to have a simple infinite light source and have it affect all of the items in the UI equally. Check out the discussion of drop shadows in Chapter 12 to see how we handle a local light source.

---

[a] Okay, so the sun is not an infinite distance away. But 93,000,000 miles is close enough to infinite in terms of the effect that its position has on items here on Earth. Objects that are several miles away from each other on Earth have virtually the same angle between themselves and the sun because their distance from each other is insignificant when compared to the distance between them and the sun.

dow background, or as if the virtual light source is actually further away in that direction. If you use drop shadow filters in your application, try playing with these and other properties to get the right feel for your UI.

3.6 Other filters

Other Flex filter classes provide other kinds of image-processing effects:

BevelFilter, GradientBevelFilter These two filters allow you to add a beveled look to your objects, giving them borders that resemble chiseled edges. The gradient version enables a more 3D look to the bevels.

GradientGlowFilter This filter builds on the GlowFilter that we discussed earlier, giving you more flexibility to set the colors in the glow.

ColorMatrixFilter This filter gives you control over the color effects in an object, allowing you to shift the hue or brightness, or to perform grayscale effects. It works by separating the red, green, and blue color channels of each pixel and manipulating each channel individually.

DisplacementMapFilter This filter lets you apply the values in an input bitmap parameter as multipliers on the filtered object. This technique allows you to shift the pixels in the filtered object by different values, according to the data in the bitmap.

ConvolutionFilter This filter is related to the BlurFilter discussed earlier. It provides a matrix of values that specify how much of the surrounding pixel values to take into account when calculating the final pixel value. But this filter lets you specify the multipliers in the matrix to allow much more custom effects, instead of just a simple blur.

We could play around with all of these filters, as they all have something to offer. But I'll leave that as an exercise for the reader. Instead, we'll just take a closer look at one of these other filters: ConvolutionFilter. This filter allows us to play around with very sophisticated image-processing techniques that you've probably seen in image-editing applications.

3.7 ConvolutionFilter

Recall in our earlier discussion of the blur filter that the final pixel value is calculated by averaging the values of the surrounding pixels. You can think of this set of input pixels being in a box around the final pixel. To average all of the pixels together equally, we multiply each pixel value in the box by one over the number of pixels in the box. So in the case of a 3×3 filter (which is the case when blurX and blurY equal three, since they specify that the final result should be blurred by three pixels in the x and y directions), each value in the box has a multiplier of one ninth.

But what if you wanted to blur the image differently? For example, a true Gaussian blur has a higher multiplier for pixels closer to the middle and lower multipliers for pixels at the edge, so that the closest pixel to the middle has more effect than the other ones used in the operation. Or what if you want a different effect entirely, and not just a blur?

That's where ConvolutionFilter comes in. It performs a similar operation to the blur we saw earlier, but it takes its multipliers for the surrounding pixels from a matrix of values. In fact, you can think of the BlurFilter as a specialized case of a ConvolutionFilter, with less flexibility in how the matrix values are set. Instead of blurX and blurY, you tell it how big the matrix is in x and y, which defines the number of pixels around each final pixel that will go into the calculation. Then you specify the values for the elements of the matrix to be multiplied by each of the surrounding pixel values.

For example, a simple convolution filter that acts the same as a 3×3 BlurFilter is specified by a matrix of nine values (3×3), each of which has the same multiplier of one ninth:

```
<s:ConvolutionFilter matrixX="3" matrixY="3"
    matrix="{[1/9, 1/9, 1/9, 1/9, 1/9, 1/9, 1/9, 1/9, 1/9]}"/>
```

Here, the matrixX and matrixY properties specify the size of the matrix in x and y and the matrix property specifies the multipliers for those elements.

The example above gives us a simple blur effect. But we've already seen blurs; how about something new?

Look sharp

One of the filtering effects that is common in image editing software is *sharpening*, where details and edges of the image become more pronounced. This technique can be used to make some details more obvious or to compensate for artifacts in an overly blurry image. Or it can be used to just make the picture look different, giving it a lot of unrealistic, bright, sharp edges.

The sharpening effect is achieved by a convolution filter. The pixels in the image are combined with each other in a way that highlights the edges. To achieve the effect, matrix elements are chosen that darken the dark pixels and brighten the light ones. In particular, we want the sharpening effect to occur at edges in the original image. Edges are areas of high contrast, where a dark color is next to a bright color. If we make the dark colors darker and the bright colors brighter in these areas, we will call more attention to these edges, thus sharpening the image.

We can achieve this result by multiplying the center pixel in the convolution kernel by a high multiplier and multiplying the surrounding pixels by a negative factor, essentially subtracting them from the final pixel value. This operation makes bright pixels even brighter because they are multiplied by the large multiplier. Dark colors are also multiplied by the large multiplier, but if the dark colors are next to bright colors, then the bright colors, multiplied by the negative factors, drag down the final pixel value for the dark colors, making the dark colors in edge areas even darker.

Instead of looking at figures and formulas, let's see an example. In the Sharpen demo, we create a ConvolutionFilter as follows:

(File: Sharpen.mxml)

```
<s:ConvolutionFilter id="sharpener"
    matrixX="3" matrixY="3"
    matrix="{0, -1, 0, -1, 5, -1, 0, -1, 0]}"/>
```

The filter is created with a 3×3 matrix, where the element in the middle is 5 and the elements beside, above, and below it are -1. This gives us the effect that we want, where the center pixel counts much more than the pixels around it and where the adjacent pixels subtract from the result. This effect is seen in in the figure below. On the left is the original image, with no filter applied. On the right, the picture has been sharpened with matrix values of [0, -1, 0, -1, 5, -1, 0, -1, 0]:

(Demo: Sharpen)

Note, in this image, how the edges of the original image are enhanced, with crisper skyline and bridge details and highlighted waves.

Now let's see what happens when we vary the amount of sharpening. The Sharpen demo has an HSlider component that allows the user to vary the multiplier of the center pixel:

```
<s:HSlider id="intensity" minimum="1" maximum="30" value="0"
    liveDragging="true" updateComplete="changeIntensity()"/>
```

A change in the slider value causes a call to the changeIntensity() function, where the convolution matrix values are calculated based on the value of the slider. We want to end up with a total multiplier of 1 from the matrix, to preserve the luminosity (the overall brightness) of the original image, so the adjacent pixels are calculated to be -(intensity.value - 1)/4, and the matrix values are set as follows:

```
private function changeIntensity():void
{
    var darkener:Number = -(intensity.value - 1)/4;
    sharpener.matrix = [0, darkener, 0,
        darkener, intensity.value, darkener,
        0, darkener, 0];
}
```

As the user moves the slider around, we see the impact of the changing values in the matrix. For example, at the highest value of the slider, we get a very distorted view of the city scene, where all of the edges have been brightened to an unrealistic amount:

We have used ConvolutionFilter only for a sharpening technique, but this flexible filter has many more capabilities. Play around with the matrix values. Look up algorithms for filtering with convolution kernels and try them out. See what effects you can get for your applications.

79

3.8   Pixel shader filters

We've seen how Flex filters make many complex image-processing operations trivial. By simply attaching a filter to an object, you can get lots of
different visual effects from glows to shadows to blurs to sharpening to many
other effects that we didn't cover. But there's still a problem with these filters: they're all you get. What if you like the approach of filters, but you
want to apply some custom image-processing algorithm that is not achiev-
able with the various filter classes that Flex provides? Well, you can't. The
set of filter classes is set. You cannot subclass the filter classes, nor can you
plug in your own implementation into the system. So while the set of filters
is rich and powerful, it's also very limited and inflexible.

Or at least it *was* limited ... until Flex 4.

Flash Player 10, which was released in the fall of 2008, included a new
filter that changes everything for Flex filters: `ShaderFilter`. Flex 4 includes
this filter and gives you infinite flexibility with filtering through the use of
Pixel Bender.

Pixel bender toolkit

Pixel Bender is a technology that shipped in 2008 with Adobe Creative Suite
4. It is available for Adobe Photoshop CS4 and Adobe After Effects CS4.
But more to the point for this book, it is also available for the Flash platform.

Pixel Bender provides *pixel shader* capabilities. This technology allows
you to provide a small program that is run for every pixel of an image, com-
puting its resulting value from various input images and parameters. For our
purposes, this means that we can provide arbitrary calculations on images
at the pixel level to derive some final result. This sounds an awful lot like
image filtering, doesn't it?

First things first: go download the Pixel Bender Toolkit application from
Adobe labs at `http://labs.adobe.com/technologies/pixelbender/`.
The toolkit is an application that lets you develop shader programs and com-
pile them for use in Flash and Flex applications.

Teaching Pixel Bender, although it is a relatively simple language with
C-like syntax, is way beyond the scope of this book, so I'll just refer you to
the toolkit and the documentation that comes with it. It's particularly helpful
to load in some of the sample shaders that come with the toolkit and play with
them to see how they work. You can start with these samples to develop your

own. You can also download other shaders from the Pixel Bender Exchange at http://www.adobe.com/go/pixelbender.

Even though I'm not proposing to teach how Pixel Bender works overall, I will go over a simple shader that we can then use in a Flex example.

Grayscaling with pixel bender

The shader we discuss in this section is used in the Grayer Flex example, which is seen here:

(Demo: Grayer)

This application lets the user drag a slider back and forth, which changes the image from completely grayscale (when the thumb is on the left) to its original color version (when the thumb is on the right). These changes are a bit lost in this book, since we are just showing the grayscale version in the figure. I suggest you go play with the Grayer application to see it in its complete, colorful form.

The grayscaler shader used by this Flex application takes an input image and a colorization parameter and produces an image that is a blend of the original image and the grayscale version of that image. The blend is determined by the colorization parameter, where a value of 1 results in the original color image and 0 results in a completely grayscaled image.

The grayscale calculation is based on a standard formula which combines the red, green, and blue channels of the original image to produce a gray pixel of a similar intensity with this calculation:

```
graypixel = red*.11 + green*.33 + blue*.55
```

81

The shader works by operating on each pixel of the original image, multiplying it times the grayscale formula to derive the gray version of that pixel, then blending that gray version with the original color pixel in the proportion determined by the colorization parameter.

The shader has three parameters:: the input image, the colorization parameter, and the output image. These parameters are declared in the shader as follows:

(File: shaders/grayscaler.pbk)
```
parameter float colorization;
input image4 image;
output pixel4 dst;
```

The only other code in the shader is the function evaluatePixel(), which is a standard function that all shaders must implement. The Pixel Bender library calls this function for every pixel of the image and takes the value of the output parameter, assigned in that function, as the result for that pixel. The function in grayscaler is as follows:

```
void evaluatePixel()
{
    float4 pixel = sampleNearest(image, outCoord());
    float4 grayPixel;
    grayPixel.r = pixel.r * .11 +
        pixel.g * .33 + pixel.b * .55;
    grayPixel.g = grayPixel.r;
    grayPixel.b = grayPixel.r;
    grayPixel.a = 1.0;

    dst = mix(pixel, grayPixel, (1.0 - colorization));
}
```

The code in the function works like this: First, we get the current pixel value in the original image, which is the image input. Then we calculate the grayPixel value according to the grayscale formula shown previously, accessing the red, green, and blue channels of the original image pixel with .r, .g, and .b notation. We set all of the red, green, and blue values in the grayPixel to that same value, and set its alpha value to 1 to make it opaque. Finally, we blend the calculated grayscale value with the original color value using the colorization parameter and the built-in mix() function. We

82

store that result in the dst output parameter, which Pixel Bender uses as the final pixel value result.

To put the shader into a format for use with Flex applications, we select the "Export Filter for Flash Player..." menu item in Pixel Bender Toolkit. This operation produces a *pbj* file, which is a binary file that the Flash player can use as a filter.

Once we have a pbj file, we can load the shader into a Flex application and create a Flex filter from it. In order to do that, we load the pbj file and create a Shader object:

```
(File: Grayer.mxml)
[Embed(source="shaders/Grayscaler.pbj",
    mimeType="application/octet-stream")]
private static var GrayscalerShaderClass:Class;
[Bindable]
private var grayscalerShader:Shader =
    new Shader(new GrayscalerShaderClass());
```

The Flex filter that uses Pixel Bender shaders is the ShaderFilter class. The only required property of this class is shader, which is a Shader object. For this property, we supply the grayscaleShader object:

```
<s:ShaderFilter id="grayscaler"
    shader="{grayscalerShader}"/>
```

We set the filter on our target object just like we do with all other Flex filters: by supplying it as an element in the object's filters array. So in order to filter our image with the shader filter, we create it with its filters property initialized appropriately:

```
<s:BitmapImage source="{GoldenGate}"
    filters="{[grayscaler]}"/>
```

Finally, to change the amount that the image is colored, we set the shader's colorization property whenever the slider changes:

```
<s:HSlider id="slider" minimum="0" maximum="1"
    snapInterval=".01" liveDragging="true"
    change="grayscaler.colorization = slider.value"/>
```

83

Note that we are setting the value on the `ShaderFilter` object, and not the underlying shader. Note, also, that the `colorization` property is not exposed by either `ShaderFilter` or the underlying `Shader` object. The only place that property exists is in the underlying Pixel Bender shader. Flex handles the details of taking any property value set on the filter and passing it through to the underlying shader. In this case, it takes the value of the `colorization` property and hands it off to the shader, which uses it internally to change the grayscale calculation in its `evaluatePixel()` function.

Note also that we never actually set the input image for the shader. So how did it know what to filter?

It turns out that the Flash player implementation of Pixel Bender supplies the first image input for the shader automatically. That image is the bitmap representation of the target object that is filtered by the `ShaderFilter`. In the case of the `grayscaler` shader, there is only one image input, so we don't need to supply anything; Flash tells the shader to use that `BitmapImage` as its input image.

The `Grayer` application is a very simple example of using Pixel Bender to create and use a custom filter in Flex. The most powerful thing about this approach to filtering is that you can really do *anything* with this technique: given the object being filtered, an arbitrary number of image inputs, other parameters you can pass in, and calculations performed in the `evaluatePixel()` function, you can get very custom, very cool, and very flexible effects. With Pixel Bender and `ShaderFilter`, you get the easy approach to image processing that Flex filters provides with the power and flexibility that Pixel Bender's programming model enables. Go check out the Pixel Bender Exchange and see what kind of effects are possible using this powerful combination.

3.9 Upon further reflection

As a final demonstration of using filters, let's reflect again upon the reflection technique. The reflection that we created in Section 2.7 was nice, but not terribly realistic. Even when we made the reflection translucent, to get away from the perfect-mirror effect of simply inverting the original image, it still didn't quite cut it for a reflection that the user would believe. That approach had a couple of distinct problems.

The first problem was that the reflection, even though it was translucent, was still a crisp, perfect copy of the original image. No surface in the real world other than a perfect mirror could produce that result. Instead, real materials are always somewhat matte and cause reflections to bounce off imperfectly, scattering the results in different directions instead of sending the reflected rays out in the exact opposite angle in which they arrived. This effect causes a more diffuse result in real world reflections.

Techniques that mimic the real world need to mimic real world surface and light interaction.

The second problem was that real reflections drop off as they get further away from the reflected object. We rarely see the entire object reflected. Instead, we see details more clearly in the part of the reflection that is closest to the reflected object, but the details get hazier the further out the reflection goes, usually disappearing entirely only part-way through the reflection.

Using what we've learned about filters in this chapter and about gradients in Chapter 2, we can fix both of these problems.

The first problem to solve is that we want the reflection surface to appear more matte and the reflection to appear more diffuse. Well, that sounds to me like a blur, and we now know how to get a blur effect very easily. We declare a `BlurFilter` like this:

(File: components/ReflexionContainer.mxml)
```
<s:BlurFilter id="blur" blurX="5" blurY="5" quality="2"/>
```

We then declare our reflection image to use the blur filter, and we're done:

```
<s:BitmapImage id="image" source="{source}" smooth="true"
        width="{imageWidth}" height="{imageHeight}"/>
<s:BitmapImage source="{source}" smooth="true"
        width="{image.width}" height="{image.height}"
        maskType="alpha" scaleY="-1" id="reflection"
        filters="{[blur]}">
    <!-- contents of BitmapImage discussed later -->
</s:BitmapImage>
```

Adding the blur gives us a more realistic reflection, seen here:

85

But the reflection is still too large, extending to the full height of the image that it is reflecting. To fix this problem and make the reflection get more diffuse the further it gets from the reflected image, we use a technique of *masking*, which is a way of constraining where and how Flex renders objects based on the properties of other objects. A simple masking operation clips an object to the bounds of some other object. The way we're going to use a mask here is a bit more involved; we're going to use the alpha channel of a mask object to tell Flex how much of the reflection image to allow through. And we're going to use a linear gradient to decrease that amount as we get further away from the reflected image. Here's the code for our mask, which is inside the reflection BitmapImage that it masks:

```
<s:mask>
    <s:Group>
        <s:Rect width="{image.width}"
                height="{image.height}">
            <s:fill>
                <s:LinearGradient rotation="-90">
```

```
            <s:GradientEntry color="white"
                    alpha="1"/>
            <s:GradientEntry color="white"
                    alpha="0" ratio=".4"/>
        </s:LinearGradient>
      </s:fill>
    </s:Rect>
  </s:Group>
</s:mask>
```

The gradient goes from fully opaque at the top to fully transparent 40 percent of the way down. This mask, coupled with the reflection's setting of maskType="alpha", ensures that the reflection is most visible at the top, next to the image being reflected, gradually disappearing and becoming completely invisible 40 percent of the way through the reflection, as seen here:

(Demo: UponFurtherReflection)

Note that the reflection for this application is handled in a separate class, ReflexionContainer. Putting the reflection effect in a separate file or class was not necessary for the demo, but it makes the technique much more flexible in general. You can simply use this component instead of any

BitmapImage and it will display the specified image with its reflection. It automatically creates a BitmapImage and a reflection of that image in a VGroup with the reflection technique developed here.

Conclusion

You can see from the examples in this chapter that Flex filters are easy to use and configure. Whether your needs involve using standard filters like drop shadows or something completely custom via Pixel Bender shaders, Flex filters make it simple to provide powerful visual effects for user interfaces.

In the next chapter, we will talk about the new "states" syntax in Flex 4, which provide a useful and powerful way of describing application and component states in your MXML code.

Chapter 4

States

Most applications enter many different states over time. An application may have different screens, for example, like a shopping site that enables searching on one screen, search results on another, and shopping cart details on another. There may be different states of individual components, like a disabled state for a button until the user has entered their billing address.

 Flex states allow you to incorporate your mental model of the different screens of your application into the application's MXML GUI code.

One of the innovative things about the Flex platform is that this concept of states is enabled by the API. Flex provides a way to describe the different states of your application and components in your MXML code directly. In this chapter, we will see how states work in Flex 4. Chapter 5 will then discuss how to use transitions to automate animations between states.

4.1   Component state

Although most of this chapter is about how to set state on an application, setting state on components is also a powerful feature of Flex 4. In fact, the feature is so useful that Flex 4 component skins use states to define the state-specific visuals of the component. So when a button is hovered over, or pressed, or disabled, the skin for that button reflects those changes by displaying different graphics depending on the button's current state. Let's

States improvements in Flex 4

The underlying concept and implementation of states did not change significantly between Flex 3 and Flex 4, but the syntax for states changed dramatically. States were a powerful mechanism in Flex 3, but writing correct state code could be very tricky, and reading even correctly written state code was a chore at best.

For developers of Flex 3 applications, I recommend using the Design View GUI builder in Flash Builder to produce state-dependent code, because it's far easier to figure out what to do in a graphical and property-value-oriented way than it is to hack the necessary MXML code. Design View produces the states block with the hierarchical structure of state-dependent override tags. You can then look at the resulting MXML code that Design View produced and be thankful that you didn't have to write it.

Fortunately, Flex 4 came along and completely changed the way that state code is written. Instead of a block of unreadable state code, we have a block of state name declarations and then state-dependent values declared directly in-line on the affected tags. Now the state code is both easy to write and read, with or without Design View's assistance.

look at an example to see how this works for components.

In the SearchMe application, which we'll see throughout this chapter, the user starts at a screen where they enter a search term into a text input box:

(Demo: SearchMe)

The search button is disabled initially because the text field is empty. The button is created this way on purpose, becoming enabled only when something is typed into the input field:

(File: SearchMe.mxml)

```
<s:Button x="115" y="121" label="Search"
    enabled="{searchInput.text != ''}"
    click="runSearch()"/>
```

When the user enters text into the input field, the button's enabled property becomes true, and the button shows up differently on the screen, indicating that it can now be clicked:

How this button state gets turned into different visuals for the button is the topic of Chapter 6, so we'll end our discussion of component states for now and learn about application state. It is sufficient to understand that everything we talk about in this chapter applies just as well to individual components and their skins as it does to entire applications. Now, let's see how states are used to define the visuals for the states of an application.

4.2   States syntax

The state of an application or a component in your application is stored as the value of the currentState property of that object. UIComponent and all of its subclasses have a currentState property, so any component in your application has a notion of "state" that can be defined and set. The way that you define information about the states is by declaring the names of states that currentState can have and by declaring different values for objects in these different states.

You put state information in your MXML code in two places: in the states block and the objects that have state-specific values.

4.3 The states block

The states block consists of an array of `State` declarations that are used in the object in which they are declared. For example, a states block that lists two states, `s1` and `s2`, looks like this:

```
<s:states>
    <s:State name="s1"/>
    <s:State name="s2"/>
</s:states>
```

In this snippet of code, the `states` tag declares the states block and each of the `State` tags declare a separate, named state. The value of the `name` property is important because it is used elsewhere in the code when creating state-specific values.

Sometimes, you may find it helpful to group states together to make it easier to declare state values that span several states. For example, you might have a panel which is the same size in several, but not all, states. Instead of setting that size for each state individually, you can specify the same `stateGroups` value for each of the states where that value is the same and use that single group to define the panel's size. The `stateGroups` property is simply a list of strings defining which "groups" a state belongs to. In the sample code below, from the demo `StateGroups`, four named states are collected into two state groups:

```
(File: StateGroups.mxml)
<s:states>
    <s:State name="s1" stateGroups="stateGroupA"/>
    <s:State name="s2" stateGroups="stateGroupA"/>
    <s:State name="s3" stateGroups="stateGroupB"/>
    <s:State name="s4" stateGroups="stateGroupB"/>
</s:states>
```

In this code, the first two states are in `stateGroupA` and the other two are in `stateGroupB`. When we refer to states in our object tags, which we will see later, we can use either the state names directly or, if it is more convenient, the state group names.

One important point to remember about the states block is that the first state in the list declares the state in which the application starts. So in both of our examples above, the application starts in state s1. This point comes in handy when defining values for objects; if you set a property to a value that is specific to that starting state, that property will have that value when the application starts. On the other hand, if there is no state-specific value assigned to that property, then the property will start out with its default value (either the non-state-specific value declared if there is one (*e.g.*, x="5"), or else whatever the default value is for that property on the object). In any case, just be aware that the first state in the states block determines the starting values for your objects and the initial view that the user sees.

4.4 Setting state values

The real functionality and power of states comes when we set state-specific values. Panels may exist in some states and go away in others. Buttons may have different locations, sizes, or text depending on the application state. Components may have different looks depending on whether the mouse is hovering over or pressing on them. These changes are encoded in the objects whose values change between states, using a simple syntax to define the different state values.

State values are set using a special syntax that is understood by the compiler, so keywords that are meaningful to the states mechanism are not actually properties on the objects themselves. For example, the includeIn and excludeFrom keywords (which we will discuss in Section 4.5) are used inside tags for objects that do not have properties with those names. Instead, the compiler sees those keywords and creates the appropriate state data.

Similarly, the syntax for specifying state-specific values (that we will also see later), such as x.s2="100", uses state syntax that is meaningful to the compiler (*e.g.*, ".s2"), but not to the object itself. So don't go looking for properties on UIComponent with these names; just know that it is some magic sauce added by the compiler when dealing with MXML code. It is this compiler magic that makes the state syntax in Flex 4 so much easier to use than the prior state syntax.

There are two categories of state information set on the affected objects: state inclusion and state values. These will be described in the remaining two sections of this chapter.

4.5 State inclusion

Often, you may want to define states in which an object exists,[1] or, conversely, states in which it does not. For example, you may want a button to be visible when the application starts up in state s1, but to go away when the application changes to state s2. To set this existence information, you use the includeIn or excludeFrom properties on the object.

The includeIn property lists the states in which the object exists; it does not exist in any other states that are not named in that list. Conversely, the excludeFrom property lists those states in which the object does *not* exist; the object exists only in states that are not in that list. You should only use one of these properties on any given object, not both.

Let's look at an example from the application SearchMe that we saw earlier in this chapter. When the user types a string into the text input box and clicks Search, the application brings up a second screen with the results:

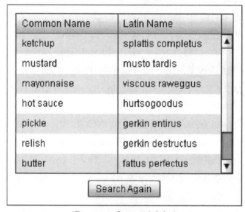

(Demo: SearchMe)

---

[1] When I talk about an object's "existence" in a state, I mean something different than simple visibility. If you want to control the visibility of a Button, for example, you can set its visible property to true (visible) or false (invisible), or you can set its alpha property somewhere between 0 (completely transparent) and 1 (completely opaque). But whether an object "exists" in a state is determined by whether the object is present in the display hierarchy of the application. For example, a Button exists in state s1 if it is a child element of its container in that state (and if the container also exists, on up the display tree). Conversely, that Button does not exist if is is not parented to any existing container in the hierarchy. With no parent in the display hierarchy, the object is not part of the hierarchy and therefore does not exist in it. It might be more correct to say "parented" instead of "exists," but I find existence a bit easier to explain.

This results screen, just like the search screen of the application, is created using states to define which elements are visible. First of all, we define the two states that we will use:

(File: SearchMe.mxml)

```
<s:states>
    <s:State name="searchScreen"/>
    <s:State name="resultsScreen"/>
</s:states>
```

Next, the includeIn syntax is used to declare which elements are visible in each state. The label, text input, and search button only exist in the searchScreen state, so they are defined together in a Group that is only included in that state:

```
<s:Group includeIn="searchScreen">
    <s:Label x="107" y="66" text="Food Item"
        fontSize="18" fontWeight="bold"/>
    <s:TextInput id="searchInput" x="86" y="91"/>
    <s:Button x="115" y="121" label="Search"
        enabled="{searchInput.text != ''}"
        click="runSearch()"/>
</s:Group>
```

Similarly, the results screen includes a DataGrid with the results, along with a button that lets the user return to the search screen:

```
<s:Group includeIn="resultsScreen">
    <mx:DataGrid x="10" y="10" width="280" height="201"
                dataProvider="{results}">
        <mx:columns>
            <mx:DataGridColumn headerText="Common Name"
                            dataField="name"/>
            <mx:DataGridColumn headerText="Latin Name"
                            dataField="latin"/>
        </mx:columns>
    </mx:DataGrid>
    <s:Button x="104" y="219" label="Search Again"
            click="currentState = 'searchScreen'"/>
</s:Group>
```

95

With these groups defined to exist in their respective states, Flex takes care of displaying the right GUI state at the right time. When the user clicks on the Search button, the application's `currentState` is set to `resultsScreen`. This causes the elements that are included only in the `searchScreen` to go away and the elements that are included in the `resultsScreen` to appear.

4.6   State-specific property values

Now that we've seen how to automate adding and removing objects from the scene, let's see how to automate changing property values between states. The idea and the syntax here are quite simple: properties have default values and you can add state-specific qualifiers to those property names to specify different values in specific states. The syntax uses the property name, followed by a period, followed by the name of a state or state group in which that property will take on the given value. For example, to set the value of x to 100 in state s1, you write `x.s1="100"`. This is far easier to understand in code, so let's look at an example, SearchMe2.

The SearchMe2 example is very similar to the earlier SearchMe example except that some elements are shared between the screens. In particular, we would like the user to be able to perform another search on the results screen without having to return to the initial search screen, so the text input and the search button will live in both states. But since these elements were in the middle of the screen in the initial `searchScreen` state, we'll have to move them out of the way to make room for the results screen. Here's what the new results screen looks like:

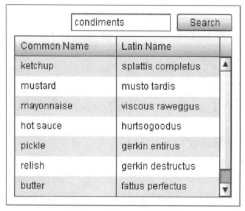

(Demo: SearchMe2)

To create this screen, we define our search screen elements a bit differently. For one thing, there is no surrounding Group that is included only in the searchScreen. Instead, we just have one element, the Label, which is included only in that state:

(File: SearchMe2.mxml)

```
<s:Label x="107" y="66" text="Food Item"
    fontSize="18" fontWeight="bold"
    includeIn="searchScreen"/>
```

We then define the text input component and the button, which now exist in both screens, to take on different position values in the two states:

```
<s:TextInput id="searchInput" x="86" y="91"
    x.resultsScreen="84" y.resultsScreen="10"/>
<s:Button x="115" y="121" label="Search"
    enabled="{searchInput.text != ''}"
    click="runSearch()"
    x.resultsScreen="220" y.resultsScreen="10"/>
```

Here, the input and the button both have default values for x and y. These define the location of the elements in the first state. But these objects also have x and y values defined that are state-specific for the resultsScreen state. These values are set on the x and y properties when the application enters into the resultsScreen state. In this way, the application defines, in a declarative way, the values that these shared elements' properties have in both states. The Flex states engine handles setting these property values whenever the application changes state.

And that's it. All this talk about how powerful the states mechanisms is and it's just a matter of some include/exclude statements and some dot-state-name property declarations. Of course, a lot is happening under the hood. The compiler is turning these simple declarations into more involved data structures internally, and the internal Flex runtime logic that changes the property and style values when states change is fairly involved, but you don't have to worry about that. You just define what your components are like in the different states of your application and you're done. Then you let Flex take care of the details of making it work correctly.

Conclusion

States are a powerful, declarative system for defining the different logical states that an application, or even a single component, can be in when the application runs. They are useful for defining anything from the different screens that a user may see during the course of using the application to the different states that a button may be in when the user hovers over it or presses it. They help define the visual differences between these states in a simple way so that you can structure your code according to how things look in the different states.

When combined with state transitions, which enable easy animations between these states, states become even more powerful, enabling the developer to create a smooth, seamless experience for the user, keeping them connected to the application. That's the subject of the next chapter.

Chapter 5

Transitions

Getting lost is always a frustrating experience. You end up wasting so much time and energy just figuring out where you are and what to do about it. Getting lost in a GUI is even worse, because it's so unnecessary.

Transitions can help.

State transitions can help your user understand where they are, how they got there, and what's happening next. By animating changes in GUI state, they help keep the user connected to the application. They help keep the user from getting lost.

5.1 Don't lose the user

How often have you found yourself using an application, or navigating a website, and the entire UI changes out from under you and you have to figure out what's where and what do do about it? The "Submit" button moved, the shopping cart total scrolled off the page, and the search results now cover the area where you thought you were supposed to enter refining search terms. This is unfortunately a common experience with GUI applications. When the application changes to a new screen, even if the new screen shares elements with the previous one, the typical application erases the current information and draws the new UI in its place, forcing the user to do the hard work of parsing all of the information in the new GUI.

This is why Flex transitions were invented; to take the user along for the ride, bringing them smoothly between the screens and states of the application. Transitions enable you to animate changes in state, which helps your users understand the changes as they happen. Applications must alter the information on the screen often during the course of being used. The more that you can bring your user along with the UI as these changes occur, the faster they will be able to understand what they need to do and the more productive they will be.

> Transitions are one of the most powerful UI mechanisms in Flex, since they enable the user to stay constantly connected to the application experience.

Transitions work hand in hand with states, which we discussed in Chapter 4. States in Flex are a powerful way to set up the changing behavior of your application. But the combination of states plus transitions makes for very compelling user experiences. Transitions provide a way to give a smooth, continuous experience to the user as they navigate the application between different states. Repositioned objects glide into their new locations, objects that go away fade out, objects that appear do so gradually. Animations can be used for every change to help the user understand the differences in the new screen.

Flex transitions make it easy to animate changes in GUI state to help the user more readily understand what these changes are. You simply declare states, define what components exist in each state and what values properties should have in each state, then define transitions between the states.

5.2   States and transitions

It might help to picture what transitions are used for. Applications typically consist of different views as the user progresses through the flow of the application. This includes different views of components as they change state (for example, a button that is depressed looks different than one that is not) as well as different screens of the overall application UI as the application changes state (for example, a search screen that accepts input and is then replaced by a results screen).

In the last example in the previous chapter, SearchMe2, we have two screens. The first screen has a label, text input box, and button:

(Demo: SearchMeTransition)

On the next screen, the label has gone away, but the input and button exist in a different location, and they are joined by a list of results:

condiments	Search

Common Name	Latin Name
ketchup	splattis completus
mustard	musto tardis
mayonnaise	viscous raweggus
hot sauce	hurtsogoodus
pickle	gerkin entirus
relish	gerkin destructus
butter	fattus perfectus

This application does not use transitions, so when it runs the label disappears, the text input and button jump to their new location, and the results suddenly appear. This change results in a discontinuous experience and the user may be left wondering how they got here and what they should do now.

We could, instead, animate those changes to make it easier to understand what's happening when the state changes. Instead of blinking the label out suddenly, we could fade it out gradually. Once the label is gone, we could move the input and button into their new locations. These animations help the user understand that the input and button are the same ones they used on the first screen. Meanwhile, instead of having the list of results mysteriously

101

pop onto the screen when the state changes, we could fade it in, helping the user to understand that it came into existence during, and because of, the change to the new state.

The resulting transition approach is in the SearchMeTransition application; we'll see the code for this later in this chapter.

Many more kinds of state changes can be transitioned, and they can be animated in a myriad of ways (many of which we will see later in the Effects chapters). But the important point for now is that we not only *can* animate these states, but that in many cases we *should* animate them, to help the user stay connected to the application. And even better, that Flex transitions make these state animations very easy.

Two elements are key to using transitions: the Transition object itself and the animation effect[1] that the transition plays.

5.3   The Transition class

The Transition class has very few properties. Its main purpose in life is to be a holder for the animation effect that will play when the state changes. But a few other important properties exist that determine when and how the transition effect plays.

The fromState and toState properties

The fromState and toState properties determine when a transition plays. The possible values for these properties are the state names specified in the states block. One other possible value is "*" which means "any state." If neither property is set for a Transition, or if both are set to "*," then the transition plays when any state change occurs (if no other transition is specified for that from/to state change). If either or both properties are set, then the transition plays when the state being transitioned from, to, or from-and-to are the same as the states named in these properties. For example,

---

[1] The topic of *effects* is a bit premature, because we have not yet talked about Flex effects, which are the mechanism used for animations in Flex. But describing how to use effects ends up requiring knowledge of transitions, so one of them had to come first. It's like looking up *engineer* in the dictionary and reading "see geek," then flipping to *geek* and reading "see engineer." Some concepts are just inseparable. If this ordering doesn't work for you, just flip ahead a few pages, read about effects in Chapters 9, 10, and 11, then come back here and catch up on transitions. Or be patient and realize that I explain the animation stuff eventually. In the meantime, I'll keep things pretty simple in this chapter.

if only toState is set, then the transition plays whenever a change occurs from any state to the state named in toState. Transitions that set these properties are of higher priority than ones that do not, so that you may have a catch-all transition that plays if no other state-specific transition kicks in, but transitions with fromState/toState values are chosen first.

For example, in the following code the second transition plays when a change occurs from any state into state s2. All other state changes cause the first transition to play:

```
<s:transitions>
    <s:Transition>
        . . .
    </s:Transition>
    <s:Transition toState="s2">
        . . .
    </s:Transition>
</s:transitions>
```

The autoReverse **property**

The autoReverse boolean flag tells the transition mechanism whether it should automatically stop and play a reverse transition if a transition that is currently running is interrupted by the opposite state change. That reverse transition is played from the point in time when the current transition stopped. For example, if an auto-reversing transition is currently playing from state s1 to state s2 and a change sets the current state back to s1, then the system plays the s2 to s1 transition from that interrupted time, if such a reverse transition exists.

Typically, a state change occurs, a transition plays, and life goes on. But sometimes, a transition may be in the middle of playing when a user or other action causes a state change to the state that the component just came from. For example, the mouse may move over a button, causing a change to the over state of that button from the previous up state. Suppose a transition exists to that over state, which plays for a half second. During that time, the user moves the mouse out of that button, causing a state change back to the up state. Both transitions can't play at the same time; that would tell the button to animate toward the over and the up state at the same time, and the results wouldn't be pretty. So Flex stops the current transition and starts the new one instead.

Prior to Flex 4, the states mechanism would simply end the previous transition and start the new one from the beginning. This is alright in many situations, but can be rather disruptive as we jump forward to the end of some effect and then start the new one. So the `autoReverse` flag was introduced in Flex 4 to create a more seamless way of turning transitions around.

When this flag is `true`, the current transition stops where it is at and the reversing transition starts from that same point (but going in the opposite direction).[2] For example, if a component is halfway through a transition moving it from x = 0 to x = 100 in the first transition and receives a message to transition back to x = 0, then the first transition stops when the button is at x = 50 and the reversing transition starts with x at that same value. The net effect is that the user sees the button stopping and turning around in place to go back to where it came from, which is much more of the experience they expect when they cause a reverse transition.

Two important caveats with `autoReverse` are important to keep in mind:

The reverse transition must exist. Flex does not actually create the reverse transition (or any other transition) for you; you have to create it yourself. So when you tell a transition that you want it to `autoReverse`, you are not telling it "figure out how to reverse when necessary," but rather "if a reverse transition exists, then start it from your stopping point if you are interrupted by it."[3]

The reverse transition must be the exact opposite. The reversing mechanism makes assumptions about the duration of both transitions; it will start playing the reverse transition at the same time as the forward transition stopped, but only if their durations are equal. For example,

---

[2] Under the hood, it's a bit more complicated. The first transition is actually ended, just as before. It ends the effect and snaps all of the values to their end positions. Then the next transition is started from the beginning, just as if the `autoReverse` flag didn't exist. But then this second transition is fast-forwarded to the same point in time as the first transition stopped at and started from that point. And since all of this is done synchronously on the single Flex thread, the user does not see any screen updates during this stop/end/start/fast-forward process, so it looks to them just as I've described it here; the reverse transition starts where the first transition ended.

[3] Automatically creating the reverse transition has been proposed as a feature for some future version of Flex, so perhaps this constraint will go away eventually. But that's not the case in Flex 4, so it's an important thing to keep in mind.

104

if a transition with a duration of 1000 milliseconds is interrupted three fourths of the way through, when it has played for 750 milliseconds, then it will start the reverse transition at the reciprocal time of one fourth of its duration. If that reverse transition also has a duration of 1000 milliseconds, then it will start 250 milliseconds into it. But if that transition has a much different duration, say 2000 milliseconds, then it will start further into it (500 milliseconds in this case), because it is only looking at the reciprocal of the proportion elapsed of the first transition. So make sure your transition effects have the same durations if they are to be reverses of each other.

Also, reverse transitions should really perform the same actions in reverse to make sure that automatically reversing will not look incorrect. For example, if a forward transition is moving then resizing an object, then the reverse transition should first resize the object, then move it. Otherwise, if the forward transition is stopped in the middle and the reverse transition is played, it will probably jump to a completely different action than the one that it was in the middle of, causing a jarring effect for the user. This requirement extends to things like start delays, where you may need to use effects like `Pause` that simply delay execution or ending of the transition effect to make it the exact opposite in functionality and timing of its reverse transition effect.

The `effect` property

This property holds the animation effect that the transition will play during the state change. We are about to discuss this topic in the next section, right about ... now.

5.4   Transition effects

The `effect` property of `Transition` defines the animation that will run when the transition is played. A transition has a just one single effect, although as we will see in Chapter 11, we can compose several effects into one overall effect through the use of composite effects.

The transition effect brings the power of states and animations together to make it easy for you to create smooth flows between states of applications, components, and arbitrary objects in the scene. The "easy" factor comes from a transition effect's ability to automatically pick up the changed values between states, without you having to specify any values. Also, that transition effect plays automatically when the state change occurs, without any extra code. As long as there is a transition declared, that transition will play whenever a relevant state change occurs.

Rather than you keeping track of the positions of an object in different states and telling a Move effect the values for those positions, you can merely declare a Move effect in the transition with no from/to values. That effect automatically determines the position change and runs the animation appropriately. Let's look at an example.

In the first state of the SimpleTransition application, the button is at the upper left of the window:

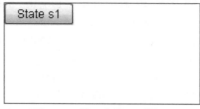

(Demo: SimpleTransition)

In the next state, the button is shifted over to the right:

The button changes location by setting state-specific values for x:

(File: SimpleTransition.mxml)
```
<s:states>
    <s:State name="s1"/>
    <s:State name="s2"/>
</s:states>
<s:Button id="button" x="0" x.s2="100"
    label="State s1" label.s2="State s2"
    click="currentState=(currentState=='s1') ? 's2' : 's1'"/>
```

This code says that the button normally lives at x = 0, but when the state changes to s2, it will be at x = 100. We then define a transition to move the button smoothly from 0 to 100 like this:

```
<s:transitions>
    <s:Transition>
        <s:Move target="{button}"/>
    </s:Transition>
</s:transitions>
```

Note, first of all, that the Move effect (which we will discuss in more detail in Chapter 9) in the code above does not give any details about *where* to move the button from and to. It simply tells the transition to move the button. When the transition plays, the transition detects where the button currently is and where it will be in the state that it is transitioning to. The transition then feeds that information into the Move effect as the values to animate between.

Through the magic of states and transitions, we get this automatic animation behavior for free. All we have to do is declare *what kind* of animation we want to have during a transition and which objects that animation acts on, and the transition takes care of figuring out how to run that animation.

 Use effects without hard-coded from/to values in your transitions; they will pick up the animation values from the states.

Also note in the previous code, just for completeness, that we have only a single transition defined, and that it plays when any state change occurs because no values are assigned to the `fromState` and `toState` properties.

5.5   Example: search transition

Now that we've seen the basics of how transition effects work, let's go back to our earlier example of the simple search application. On one screen we have the label, `searchLabel`, defined in that single state as follows:

(File: SearchMeTransition.mxml)
```
<s:Label id="searchLabel"
    x="107" y="66"
```

107

```
text="Food Item" fontSize="18"
fontWeight="bold" includeIn="searchScreen"/>
```

We also have the `searchInput` and `searchButton` elements that are located in different x and y positions in the two states:

```
<s:TextInput id="searchInput" x="86" y="91"
    x.resultsScreen="84" y.resultsScreen="10"/>
<s:Button id="searchButton" x="115" y="121" label="Search"
    enabled="{searchInput.text != ''}"
    click="runSearch()"
    x.resultsScreen="220" y.resultsScreen="10"/>
```

Finally, we have the `searchResults` data grid, which only exists in the resultsScreen state:

```
<mx:DataGrid id="searchResults"
            includeIn="resultsScreen"
            x="10" y="38" width="280" height="202"
            dataProvider="{results}">
    <mx:columns>
        <mx:DataGridColumn headerText="Common Name"
                dataField="name"/>
        <mx:DataGridColumn headerText="Latin Name"
                dataField="latin"/>
    </mx:columns>
</mx:DataGrid>
```

I'd like a transition effect that fades the label out, moves the input and button elements into place, and fades the results list in. If all of these ran at the same time, the screen would be a mess, with the various elements moving and fading all on top of one another. While simultaneous animations are appropriate in some situations, they don't work as well when the target objects are in the same area, especially when their actions are different (for example, fading versus moving).

 Animations on different objects may work better if sequenced after one another if the objects overlap or the animations are very different in nature.

I'll stagger the animations instead. First, the label will fade out. Once it is gone, the input and button elements have a clear field to move up to the top of the screen. And once those objects are out of the way, the results list can be faded into place. Here is the resulting transition:

```
<s:Transition toState="resultsScreen">
    <s:Sequence>
        <s:Fade target="{searchLabel}"/>
        <s:Move targets="{[searchInput,searchButton]}"/>
        <s:AddAction target="{searchResults}"/>
        <s:Fade target="{searchResults}"/>
    </s:Sequence>
</s:Transition>
```

Here, the transition runs automatically when `currentState` is changed to `resultsScreen`. A Sequence effect is used to stagger the animations to run one after the other (we will see more about sequencing animations in Chapter 11).

First, we run a `Fade` effect on the `searchLabel`. It fades out automatically because the transition knows that it is going away between these states.

Next we run a `Move` effect on the input and button to shift them to their new locations. This effect picks up the locations of the elements automatically and moves them to their correct positions in the new state.

Next we run an `AddAction` effect on the `resultsList` object. We'll learn more about this effect in Chapter 11, but it's there to keep the results list from appearing until we're ready to fade it in. Now that the results list is ready, we `Fade` it in. Again, `Fade` knows that it needs to fade the object in, not out, because the transition knows that the object is coming into existence, so `Fade` automatically does the right thing.

Now we've gone from an application that suddenly painted a new GUI screen to one that transitions smoothly to the new screen. Play with the application to see how it works in practice.

5.6 Example: `TransitionMultiple`

Let's look at one more example of a transition effect, `TransitionMultiple`. This time we again use a transition effect that acts upon several objects in the

GUI. We also create transitions that run both to and from the second state, to see how they differ.

In this application, we have three buttons and a panel. In the default state, s1, the three buttons are stacked up at the top, left of the screen. There is also a panel, but it is not yet visible in this state:[4]

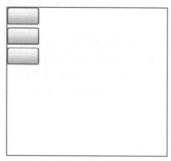

(Demo: TransitionMultiple)

In the other state, s2, the panel has entered and now occupies the same top, left area that the buttons previously did. Meanwhile, the buttons have moved to take up positions at the top/right, bottom/right, and bottom/left corners of the panel,[5] as seen here:

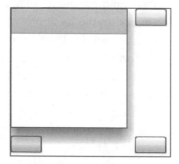

Here is the code for this UI. You can see how the property values for the panel and the buttons are declared in both the s1 and s2 states:

---

[4] It could be that the panel is too shy. But it is more probable that the buttons are in the way and the panel is waiting politely, as panels do.

[5] It's not clear whether the buttons were upset at being dislodged by the panel, but they are certainly keeping the poor panel hemmed in on all sides.

(File: TransitionMultiple.mxml)

```
<s:Button id="button1" x="0" x.s2="160" y="0" width="40"
    click="currentState=(currentState=='s1') ? 's2' : 's1'"/>
<s:Button id="button2" x="0" x.s2="160"
    y="25" y.s2="160" width="40"/>
<s:Button id="button3" x="0" y="50" y.s2="160" width="40"/>
<s:Panel id="panel" includeIn="s2" width="150" height="150"/>
```

In order to make room for the panel, the buttons have to move out of the way. This transition could work many different ways, but one reasonable approach is to move the buttons first, then fade the panel in. Or, going in reverse, fade the panel out and then move the buttons back to the upper-left.

To do this, we create a Sequence effect, which plays its "child" effects (the effects declared inside the Sequence) one after the other. The three child effects playing in the sequence are Move, AddAction, and Fade. The Move is responsible for moving the buttons out of the way. The AddAction is a helper effect that delays adding the panel to the scene until we are ready (since we do not want it suddenly appearing before the buttons have moved out of the way). Finally, the Fade effect fades in the panel. Here is the code for the transition to state s2:

```
<s:Transition toState="s2" autoReverse="true">
    <s:Sequence>
        <s:Move targets="{[button1, button2, button3]}"/>
        <s:AddAction target="{panel}"/>
        <s:Fade target="{panel}"/>
    </s:Sequence>
</s:Transition>
```

You should note a couple of important things in this code. First, the child effects act on different targets: the Move effect acts on the three buttons, while the other two effects act exclusively on the panel. The Sequence effect is merely an ordering of different effects and does not constrain its child effects to act on the same objects. Second, note that nowhere do we specify the values that we are animating from and to; these are derived entirely from the state information. For example, since button1 has an x location of 0 in the first state and 320 in the second state, then the Move effect will automatically

111

animate button1.x from 0 to 320.[6] Similarly, the Fade effect automatically determines the proper from/to values to fade the object in; it detects that the panel does not exist in the first state and does exist in the second, so it animates the transparency of the panel from fully transparent to fully opaque when it runs.

The code for the reverse transition is similar. The only differences are that the order of the child effects is different (we fade the panel out first and *then* move the buttons back) and that the AddAction effect is no longer needed because the panel goes away, so we don't need to tell the Sequence when it should be added into its container.[7] Here is the code:

```
<s:Transition toState="s1" autoReverse="true">
    <s:Sequence>
        <s:Fade target="{panel}"/>
        <s:Move targets="{[button1, button2, button3]}"/>
    </s:Sequence>
</s:Transition>
```

I have been intentionally vague here about how Flex effects actually work, because some large and interesting chapters are coming up that cover the details about effects in general and I don't want to spoil the surprise. The main point to understand for now is that a state change may cause a transition to fire, and that transition plays its effect with the values it picks up from the current state change.

---

[6] Note, too, that the other buttons are all animating from/to different values; just because the targets are specified in the same effect does not mean that they are constrained to use the same from/to values when they are derived from the state information

[7] Actually, there is a bit more here than meets the eye. It is sometimes necessary, when transitioning an object out of the scene, to use a RemoveAction effect. This effect is the opposite of the AddAction effect that we saw in the previous code snippet and tells the Sequence when its target object should be removed. By default, an object that exists in the previous state but not in the next state is automatically removed at the beginning of the transition, when all non-animated state changes occur. However, the Fade effect has logic about removing and adding items that makes it automatically keep its target object around until it is done fading it out, so the RemoveAction effect is not necessary in this particular transition. However, if the Fade effect was not at the beginning of the transition, a RemoveAction effect *would* be necessary, because the Fade would not make the object stick around from the beginning of the Sequence, but rather just for the time that the Fade is operating on the object. You'll read more about this in Chapter 11.

Conclusion

Transitions are one of my favorite things about the Flex platform. In a world where many platforms make animations hard to figure out, or difficult to use, or impossible to get right, transitions make it possible to get very powerful animated effects automatically by requiring only that the developer tell the system what they want to animate (*e.g.*, `button1`) and how (*e.g.*, `Move`), and the transition system itself figures out the details of how that object changes between states and runs the animations to get it there. It's a simple, declarative way of getting very rich GUI effects.

 Transitions make it possible to get very powerful animated effects automatically.

The next chapter covers some fundamental ideas behind animation.

Chapter 6

Skinning Components

You want your application to be familiar to users and yet be special. Flex 4 makes it much easier to customize the look of any component in a way that simply wasn't possible before. In this chapter, we'll take a look at how components interact with their skins, how you can write simple skins that perform the basic functions that components need, and how you can create completely custom component skins to get your own unique look and feel.

One of the major themes behind the whole Flex 4 release is the new component model. In Flex 4 the control of each component has been separated from its appearance. The component is now responsible for the logic of its behavior (like what a Button does when it is clicked). The component's skin is responsible for the visual appearance of the component (like what the Button's border looks like).

During the development of Flex 4, there was plenty of feedback from the Flex developer community requesting a simple mechanism to change individual, common attributes of components. The result was that the team exposed style attributes for common cases, but made custom skinning the way to go for everything else.[1]

---

[1] For example, the text color of a Button or Label is exposed as the color style. The chromeColor style lets you change the overall theme color used by a component. These are just CSS style properties that can be set either directly on the component in MXML or through CSS styling.

6.1   Components and their skins

My first task while working on the Flex 4 release was to write the new `ScrollBar` class under the new component model. When this was done, I wanted to verify that the new component really could have a custom skin that wasn't just some variation on the horizontal and vertical scrollbars that are usually used.

I wrote a `CircularScrollBar` component, whose track was a circle and whose thumb button moved back and forth along that circular track. It was a truly useless component; I can't imagine why someone would need a circular scrollbar. But the project provided a nice sanity-check that someone could, in fact, write visuals that were completely separate from the underlying logic of the component.

All components are subclasses of `UIComponent`. This means that they all share the basic elements of position, size, and events that the base class offers. But whereas in Flex 3, the components contained all of the code to display themselves (like a Button knew how to draw its border, background, and label), Flex 4 components are instead invisible objects that just handle the logic and placement of the component. The component's skin, which is a child display object of the component, is responsible for what the component looks like.

This separation enables the component to be more modular and to load the visuals from a separate object. In particular, it allows you, the application developer, to define how a component looks in a skin class and then provide that object to the component. This means that you can benefit from all of the controlling logic in the component, which you *really* don't want to rewrite yourself, while being able to completely customize the appearance of that component.

Instead of just talking about this, let's skin a `Button`, from the application `ButtonButton`. The top button looks the way you'd expect a Flex button to look and the bottom looks just like a label:

Standard Button
Just a Label Button

(Demo: ButtonButton)

As you can see in the code, the top button in the VGroup uses the default button skin and the other uses a custom skin named JustaLabelSkin:

(File: ButtonButton.mxml)
```
<s:VGroup horizontalCenter="0" verticalCenter="0">
    <s:Button label="Standard Button"/>
    <s:Button label="Just a Label Button"
        skinClass="skins.JustaLabelSkin"/>
</s:VGroup>
```

JustaLabelSkin uses the Skin object to define a group of objects in a component's skin in much the same way we use a Group object, the base container object in Flex:

(File: skins/JustaLabelSkin.mxml)
```
<?xml version="1.0" encoding="utf-8"?>
<s:Skin xmlns:fx="http://ns.adobe.com/mxml/2009"
    xmlns:s="library://ns.adobe.com/flex/spark">
    <fx:Metadata>
        [HostComponent("spark.components.Button")]
    </fx:Metadata>
    <s:states>
        <s:State name="up"/>
        <s:State name="over"/>
        <s:State name="down"/>
        <s:State name="disabled"/>
    </s:states>
    <s:Label id="labelDisplay"/>
</s:Skin>
```

This Skin file contains three important elements:

- the host component metadata,

- the states of the skin, and

- the skin parts, in this case the Label element.

In the next section we'll look at each of these elements that make up the skin.

117

6.2   The skin's elements

Any given component has a data connection that the skin can set up to grab information from its host component, a set of skin states that it expects, and a set of *parts*. These three items combine to form a contract between components and their skins.

Skin data

The first element of the component/skin contract is the data connection, which is used by the skin to retrieve data from the component. This connection is established when the skin defines some metadata that associates a hostComponent object with a particular component class. From the button example above, a connection is established from the button's skin back to the button component with this code:

```
<fx:Metadata>
    [HostComponent("spark.components.Button")]
</fx:Metadata>
```

Once this connection between skin and component is made, the skin can request data from its component, which is now available to the skin as the property called hostComponent. For example, a different version of the current skin class, JustaLabelSkin2, populates the label element of the skin with data from the hostComponent, as follows:

```
(File: skins/JustaLabelSkin2.mxml)
<s:Label text="{hostComponent.label}"/>
```

In this variation on the button skin, the label gets its text value from its button component directly, by binding to the button's label property via the hostComponent property. Compare this approach to the one in the previous skin where the label got its value by using the skin part id, labelDisplay. You can think of these two techniques as *push* versus *pull*; the button *pushing* data into the skin via skin parts versus the skin *pulling* data from the component via the hostComponent property. Both approaches work, but use different techniques to get information from one side of the component/skin gap to the other.

Be sure to add this hostComponent metadata to your skins. Even if your skin code does not access the hostComponent property directly, it still needs the metadata because Flex may need to use hostComponent internally. Also, declaring the hostComponent metadata ensures some extra compile-time checking between the component and the skin.

Skin states

A Button is put into different operational states depending on user actions. The user may mouse over the button, click on the button, or release the button. On the other hand, the button may be disabled, in which case it ignores any of these states.

As the user moves the mouse around the application UI, the button may enter into one of these states. The skin must be able to respond to that change and display the appropriate information. Even if the skin does not define graphics that are any different in any of these states, as in the example, these standard states need to be defined in the skin so that the Flex Button object can set the state value.

Part of the component/skin contract is that the skin must support the set of states that the component may use on the skin. The expected skin states are documented in metadata on the component and are reflected in the ASDocs for that class. For example, the Button class in Flex defines the four skin states up, over, down, and disabled:

```
[SkinState("up")]
[SkinState("over")]
[SkinState("down")]
[SkinState("disabled")]
```

Here's how the example button skin JustaLabelSkin fulfills this contract:

```
<s:states>
    <s:State name="up"/>
    <s:State name="over"/>
    <s:State name="down"/>
    <s:State name="disabled"/>
</s:states>
```

Even though state changes do not affect JustaLabelSkin, that skin file must still declare the required states. You'll see in Section 6.6 how to react to state changes in a component.

Skin parts

If you're going to skin a button, scroll bar, or other component, you need to know which elements are available to customize. Some components may have certain visuals that they depend on for performing whatever functionality is core to the component, or which they use if the parts are there. For example, a ScrollBar has logic about positioning a thumb part on a track part, if either part is available in the skin. These elements in the skin are called *skin parts* and are defined in the component.

Here, for example, is the part metadata from the ButtonBase class (the superclass of Button):

```
[SkinPart(required="false")]
public var labelDisplay:TextBase;
```

In this code, the component says that an optional part with the name of labelDisplay exists that must be of type TextBase (which is a superclass of Label, the component used in the JustaLabelSkin example).

A skin written for a component must, by this contract, supply any skin parts with appropriate names that are required and may also in addition supply any optional skin parts. These parts must all be of the type specified by the component.

Here's the sole skin part in the JustaLabelSkin file:

```
<s:Label id="labelDisplay"/>
```

The labelDisplay object, while not required, certainly makes the button more useful, since it displays the content of the Button component's label property, and since it is the only graphical element in the skin.[2] The name of this object, labelDisplay, is important. The Button component looks for an element of the required type in the skin with that id and, if it exists, sets its text property to be the text of the button's label property.

6.3 Better button skins

Our custom button skin in the previous example leaves much to be desired. In fact, the "button" doesn't really look like a button; it's really just a label

---

[2] A button with no visual elements at all would be truly useless. Maybe there's a corollary to the classic "if a tree falls in the forest" philosophical question; if a component has no visuals, is it really in the interface?

with some hidden button logic. A little graphics would go a long way toward fixing that problem. In fact, without some graphics to define the bounds of the button, we can't even tell what that button area is.

Let's explore how to make more interesting skins to result in better looking and more interactive components.

One of the powerful things about the new component model in Flex 4 is that the look of the component is really up to you. With the new MXML graphics tags, the easy state syntax, and the flexibility of declarative markup, you can define arbitrarily simple or complex skins, depending on what you want the component to look like. As long as you obey the skin's contract with its component that I described in the previous section, everything else is up to you.

For the rest of this chapter, we're going to develop incrementally better, or just different, skins for the button. To visualize the changes better, I created the `ButtonSkinSampler` application, which is like a playground for experimenting with new skins. This application has a single button in the middle of the window that uses the currently selected button skin. A `DropDownList` in the upper right of the window allows the user to choose between different skins for the button:

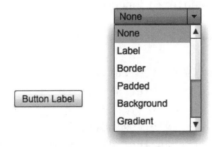

(Demo: ButtonSkinSampler)

Here's the code to place the button and the skin drop-down list:

(File: ButtonSkinSampler.mxml)
```
<s:Button id="button" label="Button Label"
    horizontalCenter="0" verticalCenter="0"/>
<s:DropDownList id="skinList" right="10" top="10"
    dataProvider="{skinDP}" selectedIndex="0"
        change="skinChangeHandler()"/>
```

121

The skin list is created with a `dataProvider` that is initialized in script code:

```
[Bindable]
public var skinDP:ArrayCollection = new ArrayCollection(
  [{label:"None", skinClass:null},
   {label:"Label", skinClass:skins.JustaLabelSkin},
   {label:"Border", skinClass:skins.BorderSkin},
   {label:"Padded", skinClass:skins.PaddedBorderSkin},
   {label:"Background", skinClass:skins.SolidBackgroundSkin},
   {label:"Gradient", skinClass:skins.GradientBackgroundSkin},
   {label:"Rounded", skinClass:skins.RoundedSkin},
   {label:"Shadowed", skinClass:skins.ShadowedSkin},
   {label:"Stateful", skinClass:skins.StatefulSkin},
   {label:"Fun", skinClass:skins.FunButtonSkin},
   {label:"Animated", skinClass:skins.AnimatedSkin}]);
```

Each item in the `dataProvider` list has both a `label`, which is the text that is displayed in the drop-down list for that item, and a `skinClass`, which is a reference to the skin class that is set on the button when that drop-down item is selected. The skin class is set when the drop-down list changes, with a call to the `skinChangeHandler()` function:

```
private function skinChangeHandler():void
{
    if (skinList.selectedItem.label == "None")
        button.clearStyle("skinClass");
    else
        button.setStyle("skinClass",
            skinList.selectedItem.skinClass);
}
```

A component's `skinClass` is set via styles, so changing the skin for the button requires setting the `skinClass` style, with a call to `button.setStyle()`. The only exception is the None item in the list that indicates that that user wants to use the default skin for `Button`. This requires clearing the style setting for `skinClass`, so `clearStyle()` is called when None is selected.

This logic around setting the skin for the button based on the drop-down list selection accomplishes a couple of things. First, it allows an easy framework in which we can add new skins and play with them to compare how they look and interact. But perhaps more importantly, at least for the purposes of this chapter, it shows that the skin class for a component is completely separate from the logic of that component. The button doesn't care what skin it is using or what that skin looks like; we can swap in any skin we desire at runtime. As long as that skin obeys the skin/component contract discussed earlier, the component couldn't care less.

Now, let's improve that ugly label-only button skin.

6.4 Adding a border

The most obvious problem in the earlier attempt at a button skin was that it really looked more like a label, and the text wasn't even centered inside that area. Labels without borders are fine because they are just informational elements on the UI. But objects that the user needs to interact with like buttons should have a more clearly defined area so that the user knows where to click the mouse. But perhaps most importantly, the user comes into any UI experience with a history of knowledge in using other UIs; you should make your interface easy for them to understand by using similar objects and UI metaphors, like buttons that look like buttons and not like floating text objects. Using our knowledge of MXML graphics tags, we can add a border to the button and then center the text inside of it.

 Don't confuse the user: custom looks in a UI are fine, but don't create entirely new metaphors for standard components or you risk confusion.

The skin class `BorderSkin` starts from the previous `JustaLabelSkin`, but adds the following object:

(File: skins/BorderSkin.mxml)
```
<s:Rect top="0" left="0" right="0" bottom="0">
    <s:stroke>
        <s:SolidColorStroke color="black"/>
    </s:stroke>
</s:Rect>
```

This rectangle draws a border around the button area, which helps define the boundaries of the component. The layout constraints `top`, `left`, `right`, and bottom are used to make sure that the border is stretched to the edges of the component. But as you can see, this doesn't actually make for a very attractive button:

Button Label

The problem is that the button has been sized to the minimum size that fits the label text, so that the border is crammed into this tight area with the text, resulting in a pretty awful looking component. We need to give these elements some space.

 Padding around text objects helps make them easier to read and avoids making the UI feel crammed and noisy.

The next drop-down item, Padded, selects the PaddedBorderSkin skin class, which adds the padding that the button needs. This skin class is a copy of the previous BorderSkin class, but modifies the labelDisplay element to the following:

(File: skins/PaddedBorderSkin.mxml)
```
<s:Label id="labelDisplay"
    left="10" right="10" top="5" bottom="5"
    horizontalCenter="0" verticalCenter="1"/>
```

The use of these layout constraints ensures both padding between the text and the sides of the component and that the text is centered within the overall component bounds:

Button Label

Now the button is beginning to look more like a button. But it's frankly pretty boring as buttons go; I remember UI widgets that looked like this on systems in the early 1980's. Surely we can do better than this dull wire-frame representation.

124

6.5   Modernizing the button

Let's dress the button up a bit and bring it into the new millennium. For starters, let's add a colored background. This at least distinguishes the area inside the button from the white background of the application. The next item in the drop-down list, `Background`, selects the `SolidBackgroundSkin` skin class. This skin class is copied from the previous `PaddedBorderSkin`, but modifies the `Rect` object to provide a fill as well as the existing stroke. Note that this `Rect` object is created before the `Label` object in the skin, which puts the background under the label instead of over it:

(File: skins/SolidBackgroundSkin.mxml)

```
<s:Rect top="0" left="0" right="0" bottom="0">
    <s:fill>
        <s:SolidColor color="0xc0c0c0"/>
    </s:fill>
    <s:stroke>
        <s:SolidColorStroke color="black"/>
    </s:stroke>
</s:Rect>
```

This skin paints the inside of the button with a gray color:

The button now stands out nicely from the window background around it. But the button is still rather dull and dated-looking, maybe circa late-1980's. Let's jazz up that background a bit.

The next item in the drop-down list, `Gradient`, loads the skin class `GradientBackgroundSkin`. This skin class is just like the previous skin class, `SolidBackgroundSkin`, but it modifies the `Rect` object's fill to use a grayscale gradient instead:

(File: skins/GradientBackgroundSkin.mxml)

```
<s:fill>
    <s:LinearGradient rotation="90">
        <s:GradientEntry color="0xf0f0f0"/>
```

125

```
        <s:GradientEntry color="0xffffff" ratio=".1"/>
        <s:GradientEntry color="0xaaaaaa"/>
     </s:LinearGradient>
  </s:fill>
```

This gradient gives the button a modern pseudo-3D look, as gradients often do, by making it seem like it has a slightly rounded shape, lit from above:

Button Label

We can modernize the button slightly more by giving it rounded corners. If you choose the Rounded item from the drop-down list, the button uses the RoundedSkin skin class. This skin is copied from the previous GradientBackgroundSkin, but adds rounded corners to the button using attributes in the Rect element:

```
(File: skins/RoundedSkin.mxml)
<s:Rect top="0" left="0" right="0" bottom="0"
        radiusX="3" radiusY="3">
   <!-- rect fill same as before -->
</s:Rect>
```

You can see that the rounded corners look less dated and dull than the previous sharp corners:

Button Label

To heighten the feeling of the button being an object with real presence in the UI, we can add a drop shadow:

Button Label

The Shadowed item in the drop-down list loads the ShadowedSkin class into the button. This is a trivial task, as we saw in Section 3.5. We simply declare a DropShadowFilter with appropriate properties:

(File: skins/ShadowedSkin.mxml)

```
<fx:Declarations>
    <s:DropShadowFilter id="shadow" strength=".3"/>
</fx:Declarations>
```

Then we add the shadow to the filters list in the Rect object:

```
<s:Rect top="0" left="0" right="0" bottom="0"
        radiusX="3" radiusY="3" filters="{[shadow]}">
```

The button is now looking pretty good; it's distinctive, it's modern-looking, it has an attractive shadow, and it has a rich gradient fill, which is very trendy in today's UIs. But try to interact with it. When you hover over the button, and then click on it, notice what happens: *nothing*. The mouse actions *are* actually having an effect; the button detects mouse hover and click actions; it's furiously dispatching events under the hood as these things happen. And the component is also telling the button skin to set its state appropriately as these actions occur. When the button hovers over the button, the skin is set to the over state, and when the mouse pressed down on the button the skin is set to the down state. But none of these exciting changes are reflected in what the user sees on the screen, so they are left wondering what's going on and whether the application has died a cruel and unusually boring death.

Let's fix this problem: let's actually tell the user what's happening in the UI. Let's use skin states.

6.6 Using skin states

Visual feedback is a critical factor in good user interfaces. UI design is not just about making things look pretty; it's about making functional, intuitive, and productive interfaces that help the user rather than confuse them.

You can help the user understand the state of the component and the state of the application overall. Give the user visual cues for simple actions. Change the look of a component when the mouse is hovering over it to communicate that the component is in a different state and is ready to accept a click action. Change the look when the mouse presses down on a component

127

to provide a clue that the user is performing that action. Don't leave the user guessing—use states to give them important visual cues about exactly what's going on.

Help the user understand what's happening in the UI by using states in your skins to give visual cues.

Now let's see how we can help the user understand the button's state. If you select the `Stateful` item in the drop-down list, the button uses the `StatefulSkin` skin class. This class starts from where the previous skin, `ShadowedSkin`, left off. Initially, the button looks identical to the previous incarnation on which it is based:

Button Label

Now move the mouse over the button. Aha! The look of the button changes as the mouse moves into the button area:

Button Label

Now click on the button. Aha, again! The button changes its appearance once more when the button is pressed:

Button Label

Let's look at the code that was added in this version of the skin to make these state indications happen:

(File: skins/StatefulSkin.mxml)

```
<s:fill>
    <s:LinearGradient rotation="90">
```

```
<s:GradientEntry color="0xf0f0f0"
    color.over="0xc0c0c0" color.down="0xa0a0a0"/>
<s:GradientEntry color="0xffffff"
    color.over="0xf0f0f0" color.down="0x808080"
    ratio=".1" ratio.down=".2"/>
<s:GradientEntry color="0xaaaaaa"
    color.over="0x808080" color.down="0xc0c0c0"/>
    </s:LinearGradient>
  </s:fill>
```

You can see that this skin code started with the same linear gradient structure from before: all of the entries, colors, and ratios are the same for the defaults. So the button looks the same when it is first shown because it is initially in the up state, in which these defaults are used. But when the button enters the over state, which happens when the mouse is over the button and the button component tells the skin to switch to that state, different colors are used for all three gradient entries. The new colors are basically darker versions of the earlier colors, so the button looks similarly lit, but darker.

When the button is clicked, the colors change again, along with the `ratio` of the second gradient entry. This time, the colors are changed to make the button have more of a pushed-in look, so that it looks like the bottom of the button is being lit from above, as it might if the button were actually concave.

The actual way in which skins reflect changes to state is completely flexible; I happened to choose this approach because it suited me, but you should experiment to find a look that you like for your components. The most important thing is to give the user some visual indication of state change. States are supported in skins for a good reason; giving the user visual cues for component state is a critical feature in good UI design.

At this point, we've completed the basics for the button. We have a skin that looks good and gives effective visual cues when appropriate. But we can keep going. Let's add some other features to the skins to have some fun.

6.7   Beyond the basics: adding sparkle to skins

Let's completely change the look and feel of the button. We currently have a pretty traditional looking button. Let's change the button so that it might fit with a game or a more "fun" UI. Let's exaggerate the graphics and text and make everything larger. Select the Fun item in the drop-down list, which loads the FunButtonSkin skin class into the button:

Several changes have been made to the skin, although none are very complicated or very different from what we had before.

First of all, the size of the button has changed by making the label text larger and bold. This increases the minimum size for the button. We also pad the label more to give more space between the edges of the button and the text, since the previous padding feels cramped with the larger text. Finally, the text color is now white, to brighten things up a bit, and the gradient colors are changed slightly to provide a better contrast with the new white text.

But the biggest change in the skin is how the button behaves. Hover over the button with your mouse. Whoa! It got bigger!

It changes colors too, like in the previous example. But resizing the button really makes it pop when the user mouses over it.

Now click it. Hey, the color changed and it grew again!

What's up with that? Buttons are supposed to stay put, right? You click them, they react, but they never move or change size. Never!

Although a moving button may be a bit over the top for a standard enterprise application, it works quite well in the context of games, especially for kid-oriented games. The cartoony feel of this interaction makes it very appealing and useful for making an interface seem more fun, friendly, and interactive.

 Physically distorting or moving a button can introduce an enhanced level of fun and interactivity to a UI.

I've seen this approach used in some games and gaming console interfaces, especially in applications designed for children. I noticed that in some situations buttons moved toward the viewer, and in other situations they moved away from the viewer. It turns out that both approaches work equally well.

You might expect all buttons to move in toward the screen, as if the button was actually being *pushed* by the mouse click. The important element is not the direction of movement, but rather that the button is moving at all. It moves in reaction to a hover even, as if to say, "Play me! I'm fun!" And it moves again in reaction to a click action, as if to say, "Alright! Let's go!"

Now let's see how it works. First, here is the new `labelDisplay`:

(File: skins/FunButtonSkin.mxml)
```
<s:Label id="labelDisplay" fontSize="20" fontWeight="bold"
    left="20" right="20" top="15" bottom="15" color="white"
    horizontalCenter="0" verticalCenter="1"
    z.over="-20" z.down="-40"/>
```

You can see, in this code, the changes made to the font, padding, and text color. You can also see how the label of the button moves for the over and down states; a new z position is used for both of those states. The ability to move objects on the z axis is part of the new 3D capabilities added in Flash Player 10. Negative values move objects out toward the viewer, positive values move them away (you can read more about the new 3D features in Section 10.5).

The background rectangle changed, too:

```
<s:Rect top="0" left="0" right="0" bottom="0"
    filters="{[shadow]}" radiusX="6" radiusY="6"
    z.over="-20" z.down="-40">
    <s:fill>
        <s:LinearGradient rotation="90">
            <s:GradientEntry color="0xd0d0d0"
                color.over="0xc0c0c0"
                color.down="0xa0a0a0"/>
            <s:GradientEntry color="0xf0f0f0"
                color.over="0xf0f0f0"
                color.down="0x808080"
                ratio=".1" ratio.down=".2"/>
            <s:GradientEntry color="0xaaaaaa"
                color.over="0x808080"
                color.down="0xc0c0c0"/>
        </s:LinearGradient>
    </s:fill>
    <s:stroke>
        <s:SolidColorStroke color="black" weight="3"/>
    </s:stroke>
</s:Rect>
```

The gradient colors changed slightly to provide more contrast to the white text, but are otherwise much as they were in the previous skins. The `radiusX` and `radiusY` values were increased to be proportional to the new, larger size of the button. And the `weight` of the stroke was increased so that the border of this button has a more pronounced, bold look.

One final change completes the illusion of this button being moved in 3D; the shadow reacts to the button movement. If we left the drop shadow alone, it would look like the window underneath the button was moving along with the button, which wouldn't be the right look at all. Instead, we need the shadow to look as if it stays in place on the background while the button moves. In fact, we need the shadow to look as if it shadows an object that is now further away from the window:

```
<fx:Declarations>
    <s:DropShadowFilter id="shadow" strength=".3"
```

```
        blurX="8" blurY="8"
        distance.over="10" distance.down="15"/>
</fx:Declarations>
```

By changing the distance of the shadow, we make it look as though the shadow reacts to the movement of the button just like a real shadow would if an object moved further away from its shadow plane. The values of blurX and blurY were also increased from their defaults to make the size of the shadow proportional to the size of this larger button.

Okay, now we have a fun button so we're done, right? Well, almost. First, I feel compelled to add some animation.[3] We have not yet covered Flex effects, which provide the animation capabilities of Flex, but I'll give a quick demo on how to add animations to skins here. I won't go into the details of how the animations work (you'll see this for yourself in Chapters 9, 10, and 11), but once you've read the later chapters and you're comfortable with effects and transitions, come back here and see how those techniques have been applied to animate the button skin.

If you select the last item in the drop-down list, Animated, you'll load the AnimatedSkin class into the button. This skin class starts where the last skin class, FunButtonSkin left off. We use all of the graphics and positioning in that skin and simply add some transition effects to animate those state changes. Go play with the application to get a feel for the animations. Animations, like chocolate, are much better when experienced directly.

To add animation to this skin file, I simply added a transitions block to declare the effects to run for the various state transitions. I also added three id properties, because in order to animate properties on an object, I need to be able to refer to that object. One of the animations changes the color on the gradient entries, so I added ids to those three objects. The rest of the objects that are animated (the drop shadow, the background rectangle, and the label) already have ids.

The transitions animate all changes between the states. We change three things when the button goes into each of the states: the color of the gradient entries for the background, the z position of the background and the label,

---

[3] After spending the entire Flex 4 release working on animation, I see possibilities for animations everywhere. I guess if I'd worked on List the whole release, I'd try to convert everything into a List instead. So maybe it's just petty rationalization justifying my pet feature in Flex 4, but I think animation adds a level of fun and interaction that goes beyond what you can get from static graphics.

and the `distance` of the drop shadow. So three animations run in parallel during each transition:

(File: skins/AnimatedSkin.mxml)

```
<s:Transition>
    <s:Parallel duration="120">
        <s:Animate target="{shadow}">
            <s:SimpleMotionPath property="distance"/>
        </s:Animate>
        <s:Animate targets="{[rect,labelDisplay]}">
            <s:SimpleMotionPath property="z"/>
        </s:Animate>
        <s:AnimateColor targets="{[ge1, ge2, ge3]}"/>
    </s:Parallel>
</s:Transition>
```

The first effect animates the `distance` property of the drop shadow filter. When the shadow moves relative to the button, it animates to its new position. The second effect animates the z property of the rectangle and the label. When the button moves out or in, that movement in z is animated. The third effect animates the `color` property of the gradient entries, so that the button animates its color change instead of switching gradient colors immediately.

Three transitions are declared for this skin: one that runs when going into the down state, one that runs when coming out of the down state, and one that runs for every other state change (the transition shown in the previous code snippet). All three transitions run essentially the same animation. The only difference between them is that the ones taking the button into and out of the down state are quicker than the transition shown in the code, with a `duration` of only 50 milliseconds instead of 120 milliseconds. This is because animating a click operation makes the button feel very sluggish if the animation is not quick enough.

Click interactions should be immediate, or at least very quick: clicking is an atomic operation that usually feels best if the UI looks like it is dispatched immediately.

In fact, no animation during a click operation is often the best approach. In some skins I've animated, I created transitions just for the other state transitions, but left the transitions from and to the down state as immediate, with no animation. In the case of this fun button, the extra magic added by animation seemed to enhance the fun feeling, so I made that action animated. Also, the button is moving so far in each direction that it seems reasonable to give it some time to get to its destination, as opposed to a more standard button where a click is not such a significant operation. But even in this case, I had to make the animation quite short to make the button usable at all. When the animation was too slow, the button felt sluggish and it would probably frustrate the user of such a component. Remember one of the most important tenets of using animations in UIs: don't piss off your user.

Don't upset the user: Use animations that help the user, not ones that may look nice but end up annoying the user.

Conclusion

You can skin many more, and much more complex, components than the simple Button covered in this chapter. For example, the ScrollBar has four optional parts to play around with, compared with Button's single labelDisplay part. You can also create skinned containers and data containers as well. We have just covered the basics here for the simple case of Button, but the same principles and skinning contract apply for every Flex 4 component, so you should be able to go from here.

In fact, a good place to start would be to read the code for the skins that ship with the Flex 4 SDK. For example, check out the standard skin for Button, in the ButtonSkin.mxml file.[4] If you think we used rich graphics

---

[4] In case you have only seen the Flex classes from the outside, as a user of the Flex APIs, you should take some time and look at the Flex framework code itself. Since Flex is an open source project, you can see the code or check out a subversion workspace at http://opensource.adobe.com. But if you don't want to go to that trouble since you probably just use the SDKs that come with the Flash Builder tool, you can also see the source code inside the sdks directory inside the folder in which you installed Flash Builder. You can even load the SDK projects into Flash Builder to make browsing the source code easier.

in the custom skin examples in this chapter you should see what goes into the default skins in Flex. This may give you ideas of how to design your own skins. It may also be a good place for you to start with your custom skin development by copying that code and modifying it to give your components their own unique look.

The main point is that you have easy access to the Flex source code and you should look at it to learn how things work, such as examining the skin files that ship with the standard components to see how you might create your own custom skins.

Chapter 7

Animation

Users are very much alive—shouldn't their applications be alive as well? Animating elements in the UI creates a rich, lively environment in which the user can work. Even better: these techniques can help the user actually *enjoy* using the application. More importantly, animation can be used to help the user understand what could otherwise be a complex and confusing user interface, helping connect them to the different states of the application and understand what they need to do.

In order to write these kinds of dynamic interfaces, we first need to understand something about animation.

7.1 Animation defined

Animation is, essentially, the changing of values over time. Typically, especially as far as GUI applications are concerned, animation changes visual properties of the objects on the screen, such as their location, size, and translucency.

Although we think of animation as being moving objects, in reality it is a series of static images that we interpret as motion. For example, animation on a computer screen happens by updating static images on the screen as fast as the refresh rate of the display allows, which is typically about 60 times per second. Fortunately, our brain is good at lying to us and interprets a series of images as fluid motion if the animation is done right. This crossover from images to perceived continuous motion is the premise of flip-book animation. It is also how movies work, since movies are also just a series of static images, typically shown on the screen at 24 frames per second. In fact, think

---

Animation and Flex effects

Flex developers generally create animations using Flex effects, which are discussed in Chapters 9, 10, and 11. But in order to understand these higher-level capabilities, I find it helpful to understand the fundamental concepts and classes that effects use internally. And chances are, since you went out and invested in a book on how to do this kind of stuff, you are probably interested in how it all works. So consider this chapter and the next one, Chapter 8, as steps toward learning how to use Flex effects *effectively*. The current chapter on animation covers the fundamental concepts behind animation. The next chapter, Chapter 8, covers the capabilities of the `Animation` class that is used by Flex effects internally for running their animations. Consider both of these chapters as getting the fundamentals down so that the material in the effects chapters makes more sense.

---

about the meaning of the old word for movies: "moving pictures," which is exactly what they are: a series of still images shown in rapid succession that give the illusion of motion.

If animation is a process of changing values over time, then in order to perform computer animation we need to figure out how to calculate the values appropriately to create convincing animations. It is easy in Flex to change properties, like the x property of a `Button` to change its location. We do this by simply setting the property, like this: `button.x = 5`. But how do we continually change the property x over time? Well, we could start with a mechanism for handling periodic callbacks.

7.2   Periodic callbacks

All GUI toolkits that I've worked with, including Flex, offer some facility to call back into application code at some specified frequency. As you saw before, animation in computer systems is about changing properties over time. The technique used for changing these properties is typically setting up a timer to call back into application code at regular intervals, at which time the application figures out the proper value for the object to have at that time and sets that value on the object. The typical approaches to handling periodic callbacks in Flex are the `enterFrame` event and the `Timer` class.

Periodic callbacks with `enterFrame`

Every Flex application has a `frameRate`, which is a property on the application itself. Flex's default `frameRate` is 24, which means that the application window is updated 24 times per second (or as close to that as the Flash player can handle, given system constraints). But you can change that value in the `Application` tag for your application. For example, the following code sets up an application to run at a rate of 10 frames per second:

```
<s:Application xmlns:fx="http://ns.adobe.com/mxml/2009"
    xmlns:s="library://ns.adobe.com/flex/spark"
    frameRate="10">
</s:Application>
```

Whenever the Flash player is about to draw the next frame of the application, it dispatches an `enterFrame` event to any listeners. This is a natural place for applications to plug into if they want to get periodic callbacks. Listeners of this event are guaranteed to get called back at the current rate of the application, which is typically good enough for most animations.

To be called on the `enterFrame` event, you simply add a listener for this event to any component or container that you wish to listen to, or to the underlying Flash `stage` itself. For example, to get `enterFrame` events for the application example above, we could add an event listener to the `Application` tag as follows:

```
<s:Application xmlns:fx="http://ns.adobe.com/mxml/2009"
    xmlns:s="library://ns.adobe.com/flex/spark"
    frameRate="10"
    enterFrame="enterFrameHandler(event)">
</s:Application>
```

We then need to create a function to handle the `enterFrame` event callback, which is listed in the code above as `enterFrameHandler()`. In our handler function, we can update our components according to however we want to animate them. Let's look at an example.

Moving a button with `enterFrame`

In the `EnterFrameMover` application, seen in the figure below, we have a single button:

139

(Demo: EnterFrameMover)

The button, when clicked, adds an event listener for the `enterFrame` event so that the event results in a call to `enterFrameHandler()`:

(File: EnterFrameMover.mxml)

```
<s:Button id="button" label="Move Me"
    click="addEventListener('enterFrame', enterFrameHandler)"/>
```

Note that we add the event listener when the button is clicked instead of in the `Application` tag, as we did in the earlier code snippet. Adding the event listener on a button click event gives us two advantages. First, it allows more flexibility about when we start the animation. The animation starts only when the user clicks on the button, instead of automatically at application creation time. Second, it guarantees that the application and button are in a reasonable state to be moved when our handler function is initially called.

Here is the event handler code that moves our button:

```
private var moveIncrement:Number = 10;
private function enterFrameHandler(event:Event):void
{
    button.x += moveIncrement;
    if (button.x + button.width > width)
    {
        button.x = width - button.width;
        moveIncrement = -moveIncrement;
    }
    else if (button.x < 0)
    {
        button.x = 0;
        moveIncrement = -moveIncrement;
    }
}
```

This code moves the button by `moveIncrement` pixels every time. When the button goes beyond the window boundaries, the button is placed back inside the window and our increment variable is negated. This change reverses the direction of further button movement until the button hits the window bounds on the other side.

This seems pretty easy, right? We just set up an event handler, handle the callbacks, and make any property changes that we want to animate our UI objects. Ten lines of code later and there's a moving button in our application. Of course it's far from an animated interface that anyone wants to actually use, but you can start to see how we might get there. Things are at least starting to move around on the screen. Now let's see how to do the same thing with the `Timer` class.

Periodic callbacks with `Timer`

Using the `Timer` class is similar to using the `enterFrame` event. The main difference is that the `enterFrame` event is already set up to be sent around the system. All we have to do to animate via `enterFrame` is to plug into that existing system by adding a listener and implementing our event handling function. Using the `Timer` class requires a bit more effort because we have to set up and start the `Timer` before it dispatches the events we care about. But this little bit of added work also brings added flexibility. Using `Timer` allows us to break away from the application frame rate and use an animation rate that is more tailored to our requirements.

The main elements of a `Timer` object are its `delay`, its `repeatCount`, and its event listeners:

`delay` This property sets the amount of time, in milliseconds, between timer events. This is the rate at which an event handler is called while the timer is running. For example, a value of 20 means that the timer attempts[1] to call its listeners every 20 milliseconds, or about 50 times per second. You should set the `delay` to be a value that provides rea-

---

[1] I say "attempts" because the actual rate at which the timer's listeners are called is determined by a combination of the `delay` rate plus any constraints of the operating system and possibly the browser that your application is running within. For example, the maximum timer rate in Internet Explorer on Windows is currently about equivalent to the refresh rate of the computer monitor, typically 60 frames per second, or just over 16 milliseconds between events ((1000 milliseconds) / (60 frames per second) = 16.67). This means that a delay of anything less than 16 is irrelevant, because 16 milliseconds is the smallest delay that the Flash player can handle in this situation. This may seem arbitrary or too constrictive, but think about it: why would you want to waste CPU cycles on the user's machine running an animation faster than the user can possibly see updates to the screen?

sonably smooth animations without running so fast that you're wasting CPU cycles needlessly.

repeatCount This property specifies the number of times that the timer calls its listeners before ending. For a typical animation, you set this to 0, which means that it continues until you actually stop the timer with a call to stop(). If you just want to perform an action once with some initial delay, a repeatCount of 1 makes sense, but for typical animations you want the timer to keep calling your handlers until you are done with your animation and ready to stop it.

Other than these properties, the start() and stop() functions exist to get the timer going or to stop it.

The way you typically use a Timer is by creating it, assigning appropriate values for delay and repeatCount, adding your event handler(s), and calling start(). Then later, when you want to end the animation, you call stop(). And that's about it—the rest of it is up to your timer event handler.

Moving a button with Timer

The observant section-heading reader may have noticed that this section bears a striking resemblance to the demo section in the earlier enterFrame discussion. This is not mere coincidence; we are going to perform the same amazing button-movement animation as before, only this time we use the Timer class so that you can see the differences in the two approaches. If you want to picture the application, see the screenshot in that previous example; it's a picture of the application that uses enterFrame, but trust me: the Timer version of the application looks exactly the same.

If you look at the TimerMover code, you see that the button is declared a bit differently. Instead of adding a listener to the existing enterFrame event as we did before, we use the click event to call a new startAnimation() function to set up our animation:

(File: TimerMover.mxml)

```
<s:Button id="button" label="Move Me"
        click="startAnimation()"/>
```

The startAnimation() function starts the animation by creating, setting up, and starting our timer:

```
private function startAnimation():void
{
    var timer:Timer = new Timer(20, 0);
    timer.addEventListener(TimerEvent.TIMER, timerHandler);
    timer.start();
}
```

The Timer is constructed with two values: a delay of 20 (which results in an effective frame rate of 50 frames per second) and a repeatCount of 0, which causes the timer to run indefinitely. We then add our event handler to the timer by listening to the TIMER event on TimerEvent. This event listener tells the timer that we want our timerHandler() function called every delay milliseconds. Finally, we start() our timer, which causes the timer to run and start calling our event handler at periodic intervals.

Our event handler code is exactly as it was before, but the function has been renamed to make it clear that it handles timer events:

```
private var moveIncrement:Number = 10;
private function timerHandler(event:Event):void
{
    button.x += moveIncrement;
    if (button.x + button.width > width)
    {
        button.x = width - button.width;
        moveIncrement = -moveIncrement;
    }
    else if (button.x < 0)
    {
        button.x = 0;
        moveIncrement = -moveIncrement;
    }
}
```

If you run the application, you see just about the same thing as you saw before: the button, when clicked, starts moving back and forth between the left and right boundaries of the window. Of course, we are still far from having a cool UI experience, but it is at least the beginnings of some kind of animated interaction.

143

Now run both applications, side by side, and look at the animation. Do you notice any difference? There should be a significant speed difference between the two buttons; the one in the TimerMover application is moving along much faster than the button in the EnterFrameMover application. It's easy to understand why this is the case; the EnterFrameMover animation is running at the frameRate of that application, which defaults to 24 frames per second, while the TimerMover button is moving at the rate declared in the Timer constructor, which is about 50 frames per second. We could change these values to make the rates match, but the difference scratches at the surface of a large issue: frame-based versus time-based animation.

7.3   It's about time: frame- versus time-based animation

In the previous two examples, the button moved at different speeds, depending on the event-handling rate of the underlying animation. In the EnterFrameMover case, the button moves ten pixels every $\frac{1}{24}$th of a second. In the TimerMover example, the button moves the same ten pixels for every $\frac{1}{50}$th of a frame. To vary the speed of the button's movement, then, we can change the underlying rate of the animations. For example, we can set a frameRate for the enterFrame example to 50 to give it the same rate as the Timer example. Or we could change the delay property for the Timer example to match the frame rate of the enterFrame example.

As an example, take a look at the TimerMoverVariableDelay demo application, as seen here:

(Demo: TimerMoverVariableDelay)

The TimerMoverVariableDelay application is based on the previous TimerMover application, but it adds an HSlider that you can use to control the Timer's delay property, and hence the speed of the button as it moves back and forth:

(File: TimerMoverVariableDelay.mxml)
```
<s:HSlider id="slider" minimum="1" maximum="250" value="20"
    change="timer.delay = slider.value"/>
```

144

The only other change from the original application is that the `timer` variable is declared outside of the `startAnimation()` function so that its `delay` property can be changed with the slider. The functionality of this version is the same as before—the button moves back and forth when clicked. Run the application and play with the slider. Notice how changing the slider's value changes two things in the animation: the overall speed of the button moving back and forth and the number of times the button changes position each second. These changes are linked, because the number of frame updates per second determines the speed of the button, since we are moving the same amount of pixels per update. The more updates there are, the further the button moves.

But this approach has a problem: what if our animations do not run at the exact rate that we anticipate? For example, what if we run the `TimerMover` example on a horribly slow machine and don't get anywhere near the requested `delay` rate? Then we would see the button move at a much slower speed than the speed we wanted when we set up our animation.

Even worse (and yet very common), what if the machine we are running on is intermittently busy doing things more CPU-intensive and arguably more important than animating our button, and Flash doesn't get around to servicing our callbacks at a constant rate? Then we would see the button move at unpredictable speeds, sometimes slower, sometimes faster, depending on how quickly the system got around to servicing the animation events.

This unpredictability of speed from system to system, or even from frame to frame on a busy system, is far from ideal. We want our animations to have the same feel no matter when or where they run. Without some kind of predictable behavior, it is difficult to design a user experience that feels consistent and robust across potentially vastly different situations. So how do we fix this problem?

The answer will come in time. That is, we need to account for *time* in our animation calculations. The animations so far have used a static amount of movement between frames, so the speed of the animated object was dependent on the rate at which those frames were serviced. This is known as frame-based animation. We need to move to a time-based system instead, where the speed of objects is based on the actual time elapsed at each frame. We can make the object appear to move at a constant rate, from frame to frame and across entire systems, by always calculating the object's position according to the time elapsed instead of just how fast the system was able to service the next animation frame.

Account for time in animation calculations; update objects based on elapsed time, not just elapsed frames.

The concept behind time-based animation is simple: with each frame update, you calculate the amount of time that has elapsed since the previous position, account for the speed that you want the object to move, and calculate the new position based on this elapsed time and speed. For example, if you want the button to move at a speed of 500 pixels per second (where one second equals 1000 milliseconds), then for an elapsed time of 20 milliseconds you calculate that the button should move a total of ten pixels (20 ms/ 1000 ms/sec) * 500 = .02 * 500 = 10).

Let's look at another example. For this example we use the Timer mechanism because I find it to be more flexible than the enterFrame mechanism, but you could apply the same approach to either mechanism.

Demo: time-based motion

For this new application, TimeBasedMover, we start from the previous application, TimerMoverVariableDelay, which gives us the slider to control the amount of time between frame updates. That way, we can see the effect that a varying frame rate has on the overall button speed. The application looks just like the one in the previous example, with a slider to control button animation.

In order to create a time-based version of the animation, we need a couple more variables for use in our calculations:

speed We need some idea of speed or velocity. This is the amount of movement per time period that we use to calculate the actual amount moved each frame, depending on how much time has elapsed. In the application code, this is a constant that we call pixelsPerSecond, indicating how many pixels the object moves in an entire second. For any amount of time that has elapsed, we simply calculate the elapsed fraction of a second and multiply it times our pixelsPerSecond constant to get the actual pixels moved in that frame.

elapsed time For every frame, we need to calculate how much time has elapsed since the last frame. This requires two new things in our code: a "current time" variable (and a way to measure that current time) and a "previous time" variable, which was the time at the previous frame. For the current time (cleverly called currentTime in our application), we call the Flash function getTimer(), which simply returns the number of milliseconds since some irrelevant time in the past. It really doesn't matter what the return value is; it is only useful when comparing it to other values, to determine the elapsed time between two measurements. In order to compare the current time against the time in the last frame, we store each frame time, after we're done with it, in a variable called prevTime. When we first start our animation, we store the current time in this prevTime variable and thereafter use that variable to calculate the time delta between the last frame and the current one.

Since the button is now moving a variable number of pixels per frame, we need a slightly different mechanism for incrementing the button each time and determining whether it is moving right or left. We now have a boolean variable, movingRight which tracks whether the button is moving to the right or not. When we detect that the button has gone past the window bounds to the right, we set this to false so that the button moves left. Then for every frame we calculate the number of pixels the button should move, according to its speed and the elapsed time since the last frame. We then either add or subtract that number of pixels based on the movingRight boolean.

Now let's see the code. The GUI elements, the button and the slider, are exactly the same as they were in the previous example; it is just the variables and the timerhandler() function that have been updated to handle the new time-based animation capability:

(File: TimeBasedMover.mxml)

```
private const pixelsPerSecond:Number = 500;
private var prevTime:Number;
private var movingRight:Boolean = true;
private var timer:Timer = new Timer(20, 0);
private function timerHandler(event:Event):void
{
    var currentTime:Number = getTimer();
    var deltaTime:Number = currentTime - prevTime;
    var pixelsToMove:Number =
        pixelsPerSecond * deltaTime/1000;
```

```
    var overshoot:Number;
    if (movingRight)
    {
        button.x += pixelsToMove;
        if (button.x + button.width > width)
        {
            overshoot =
                button.x + button.width - width;
            button.x =
                width - button.width - overshoot;
            movingRight = false;
        }
    }
    else
    {
        button.x -= pixelsToMove;
        if (button.x < 0)
        {
            overshoot = button.x;
            button.x = -overshoot;
            movingRight = true;
        }
    }
    prevTime = currentTime;
}
```

The startAnimation function is similar to the one in the earlier application, TimerMoverVariableDelay, but this time we also initialize the new prevTime variable to the current time when the animation starts:

```
private function startAnimation():void
{
    timer.addEventListener(TimerEvent.TIMER, timerHandler);
    timer.start();
    prevTime = getTimer();
}
```

Much of the logic is similar to what it was before, moving the button around according to the number of pixels that we calculate. This calculation is just as we explained earlier: we figure out the amount of milliseconds elapsed since the last frame and calculate the number of pixels to move based on the speed of the button (pixels per second) times the fraction of a second that has elapsed.

The turn-around logic has been upgraded a tad since the previous version of the application to take into account the overshoot, or the number of pixels past the boundary that the button went in the last move. This allows us to calculate the position of the button as if it had bounced off the edge, instead of simply placing it at the edge when it changes direction. This nuance does not matter much for high frame rates because the button doesn't overshoot by much when little time passes between frames. But for high delays (low frame rates), this can be a significant impact on the overall speed of the button, so I upgraded the logic to account for it. It is particularly noticeable in this version of the application because we now have a variable amount of movement each frame depending on the delay. In the previous versions, the button moved ten pixels every frame regardless, so the overshoot value in those cases could only reach a maximum of ten pixels, which didn't have much impact on the visual results.

Other than the changes noted above, the code is much as it was before. We move the button by the appropriate number of pixels and perform some logic to turn it around at the boundaries. But the best part is that now our button is moving at a constant speed, regardless of the frame rate. To see the impact that this has, run `TimeBasedMover` and play with the slider. Note that the button always moves at the same overall rate, even at the extremes with either very small or very large delays. Yes, a large delay makes the animation very chunky, but still the button manages to get where it's going in the same overall amount of time.

Time-based animation: it's the only way to go for smooth, predictable, and pleasing animations.

Conclusion

We've seen a lot of information about how to move objects (or at least buttons) around on the screen. We've seen how you can hook into the event system of Flex in a couple of different ways and how you can use time-based animation techniques to get smooth and robust animations.

So we're done, right?

Well, not quite. We've seen how you can make things move on the screen. But even though there wasn't much code there, it's still more boilerplate code than I would like to write every time I want to animate anything. That's why Flex provides animation facilities for developers such as the Animation class, which you'll see in the next chapter.

Chapter 8

The Animation Class

In the animation examples in the previous chapter, we set up set up a `Timer`, added an event handler to listen for timing updates, and waited around to get called back in our handler to then calculate the object's new position and move it. Although the code wasn't too difficult to write, we would have to rewrite that same kind of code every time we wanted to run an animation, and that gets a bit tedious. In addition, other important animation techniques exist that we didn't get to in those examples, like stopping an animation after a specified time period. Finite animations are more common in real UI animations than the infinite animations in the earlier examples. And perhaps more significantly, the animations in the previous chapter were not really that compelling; shifting a button back and forth doesn't make for an exciting user interface. For the kinds of animations that compelling UIs demand, we need more complex animation capabilities that would be very time-consuming to write with just the techniques that we saw in Chapter 7.

Luckily, Flex provides a timing engine that is a big step up from the `Timer` class to handle much of this functionality for us: the `Animation` class. You create an instance of the `Animation` class, tell it the duration you want it to have, hand it the start and end values, tell it how to call you back, and it goes off and does the whole thing for you. It still calls your code because you still need to set the position of the button, but the `Animation` class even handles the calculation of that button position for you. `Animation` has all of the logic for time-based animation built into it, and only needs to know the duration and the start/end values and it can figure out everything else. And the animation automatically finishes when the full duration has elapsed (or you can set it up to run indefinitely, just like the `Timer` in the last chapter's

151

examples). All you have to write is the code to set up and start the animation and to handle the callbacks to set the calculated values on the target object.

For example, to construct and play an `Animation` that animates the x property of our button object from the left side of the window to the right over a period of 500 milliseconds, we might do the following:

```
var anim:Animation = new Animation(500, "x", 0,
    width - button.width);
anim.play();
```

But notice that we haven't yet told our animation how to contact our code with animated values as the animation runs. For that, we need to work with the `IAnimationTarget` interface.

8.1   Animation targets

`IAnimationTarget` is an interface in Flex that clients of `Animation` need to implement. This approach provides a standard way for classes to declare that they implement all of the callback methods that `Animation` may need to call during the course of an animation. All we've seen in our previous examples are cases where an animation sends out update events while running, but other events exist in more interesting animations that are useful to listen in on, such as when the animation starts, when it ends, and when it repeats. The `IAnimationTarget` interface declares all of the necessary callback functions and any object that wants to receive callbacks from `Animation` needs to provide a class that implements these functions. Here is the interface:

```
public interface IAnimationTarget
{
    function animationStart(animation:Animation):void;
    function animationStop(animation:Animation):void;
    function animationEnd(animation:Animation):void;
    function animationRepeat(animation:Animation):void;
    function animationUpdate(animation:Animation):void;
}
```

This interface encapsulates the functions that are called throughout the life of a running `Animation`:

152

animationStart() This function is called when the animation actually begins. Typically this happens when the animation's start() function is called, but a property on Animation called startDelay provides an optional delay mechanism for animations (which is useful for sequencing multiple animations together). If a positive startDelay is declared on the animation, animationStart() is called only after that delay expires and the animation actually begins actively playing.

animationStop() This function is called only if the animation is forcibly stopped, which happens if the animation's stop() function is called. This causes the animation to stop in its tracks, sending out this call followed by an animationEnd() call.

animationEnd() This function is called when an animation ends, which can happen in one of three ways: The animation's stop() function may be called, which stops the animation in its tracks. The animation's end() function may be called which, unlike stop(), sends out a final update call with the end values, even if the animation's full duration was not yet reached. Or, finally, the animation may come to a natural end when its declared duration has elapsed.

animationRepeat() We will see more about repetition later, but briefly this function is called when a repetition cycle of the animation begins.

animationUpdate() This function is the most important one in the interface, and is the equivalent of the event handlers in the animation examples in the previous chapter. This function is called for every frame of the animation, and provides the means for the recipient to set the animated values calculated by Animation on target object(s).

Each of these functions has just a single parameter; the Animation instance that called the function. The animation object holds the information that the handler needs, such as the calculated values during an animationUpdate() call. For example, to retrieve the calculated value for x during a call to animationUpdate(), you access the currentValue property, like this:

```
var xValue:Number = animation.currentValue["x"];
```

But enough talk—let's see how the Animation class works in practice.

8.2   Demo: moving a button with the `Animation` class

This example, `AnimationMover`, is seen here:

(Demo: AnimationMover)

For this application, we need more than a single MXML file because we need a separate class that implements the `IAnimationTarget` interface. I've created an ActionScript class named `AnimationTargetDispatcher` that does just this. `AnimationTargetDispatcher` is a utility class that turns the function calls into dispatched events, in order to make it easier to deal with just the animation events we care about. To get a callback just for specific events, like the update events that we care about, we just need to add an event listener to an instance of this class, then set the `animationTarget` property of `Animation` to that instance. Then for every call to `animationUpdate()` in `AnimationTargetDispatcher`, we get a callback to our event listeners for the update event. An `AnimationEvent` class is found in the same `utils` directory that is used by the dispatcher to encapsulate the event constants (START, END, *etc.*) and the underlying `animation` property that holds the animated values. To create our animation target, we declare it as an MXML object as follows:

(File: AnimationMover.mxml)

```
<local:AnimationTargetDispatcher id="animTarget"
    update="updateHandler(event)"
    end="endHandler(event)"/>
```

This declaration tells our dispatcher to call us whenever an update or end event occurs. The update event is the one that deals with turning the animated value into the new button position. We need the end event to handle turning the button around and animating it in the other direction. But before we look at these functions, let's first see how we finish setting up our animation object.

Our button looks the same as it did in some of the examples in Chapter 7:

```
<s:Button id="button" label="Move Me"
        click="startAnimation()"/>
```

154

AnimationTargetDispatcher

I created the `AnimationTargetDispatcher` class just to simplify this demo. But the class is a general-purpose utility that you should consider using if you ever need to use the `Animation` class directly. The higher-level Flex effects classes, which we will see in later chapters, are probably the main animation classes that you will use in your development. To a great extent, the `Animation` class is just an implementation detail of those classes. But in some cases you may want a lower-level class that just runs the timing engine without the added capabilities of effects. And in that case, you may want a quick way to plug into the animation events that the class sends out. `AnimationTargetDispatcher` comes in handy for that situation.

The `startAnimation()` function creates and starts the animation:[1]

```
private function startAnimation():void
{
    if (button.x == 0)
        anim = new Animation(500, "x", 0,
            width - button.width);
    else
        anim = new Animation(500, "x",
            width - button.width, 0);
    anim.animationTarget = animTarget;
    anim.play();
}
```

The animation is declared with a duration of 500 milliseconds. It operates on the x property (this determines the lookup key by which the animated values are stored and retrieved from the animation), which takes the but-

---

[1] You can also create `Animation` instances in MXML, just like I did for the `AnimationTargetDispatcher` instance. I chose to not do so for this example because the constructor for `Animation` allows a convenient way to set the parameters that we care about in this example. If we declared the class in MXML instead, we would need to set up the start and end values a bit differently, using classes and concepts that we haven't yet seen. In the fullness of time and thickness of this chapter, we will discuss these other concepts. At that time, it will be easier to describe how to set up `Animation` in MXML. But for the purposes of these demos and this description, we'll stick with the handy ActionScript constructor.

155

ton from one side of the window to the other. Some logic exists for detecting whether the button is currently on the left of the window (if button.x == 0), which is used to determine whether to animate from left to right or right to left. This logic is used later when reversing the animation. The animation uses our AnimationTargetDispatcher instance as its animationTarget, which ensures that the handler functions are called for update and end events. Finally, we play() our animation.

The update handler function is simple:

```
private function updateHandler(event:AnimationEvent):void
{
    button.x = event.animation.currentValue["x"];
}
```

Notice how much shorter this code is than the update handling code in the examples in the previous chapter, before we learned about the Animation class. Instead of calculating elapsed time and movement, we simply use the value that the animation has calculated for us. Also, we do not need to worry about the turn-around logic in this handler because we know that the animation only runs from one side of the window to the other. The animation has a set duration, after which it simply ends and sends out a final x location in the correct place at the window's edge.

Since the animation runs only once in a single direction, we need some additional logic to handle the back-and-forth behavior from our previous examples. To perform this action, we need to detect when the animation ends, which must mean that the button is at the edge of the window, and then restart the animation going in the other direction. We handle this logic in the handler for the end event:

```
private function endHandler(event:AnimationEvent):void
{
    startAnimation();
}
```

The code in endHandler() is simple; we just call the startAnimation() function that we saw earlier, which already has the logic to determine the correct direction in which to move the button.

8.3   Repetition, repetition, repetition

The `AnimationMover` application is pretty slick for an application that performs the awesome task of moving a button back and forth. In just a few lines of code and a couple of functions we were able to get the same behavior that we saw in the previous chapter's examples, but with less code than those earlier examples, which had to account for all of the timing details. Clearly, the `Animation` class is saving some effort in creating and running simple animations.

But some tedious details are still in this code that I would rather see handled elsewhere. In particular, the logic about detecting the turn-around of the button and restarting the animation seems like something that ought to be part of our timing engine. Wouldn't it be great if `Animation` knew how to perform repetition logic?

Allow me to introduce the repetition behavior logic in `Animation`. This set of properties tells an animation how many times to run, what to do when it repeats, and how long to wait before starting each repetition cycle:

`repeatCount` This property, along with the `duration` property, how long the animation runs. Each iteration lasts for `duration` milliseconds, with the `repeatCount` being a multiplier of that duration. An animation with a 500 millisecond `duration` and a `repeatCount` of 3, for example, runs for a total of 1500 milliseconds. As with `Timer`, a value of 0 means the animation should repeat indefinitely. The default value is 1, which means that the animation does not repeat.

`repeatBehavior` This property tells the animation how to repeat each time. Two values are possible, declared as constants in the `RepeatBehavior` class: LOOP and REVERSE. A value of LOOP means that the animation repeats by setting the properties back to their start values and running again in the same direction to the end values. In our button example, this means the button always animates from the left to the right side of the window. A value of REVERSE means that the animation switches the direction of movement with each repetition. In our button example, REVERSE reverses the start and end values and moves the button in the opposite direction each iteration.

`repeatDelay` This property is an optional delay value that tells the animation how long to pause before each new repetition cycle. The default value is 0, which means that the next repetition cycle begins immediately after the previous one ends.

This repetition behavior is exactly what we need for our animating button example to get the button to move back and forth. Let's see how it works in code, from the AnimationRepeater example. The application UI looks exactly like the previous AnimationMover example, so check out the screenshot on page 154 if you need to refresh your memory.

Two changes were made to the earlier AnimationMover application to use the repetition logic of Animation. First, the code in startAnimation() was simplified by removing the turn-around code, where it set up each animation to move to the right or left depending on the current position of the button. Instead, the code now sets up a single animation to run forever and to reverse at the end of each cycle:

(File: AnimationRepeater.as)

```
private function startAnimation():void
{
    anim = new Animation(500, "x", 0, width - button.width);
    anim.repeatBehavior = RepeatBehavior.REVERSE;
    anim.repeatCount = 0;
    anim.animationTarget = animTarget;
    anim.play();
}
```

Notice the single initializer for anim compared to the previous examples where there were two initializers; the animation is always created to run from left to right. The repeatBehavior value of REVERSE tells the animation to reverse each time and switch its start and end values for each iteration. A value of 0 for the repeatCount tells the animation to run indefinitely.

The only other change to the previous AnimationMover example is the removal of the endHandler() function. This function existed only to restart the animation each time it ended. But now that the animation is performing the reversal for us, we no longer need that function and can remove the handler. Also, our AnimationTargetDispatcher need only dispatch update events, since we no longer have the handler for end events:

```
<local:AnimationTargetDispatcher id="animTarget"
    update="updateHandler(event)"/>
```

8.4 Motion paths: more is better

Interesting animations usually involve animating several properties at once, like the width *and* height of a resizing object, or the x *and* y location of a moving object, or several of these and other properties in parallel. All of the examples using Animation that we have seen so far have used constructor arguments for the class to pass in the property name and values used, which constrained our examples to use just the one property allowed in the constructor. But Animation can actually animate several properties in parallel using motionPaths.

The motionPaths property is a Vector of MotionPath objects. You can supply any number of MotionPath objects to a single Animation, where each separate MotionPath describes the attributes for a single property. The Animation then acts on all of these objects in parallel, calculating values for each specified property on every frame of the animation, according to the information in the property's MotionPath.

MotionPath is the more powerful, and more general, class, but we will start with its more commonly used subclass, SimpleMotionPath.

The SimpleMotionPath **class**

SimpleMotionPath is a data structure that provides a property name and a set of from/to/by values. This information encapsulates everything that an Animation needs to know about a property to calculate values for the property at each frame of the animation.

property This variable holds the name of the property being animated.

valueFrom This variable holds the value that the property starts at when the animation begins.

valueTo This variable holds the value that the property animates to and therefore ends at when the animation is complete.

valueBy This optional variable holds the amount of change in the property between its start and end values. valueBy is optional because if both valueFrom and valueTo are supplied, then valueBy is ignored. But if it is more convenient in your situation to declare the amount

159

of change and either `valueFrom` or `valueTo`, then `Animation` calculates the unsupplied value by adding or subtracting `valueBy` from the from/to value that is supplied.

As an example, the application `AnimationRepeater` has been rewritten using `SimpleMotionPath`, resulting in `SimpleMotionPathAnimation`. The application UI looks like just it did in the first example, seen on page 154.

Previously, we had to call into ActionScript code to create the animation:

(File: AnimationRepeater.as)

```
private function startAnimation():void
{
    anim = new Animation(500, "x", 0,
        width - button.width);
    anim.repeatBehavior = RepeatBehavior.REVERSE;
    anim.repeatCount = 0;
    anim.animationTarget = animTarget;
    anim.play();
}
```

This use of ActionScript was necessary because it was the only way to pass the `property` and value arguments into the animation (because MXML declarations call a no-argument constructor). But with `SimpleMotionPath`, we can now declare our `Animation` in MXML instead:

(File: SimpleMotionPathAnimation.mxml)

```
<s:Animation id="anim" duration="500"
    repeatBehavior="reverse" repeatCount="0"
    animationTarget="{animTarget}">

    <s:SimpleMotionPath property="x" valueFrom="0"
        valueTo="{width - button.width}"/>

</s:Animation>
```

To play the animation, we just call `play()` from our button click handler:

```
<s:Button id="button" label="Move Me" click="anim.play()"/>
```

You can see from this example that motion paths allow us to take a more declarative approach to animations and to create our `Animation` object in

MXML. We just need to set up our `Animation` object with appropriate property values, including motion paths,[2] and our animation is ready to go.

As another simple example, let's extend our button animation to operate in two dimensions, animating x to the right side of the window and y to the bottom of the window, as seen here:

(Demo: SimpleMotionPathAnimationXY)

Two changes must be made to the previous example, as seen in the example `SimpleMotionPathAnimationXY`. First, we need to declare another `SimpleMotionPath` to hold the information about y, so our new `Animation` declaration, including both motion paths, looks like this:

(File: SimpleMotionPathAnimationXY.mxml)

```
<s:Animation id="anim" duration="500"
    repeatBehavior="reverse" repeatCount="0"
    animationTarget="{animTarget}">

    <s:SimpleMotionPath property="x" valueFrom="0"
        valueTo="{width - button.width}"/>
    <s:SimpleMotionPath property="y" valueFrom="0"
        valueTo="{height - button.height}"/>

</s:Animation>
```

The second motion path ensures that the animation calculates new values for y, just as it does for x. The only other thing needed is to grab those calculated values and set them on the button object. I've added one more

---

[2] Note that the `motionPaths` tag is implicit around the `SimpleMotionPath` tag, because `motionPaths` is the default property of the `Animation` class. Default properties help make MXML code more terse and readable, so I use them when I can.

line to updateHandler(), resulting in this new function that sets both x and y properties:

```
private function updateHandler(event:AnimationEvent):void
{
    button.x = event.animation.currentValue["x"];
    button.y = event.animation.currentValue["y"];
}
```

SimpleMotionPath is like the name says: simple. It's just about providing from/to information to an animation for a particular property. But since this is essentially what an animation does, animating a property from one value to another, it is quite important and useful. Next we'll see how to create more complex and flexible animations using the MotionPath class.

The MotionPath class

The main difference between SimpleMotionPath and its superclass is that MotionPath allows you to specify multiple values that a property animates between over the course of an animation. Like its subclass, MotionPath has a property variable. But instead of defining single from/to values, it takes a set of Keyframe objects that define several points along a path, which is an excellent segue to the next section.

The Keyframe class

The word *keyframe* comes from old cartoon animation, where each frame of a cartoon was hand-drawn. The typical process for any particular scene or action was that the senior animator would draw the "keyframe" poses which really defined the action, and then the junior animator would draw all of the frames in between (called, not surprisingly, "in-betweens").

Similarly, in computer animation, we provide start and end values for object properties and let the animation engine calculate all of the in-between values. We've already seen this with our animation examples so far; we provide the from and to values and the Animation class calculates the in-between values. So really, keyframes are nothing new to us. It's just that we have only seen situations with two keyframes so far: one at the beginning and one at the end.

162

But for more flexible animations, you really want the ability to define potentially several values along the way during an animation. In this model, each value you define can be considered another keyframe, and the intervals in between these keyframes are the times in between when the values are calculated by the animation.

In order to define these keyframes, you need some kind of data structure to hold the information. Each keyframe is really a time/value pair; it defines the time at which you want the property to have that value. Our earlier use of implicit keyframes, with the from/to pairs, did not need a time property because the time for each keyframe was assumed. The first keyframe was at time = 0 and the second was at the full duration of the animation. But when you have a sequence of several keyframes, you need to know for each one the time at which the property should be at that value. The Keyframe class is that data structure.

The Keyframe class has these two properties:

time This is the number of milliseconds from the start of the animation.

value This is the value of the property at the given time.

An optional valueBy property exists, like the similarly named property in the SimpleMotionPath class, that gives an offset of the value. The system computes the actual value when the animation is run so that the value equals the value at the previous keyframe plus this valueBy value. But typically, keyframes just use a time/value pair.

An important point to note is that the value and valueBy properties are Objects, not numbers. Most animations work on numeric values, especially GUI animations that are moving objects around or changing their size or fading them in and out. But it is possible to create animations that use non-numeric or complex data types. We will see more about this in the Section 8.5. For now, just think of the value as a number because it's easier to think of it that way and the values are usually numbers anyway.

Now that we know what a Keyframe is, we can see how MotionPath uses keyframes to define the animation of a given property. MotionPath has a property, keyframes, which is a Vector of Keyframes, which define the set of values that the property animates between over time. This is probably easiest to see with an example:

(Demo: MotionPathAnimation)

In this application, `MotionPathAnimation`, I have defined a complex path for the button to follow. The code is mostly copied from the previous example, `SimpleMotionPathAnimationXY`, which moved the button in a straight line from the upper left to the lower right with these two `SimpleMotionPath` objects:

(File: SimpleMotionPathAnimationXY.mxml)

```
<s:SimpleMotionPath property="x" valueFrom="0"
    valueTo="{width - button.width}"/>
<s:SimpleMotionPath property="y" valueFrom="0"
    valueTo="{height - button.height}"/>
```

`MotionPathAnimation` moves the button over to the right, then down, then back to the left with two `MotionPath` objects that animate the button's x and y properties in three stages:

(File: MotionPathAnimation.mxml)

```
<s:MotionPath property="x">
    <s:Keyframe time="0" value="0"/>
    <s:Keyframe time="500"
        value="{width - button.width}"/>
    <s:Keyframe time="1000"
        value="{width - button.width}"/>
    <s:Keyframe time="1500" value="0"/>
</s:MotionPath>
<s:MotionPath property="y">
    <s:Keyframe time="0" value="0"/>
    <s:Keyframe time="500" value="0"/>
```

164

```
<s:Keyframe time="1000"
    value="{height - button.height}"/>
<s:Keyframe time="1500"
    value="{height - button.height}"/>
</s:MotionPath>
```

We set up keyframes for x and y at time 0 to start our animation from the appropriate values. In the interval leading up to time 500, the button moves toward the right of the window. In the next interval leading up to time 1000, the button moves down toward the bottom right of the window. And leading up to the final interval at time 1500, the button moves back toward the bottom left of the window. Like the earlier examples, this is a repeating/reversing animation, so the button reverses course at the end and retraces its multiple steps back to its starting position.

Note that although we use the same time values in this example for both of these properties, this is not a requirement; it just depends on what you want your animation to do. For example, if we eliminate the two Keyframe objects in the middle for our y property, we get an animation that moves y constantly downward, independent of where the first MotionPath is positioning the button in x.

The eventual goal for keyframe animation in MotionPath is to allow more complex, curved animations, where you can define not only multiple steps along the way, but also more complex paths that the objects take between those points. For now, objects travel in a purely linear fashion between these points. So the advantage of having keyframes is more to simplify animations that otherwise would have been composed of several linear animations into one single segmented path. This composition saves some code and complexity over running several animations to do that task.[3]

We have now seen how to get more complex animations by using motion paths to animate over several properties in parallel, and potentially through several intervals along the way by using keyframes. Along the way, we mentioned that we could animate properties that were not just numbers. The next section on interpolation shows how this is possible.

---

[3] Keyframes actually came out of a Flex 4 SDK requirement that will be discussed in Chapter 9 to combine multiple parallel transform effects into a single running animation. This combination of effects is handled by creating multi-step keyframe sequences. Since Flex needed this capability internally, it made sense to expose the functionality externally for other developers to use, to create more complex multi-step animations of their own.

8.5   Interpolation: when numbers just aren't enough

Interpolation, or calculating values between other known values, is a critical piece of an animation engine. Without the ability to determine those in-between values, the animation engine would not be able to determine the values to set properties to during an animation.

One of the important, new capabilities of effects in Flex 4 is the interpolation of non-numeric types. Prior to Flex 4, Flex animations assumed and operated on purely numeric values. You could animate any property you wanted ... as long as it was of type `Number`. But sometimes you want to animate objects that aren't numbers, like `Points` or `Rectangles`. Or sometimes you may want to animate numbers, but in a way that doesn't just calculate the animated values by linear interpolation of the numeric endpoints. We will see why this is sometimes necessary when we discuss color animation in Section 9.5.

The tricky part with interpolating arbitrary types is that Flex has no idea how to interpolate a random property type for which it is given start and end values. If you give an animation a start `Rectangle` and an end `Rectangle`, what should the system do? Or to make the problem even trickier, if you give it an `Object` for each endpoint, how does it know what kind of `Objects` they are, much less how to calculate in-between values for them?

To handle this functionality, Flex has introduced the concept of type interpolation for effects, via the new **IInterpolator** interface. You can now create animations with arbitrary objects and types by implementing this interface. Since Flex cannot possibly know how to interpolate between any arbitrary typed endpoints, you can tell it how to do so. You supply the interpolator and Flex calls your code to perform the interpolation. Flex handles the rest of the animation calculations to determine the fraction elapsed of an animation. Then when it is ready to turn that fraction into an actual value for a given property, it calls the interpolator to calculate the value.

By default, Flex uses the built-in `NumberInterpolator` so you don't have to worry about supplying an interpolator for typical situations involving numbers. But for any situation that requires custom interpolation, you supply an interpolator and Flex calls that object to perform the calculation.

An example will help explain how this works. Take a look at the demo application `PointAnimation`, seen here:

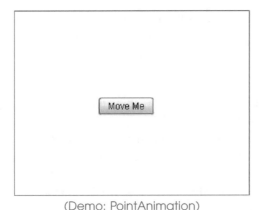

(Demo: PointAnimation)

This application is based on SimpleMotionPathAnimationXY, which we discussed earlier. In the previous version of the code, we animated both x and y using two separate SimpleMotionPath objects to describe their motion paths:

(File: SimpleMotionPathAnimationXY.mxml)

```
<s:SimpleMotionPath property="x" valueFrom="0"
    valueTo="{width - button.width}"/>
<s:SimpleMotionPath property="y" valueFrom="0"
    valueTo="{height - button.height}"/>
```

In the new version, PointAnimation, we use just one SimpleMotionPath to achieve the same effect:

(File: PointAnimation.mxml)

```
<s:SimpleMotionPath property="location"
    valueFrom="{startPoint}" valueTo="{endPoint}"/>
```

We need only one SimpleMotionPath because we are now animating a single Point object, which encapsulates both the x and the y properties in the target object:

```
[Bindable]
private var startPoint:Point = new Point(0, 0);
[Bindable]
private var endPoint:Point = new Point(200, 200);
```

Of course, Animation does not know how to animate Point objects by default, so we have to tell it how to do so. First, we need a custom interpolator, which I've called PointInterpolator:

(File: utils/PointInterpolator.as)

```
public class PointInterpolator implements IInterpolator
{
    public function interpolate(fraction:Number,
        startValue:Object, endValue:Object):Object
    {
        var startPoint:Point = Point(startValue);
        var endPoint:Point = Point(endValue);
        return new Point(
            startPoint.x + fraction *
                (endPoint.x - startPoint.x),
            startPoint.y + fraction *
                (endPoint.y - startPoint.y));
    }

    public function increment(baseValue:Object,
        incrementValue:Object):Object
    {
        var basePoint:Point = Point(baseValue);
        var incrementPoint:Point = Point(incrementValue);
        return new Point(basePoint.x + incrementPoint.x,
            basePoint.y + incrementPoint.y);
    }

    public function decrement(baseValue:Object,
        decrementValue:Object):Object
    {
        var basePoint:Point = Point(baseValue);
        var decrementPoint:Point = Point(decrementValue);
        return new Point(basePoint.x - decrementPoint.x,
            basePoint.y - decrementPoint.y);
    }
}
```

This class implements the IInterpolator interface, which has the three functions implemented in our PointInterpolator class. The most important function is the first one: `interpolate()`. It is this function which `Animation` calls every frame to calculate the animated value for the current elapsed fraction of the animation. The function is called with three values:

`fraction` This is the elapsed fraction of the animation. For example, if 250 milliseconds has elapsed in an animation with a duration of one second, then `fraction` equals `.25`.

`startValue, endValue` These are the values of the property at the start and end of the animation.

Note that in the case of animations with more than two keyframes, as we discussed in the previous section, the `fraction`, `startValue`, and `endValue` values passed into the `interpolate()` function are for the current animation interval, not the overall animation.

Given these function parameters, we can calculate the current animated value. The approach used in `PointInterpolator`'s `interpolate()` function is a typical parametric calculation in both x and y, where the animated value is simply the start value, plus the fraction, times the difference between the start and end values.

The other functions in `PointInterpolator`, and in any `IInterpolator` implementation, are used when an animation is created with a "by" value, such as the `valueBy` property of `SimpleMotionPath`. These functions enable `Animation` to calculate the actual start or end value given one or the other plus the "by" value. Just as `Animation` doesn't know how to calculate interpolated values for arbitrary types, it doesn't know how to calculate some delta from a supplied start or end value if it does not understand the type. So it relies on a supplied interpolator to perform that calculation.

Now that we have defined our interpolator, we create an instance of it and give it to the `Animation` object:

(File: PointAnimation.mxml)

```
<utils:PointInterpolator id="pointInterpolator"/>
<s:Animation id="anim" duration="500" repeatBehavior="reverse"
    repeatCount="0" animationTarget="{animTarget}"
    interpolator="{pointInterpolator}">

    <s:SimpleMotionPath property="location"
        valueFrom="{startPoint}" valueTo="{endPoint}"/>

</s:Animation>
```

Here, we create an instance of our interpolator, `pointInterpolator`, and then supply it to the `Animation` by setting the `interpolator` property. By default, `interpolator` is set to an instance of `NumberInterpolator`, so numeric interpolations happen with no intervention required. But by supplying our own `interpolator`, we ensure that the animation calls our code to figure out how to interpolate between our `Point` values.

The end result of the `PointAnimation` application is the same as the earlier `SimpleMotionPathAnimationXY` example; it animates the button from the upper left to the lower right. In fact, since we could do this animation before with just two `SimpleMotionPath` objects acting on x and y individually, the extra effort in writing a custom interpolator to animate the `Point` value doesn't really seem worth it. Of course, the example was written mostly to demonstrate how you might write and use a custom interpolator when you actually need to, and the `PointInterpolator` was simple to understand. But in some cases, you might want to take this approach instead of animating separate properties. For example, I recently wrote an application where animating the size and location of an AIR application required using a `Rectangle` interpolator on the window's bounds. In that case, the custom interpolator was needed because setting the individual x, y, `width`, and `height` properties on the window caused the window to jerk around on the screen as each property update was handled immediately by the native window. It worked far better to animate the bounds structure and set the rectangular native window bounds structure atomically, which was only possible by animating the more complex `Rectangle` structure instead of the individual properties.

 Interpolators are useful when a type is not understood by the system or when you need to combine multiple property animations into single data structure animation.

Note that interpolators are not just used at the `Animation` level; you can also supply a custom interpolator to a `MotionPath` or `SimpleMotionPath` object. Each motion path being animated by a single `Animation` is responsible for calculating the animated values for its property, so interpolation happens at that level. So it is possible to animate, say, a numeric value like the width of an object at the same time as animating a `Point`-based location value inside the same `Animation`. Also, as with many of the other properties, Flex effects (which we will discuss starting in the next chapter) accept custom interpolators, so you don't have to dive down to the `Animation` level to get custom interpolation.

We've seen how to handle animating arbitrary types in Flex animations, which was one of the new capabilities introduced in Flex 4. Now let's see another new element in Flex 4 animations: easing.

8.6 Easing does it

In the real world, objects accelerate when they fall with gravity and decelerate when moving against gravity. Friction slows objects down. People accelerate into a steady walking speed and decelerate when coming to a stop. Vehicles accelerate and decelerate when starting and stopping. All of these motions use non-linear timing. Anything that moves linearly in time, starting, moving, and stopping with the same speed, looks unnatural and robotic.

If we want our applications to feel natural to our users, then we should use non-linear timing in our animations. Otherwise, the animations simply look and feel wrong, like a poor attempt to make something whizzy on the screen, rather than a fluid motion that attempts to integrate with the user's real world experience.

 Good animations use non-linear timing to achieve natural motion.

Non-linear timing is the concept behind *easing*: the ability to change the timing of how things are moved about on the screen. Acceleration, deceleration, bouncing, springing; all of these and more can be applied to different UI situations to get an appropriate feel for the application.

Easing was already a powerful capability in Flex effects prior to Flex 4. You could pick one of several built-in easing functions and tell an animation to use that easing function when calculating the target values for its objects.

Flex 4 has expanded on that earlier system to provide one that has similar capabilities, but much more flexibility. The flexibility is both in terms of the built-in easing classes that you can use by default and in a simple API that you can implement to provide your own custom easing. First, let's talk about the classes that come with the Flex SDK and how to use them in your applications. Then we'll see how to implement your own easers if you want to go beyond the classes that Flex supplies by default.

The ins and outs of easing

Some of the easing classes provide the functionality of easing in and/or out of an animation. Or if you really want linear timing, the Linear class also provides the capability of no easing at all. Whether and how much you want to accelerate in, decelerate out, both, or neither, one of these classes should suit your needs.

Linear This class provides linear timing, which results in constant motion, if that's what you need. Linear timing is equivalent to using the elapsed fraction of an animation (effectively providing no easing at all). However, two properties exist on this class that enable accelerating into the motion (easeInFraction) and decelerating out of it (easeOutFraction). Using these properties creates a motion that starts off slow, accelerates to some constant speed, and then slows down at the end.

Sine This class, the default used by Animation and the Flex effects that we will see in upcoming chapters, provides a gentle acceleration into the motion and deceleration out of it. Unlike Linear, this class provides easing that is always either accelerating or decelerating; there is no period of constant motion. The easeInFraction controls the percentage of time spent accelerating; the rest of the time is spent decelerating. For example, a value of .5 causes the object to accelerate for the first half and decelerate for the second half (this type of motion is sometimes called "ease in-out"). A value of 1 causes the object to start slowly and accelerate all the way through the animation. And a value of 0 causes the object to start out fast and decelerate throughout the entire animation.

Power This class, like Sine, provides the ability to accelerate into and then decelerate out of the motion, using the same easeInFraction to control how much time is spent in either phase. But an additional parameter, exponent, controls the shape of the acceleration/deceleration curves. The internal calculation multiplies the elapsed fraction of the

172

animation by itself exponent times. The higher the exponent, the greater the acceleration/deceleration curve. For example, an exponent of 2 provides a very gentle quadratic acceleration/deceleration motion, which starts immediately and gradually accelerates, whereas an exponent of 5 starts out much slower but accelerates much faster.[4]

Fun easing classes

The other two easing classes in Flex 4, Bounce and Elastic, provide a more fun easing experience, causing objects to appear more lifelike as they bounce against or wobble around the end value of an animation. These easing classes are not appropriate for all situations, but they can help liven up a UI experience by making it seem more organic and enjoyable:[5]

Bounce This class causes the object to accelerate toward the end point and bounce against it several times before stopping.

Elastic This class is like Bounce except instead of bouncing off the endpoint, it shoots past and wobbles around the end like it's on a spring, gradually decreasing its oscillations and stopping at the endpoint.

 Lifelike motions like bouncing can add fun to an application.

---

[4] If you used the Flex 3 easing classes, you may wonder what happened to the old Quadratic, Cubic, Quartic, and Quintic classes. Theses classes don't exist explicitly in Flex 4 effects, but their functionality has been subsumed into the single Power function. By using the exponent property, you can achieve the same behavior as any of these classes. But since exponent has no limit, you can also achieve any higher-order function instead of being constrained to the previous level of Quintic. And by setting the easeInFraction appropriately, you can achieve the old easeIn, easeOut, and easeInOut function behavior, but since you can set the fraction to anything between 0 and 1, you have much more flexibility for setting the inflection point between the accelerating and decelerating curves. So the old functionality of these classes didn't go away, only the classes did.

[5] Whenever I give a presentation with a demo that uses a bounce effect, I never fail to get smiles or even laughter from the crowd. There is something inherently fun about seeing objects on the screen mimic lifelike behavior. Just adding a simple bounce to an object can imbue it with life and happiness in a way that no other amount of smooth gradients, drop shadows, and beautiful design can. I think this is one of the things that makes cartoons so enjoyable; it's inexplicably fun to see simple objects on the screen taking on the attributes and physical interactions of objects in the real world.

To use any of these easing classes, you simply create the object, supply property values as appropriate, and then supply the instance to your Animation object. We can see this in the BounceAnimation example:

(Demo: BounceAnimation)

This example is based SimpleMotionPathAnimation, we which discussed earlier. First, we declare our Bounce object:

(File: BounceAnimation.mxml)
```
<s:Bounce id="bounce"/>
```

Next, we supply this object to the easer property of our Animation. Note that we have changed this Animation slightly from the version in the earlier SimpleMotionPathAnimation example. For one thing, it animates the y property of the button instead of x, and it uses a Bounce easer to give it a gravity bounce feel as it animates toward the bottom of the window and bounces against it. Also, we have removed the repetition behavior of the button to make the example simpler (and because a repeating bounce simply doesn't look right):

```
<s:Animation id="anim" duration="1500"
    animationTarget="{animTarget}"
    easer="{bounce}">

    <s:SimpleMotionPath property="y" valueFrom="0"
```

174

```
        valueTo="{height - button.height}"/>
</s:Animation>
```

Our `updateHandler()` function was also updated slightly from the previous version in order to handle animating y instead of x:

```
private function updateHandler(event:AnimationEvent):void
{
    button.y = event.animation.currentValue["y"];
}
```

And that's it: all we have to do to get any custom easing behavior is create and supply an instance of the appropriate easing class to our `Animation`. Internally, the `Animation` class calculates the real elapsed fraction of the animation, then calls into its `easer` implementation (the default is `Sine` with an `easeInFraction` of .5) to get the eased fraction, and then passes that fraction into the interpolator to calculate the animated, eased value for that animation frame.

The simple part of easing is writing the code that uses the classes. The trickier part is picking the appropriate easing class for your situation. It helps to be able to visualize the behavior of the easing classes, which is best done by watching them in action.

Run the `EasingSampler` application, seen here:

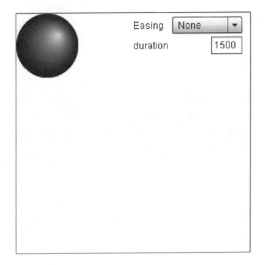

The code is based on the earlier example, BounceAnimation, except for the additional code to handle setting up the animation and animating a ball instead of the button.[6] But the logic of creating and running anim is the same as before; we simply animate the y property of the ball.

The application allows you to set up an animation with any of the built-in easing classes and to set the properties of those easers. Here we can see the drop down list showing the easing classes that are available in the SDK and in the application—Sine, Power, Linear, Bounce, and Elastic (None indicates no easing):

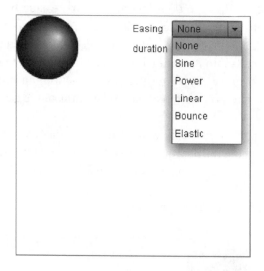

Once a selection is made, UI controls will appear that allow us to set the various properties of that easer. For example, if we choose the Power easer from the drop down list, we see fields for both easeInFraction and exponent, which allow us to configure these parameters for the resulting Power instance:

---

[6] Somehow, a ball accelerating toward the bottom of the window just looks better than a button doing the same thing. Maybe because in the real world we grew up bouncing balls on the ground and not UI controls.

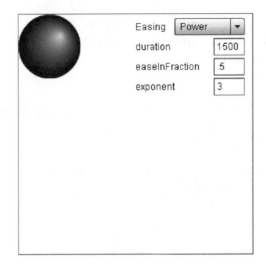

Each of the possible easers is set up with data bindings to its properties in the various input fields:

(File: EasingSampler.mxml)

```
<s:Sine id="sine" easeInFraction="{Number(easeInInput.text)}"/>
<s:Power id="power" easeInFraction="{Number(easeInInput.text)}"
    exponent="{Number(exponentInput.text)}"/>
<s:Linear id="linear" easeInFraction="{Number(easeInInput.text)}"
    easeOutFraction="{Number(easeOutInput.text)}"/>
<s:Bounce id="bounce"/>
<s:Elastic id="elastic"/>
```

The Animation is set up with no easer to begin with, but the current selection in the drop down list causes that property to be configured whenever the value changes (including when the drop down list is first instantiated and the value of None is set):

```
<s:DropDownList id="easingList" selectedItem="None"
    width="90" change="easingChangeHandler()">
    <s:ArrayCollection>
        <fx:String>None</fx:String>
        <fx:String>Sine</fx:String>
        <fx:String>Power</fx:String>
        <fx:String>Linear</fx:String>
```

```
        <fx:String>Bounce</fx:String>
        <fx:String>Elastic</fx:String>
    </s:ArrayCollection>
</s:DropDownList>
```

Changes to the drop down list result in a call to easingChangeHandler():

```
private function easingChangeHandler():void
{
    currentState = easingList.selectedItem;
    switch (easingList.selectedItem) {
        case "None":
            anim.easer = null;
            break;
        case "Sine":
            anim.easer = sine;
            break;
        case "Power":
            anim.easer = power;
            break;
        case "Linear":
            anim.easer = linear;
            break;
        case "Bounce":
            anim.easer = bounce;
            break;
        case "Elastic":
            anim.easer = elastic;
            break;
    }
}
```

This function first sets the currentState of the application, which is used by the various input fields to determine whether they should be visible, according to whether they are used by the currently selected item in the easing list.[7] Then the easer property of the animation is set according to the selected item in the drop down list. The item is already configured with the

---

[7] In case I didn't make this clear in Chapter 4, I love states in Flex. In particular, I love the new states syntax in Flex 4, which makes UI code like this so easy to write and read.

178

various settings in the input fields because its values are set through data binding to those field values. So as soon as we set the easer property, we're ready to go. Now we just click on the ball and watch it move.

The first setting is "None," which causes the animation to have a simple linear ease with no acceleration or deceleration (this is the default behavior for Animation if you pass in null for the easer property). You can see that the motion of the object is very unnatural and just cries out for something more lifelike, with some natural acceleration and deceleration.

Play with the application, get a feel for how the various easing behaviors change the nature of the animation. Play with the duration field too; some of the easing behaviors feel more natural with longer or shorter durations. For example, Elastic easing benefits from a longer duration, probably because it is moving much more during the animation, so a short duration ends up making it feel unnaturally fast.

 No single animation behavior fits all situations; experiment with different approaches to find the motion that works.

Custom easing

Sometimes, the easing behavior you want for your application may not be possible with the built-in classes. Maybe it's a variation on the one of the built-in classes, or maybe it's something entirely new. In either case, providing your own custom easer for an animation is a trivial task. All you have to do is write an implementation of the IEaser interface. The interface has just one function that takes a single argument and returns a value:

```
public interface IEaser
{
    function ease(fraction:Number):Number;
}
```

During each update of an animation, the Animation calculates the elapsed fraction of its duration and passes that fraction, a number between 0 and 1, into its easer. That easer calculates a new fraction, based on its easing function, and returns that value. Usually, the return value is also a value between 0 and 1, although the `Elastic` easer returns values greater than 1 when it overshoots the endpoint to get its springy effect.

All you have to do in your custom easer is figure out how you want to alter the elapsed fraction to get the kind of easing effect that you desire. For example, look at the `CustomEaseAnimation` application:

(Demo: CustomEaseAnimation)

This application is exactly like the earlier `BounceAnimation` example, except that instead of creating and using a `Bounce` easer, we use our own easer, `CustomEaser`:

(File: CustomEaseAnimation.mxml)

```
<utils:CustomEaser id="customEaser"/>
<s:Animation id="anim" duration="1500"
    animationTarget="{animTarget}"
    easer="{customEaser}">

    <s:SimpleMotionPath property="y" valueFrom="0"
        valueTo="{height - button.height}"/>

</s:Animation>
```

`CustomEaser` is an implementation of `IEaser`, where I've written my own `ease()` function to return an eased fraction. By default, the function simply returns the `fraction` passed into the function:

180

(File: utils/CustomEaser.as)

```
public function ease(fraction:Number):Number
{
    return fraction;
}
```

This behavior is equivalent to a linear ease, or no ease at all; the eased fraction equals the elapsed fraction of the animation. No acceleration, deceleration, or other timing behavior is applied. But the point of this example is not the behavior of the default CustomEaser, but rather to be a shell for you to write and experiment with your own easing behavior. For example, if you want an easer that reverses the direction of the animation, you could rewrite ease() to invert the value of the elapsed fraction:

```
public function ease(fraction:Number):Number
{
    return 1 - fraction;
}
```

Or if you wanted some power function, you could multiply the fraction by itself. For example, this function calculates a cubic, accelerating result:[8]

```
public function ease(fraction:Number):Number
{
    return fraction * fraction * fraction;
}
```

You can really do anything you want in a custom easer to come up with easing behavior that makes sense for your application. The main constraint is that you should try to make your fraction map to values between 0 and 1, since the return value is used to calculate the amount of change between the start and end points of the animation, and values wildly outside of that range may not give a sensible result.[9] But even this constraint is soft, as we saw with the Elastic easer, which returns values beyond 1 as it wobbles

---

[8] Of course, you don't need to write your own easer to get this cubic functionality; just use the built-in Power class with an exponent of 3. But you get the idea.

[9] For example, imagine if you are animating a color value between black (0) and blue (255). If your easer implementation returns a value of 2, the resulting color would be 510 (twice the end value). I don't know what that would look like, but it wouldn't be blue.

the animation past the end point. So go: edit the `CustomEaser` code, play around with it, and have fun.

Like we discussed earlier for type interpolation, easing capability is not limited to just the `Animation` class. You can supply custom easing to any `Keyframe` object to get different easing during a single interval of a multi-step motion path. And the `easer` object is also used at the effects level, which is discussed in the coming chapters. The actual implementation of the property and functionality is at the `Animation` level, but typical users of easers supply them at the higher effects level, then the Flex effects pass them down to the `Animation` objects they use internally.

8.7 The `Animation` class and Flex effects

The motion paths, interpolation, and easing capabilities discussed in this chapter are on the `Animation` object. But this functionality is also found, and more commonly used, at the Flex effects level. We covered these features in this chapter to show how they work at the underlying `Animation` level. But Flex effects expose these same features, and then supply them to their underlying `Animation` objects.

In the upcoming chapters on effects, we will see how some of the effects like `Animate` use motion paths directly to declare the properties that they operate on. We will also see how the `AnimateColor` effect uses custom type interpolation under the hood to animate values that cannot be interpolated by straight numeric interpolation. And the easing behavior we discussed in the previous section can be used on any effect by supplying a value to the `easer` property to that effect. So while we showed all of these properties in the context of the `Animation` class, which is probably a lower level of Flex effects than most Flex developers use, you can and should apply these same techniques to the higher-level Flex effects to get the same powerful functionality for your applications.

Conclusion

In this chapter, we've seen some interesting aspects of the `Animation` class. In particular, we've seen not only how `Animation` simplifies the code needed to run animations, but also how it offers powerful features such as custom type interpolation and easing. In fact, this is exactly the purpose that

Animation serves for Flex effects; it is the underlying timing engine of those effect classes.

Now that we've seen what's going on at the Animation level, it's about time we talked about Flex effects, which is the subject of the next chapter.

Chapter 9

Flex Effects: The Basics

Flex effects are a set of classes providing task-based ways of animating target objects, like Move to move objects around, Resize to change objects' dimensions, and Fade to fade objects in and out. The effects are, like many Flex objects, declarative in nature, and make it easy to write MXML code that creates the effect which can later be played on its target object.

You can think of Flex effects as combining the capabilities and API of Animation, which we discussed in Chapter 8, with the functionality of actually setting animated values on target objects (which we had to handle ourselves in those Animation examples). In fact, as I mentioned in the previous chapter, Flex effects use the Animation class internally to run the actual animations that calculate the property values for the effects. But once the values are calculated for each animation frame, the effect takes care of setting those values on its target object so that you don't have to get involved once you've created and started the effect.

Flex effects also provide utility properties to make it easier to supply effect-specific values. For example, since the Move effect is all about changing x and y values, it exposes the properties xFrom, yFrom, xTo, and yTo, rather than making you create and populate the underlying motionPaths object with a list of SimpleMotionPath objects that do the same thing.

Finally, Flex effects have extra logic built into them that builds on what they know about Flex GUI objects. The Animation class is Flex-agnostic;[1] it exists just to run a timer and calculate animated values. But Flex effects use knowledge of Flex to create more useful and powerful animations. For

---

[1] In fact, I built a library with Animation and its helper classes that has no dependencies on the rest of the Flex toolkit and posted the resulting "Flexy" library to my blog.

example, the Fade effect can figure out whether to fade an object in or out based on state information about the object's existence or visibility.

Most of the work of effects is done by the Animate class, which is the superclass of all of the Flex 4 effects. The subclasses of Animate provide differing types and amounts of added functionality, from simple utility wrappers that expose convenience properties to more complex systems to handle effect-specific features. We will see some of the simpler and more common effects in this chapter and then take a look at the more advanced effects in Chapter 10. But first, here's a little background.

Flex 4 vs. Flex 3 effects

The effects system in Flex was rewritten in Flex 4 to suit new requirements for the platform: Flex needed to support animation of arbitrary objects and arbitrary types.

Previously, except for some corner cases, Flex effects enabled animation on components only, calling specific functions on those components to change their properties appropriately. For example, the Move effect in Flex 3 called the move() function on its target objects to change their (x, y) positions. This worked fine in Flex 3, where UIs were constructed only of components and such assumptions were always true.

But in Flex 4, different kinds of objects inhabit the UI, such as the new graphic elements that we saw in Chapter 2. In addition, a new tool exists for creating Flex applications, Flash Catalyst, which designers can use to create and animate UI elements, including these graphics objects. It is no longer possible to assume that animations target only components. Instead, Flex needed a more general animation system that allows these other non-component objects to be animated as well.

Also, the former effects system was somewhat constraining because it could only animate specific types of values. In particular, it only dealt with Number values. This works fine in the common case, where an application animates numeric values such as the width or x location of an object. But what if you want to animate a String object for some specific effect? Or some more complex data structure object? Or some arbitrary type specific to your application? Or what if your type is a numeric value but you want to interpolate in-between values in a way that is not just a linear interpolation between the endpoints? For example, colors are represented as unsigned integers, but interpolating colors should not be done by straight numeric interpolation. Instead, the interpolator should break the color into its component channels and interpolate those channels separately. If Flex 4 is to support a wide variety of applications and appeal to designers for creating more rich user experiences, clearly it needs to support animating arbitrary types as well as arbitrary objects.

So the effects system in Flex 4 was written to support these goals, building upon a new framework that allows animation of arbitrary types and objects. The arbitrary type interpolation capability is provided by the underlying Animation class that effects use, as we saw in Chapter 8. The ability to animate arbitrary objects comes from the new Animate class.

9.1   The Animate effect

Animate is the superclass of the new effects classes in Flex 4, providing common functionality that is used by the new effects, including the ability to target arbitrary objects and types and the creation and playing of the underlying Animation class that we discussed earlier. Animate can also be used directly to animate properties on target objects.

Creating and playing an Animate effect is easy: you provide one or more target objects to be modified, the names of the properties on the targets to be animated, and the values that the properties animate between while the effect plays. You also set some optional parameters on the effect, such as the duration that the effect should last. Finally, you call play() to start the effect, or have the effect start automatically as part of a state transition, as we saw in Chapter 5.

Let's take a look at an example, AnimateButtons:

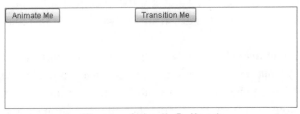

(Demo: AnimateButtons)

The Animate effect in this application operates on the x, y, and width property of the button simultaneously:

(File: AnimateButtons.mxml)

```
<s:Animate id="mover" target="{button}">
    <s:SimpleMotionPath property="x"
        valueFrom="0" valueTo="100"/>
    <s:SimpleMotionPath property="y" valueTo="100"/>
    <s:SimpleMotionPath property="width" valueBy="100"/>
</s:Animate>
```

The button object is defined as follows:

```
<s:Button id="button" label="Animate Me"
    click="mover.play()"/>
```

Note that the underlying Animation uses motion paths as its mechanism of supplying properties and values, as we saw in Section 8.4. Most of the Flex effects, like Move and Resize, expose properties that wrap motion paths internally. But the general-purpose Animate superclass uses motion paths, and typically SimpleMotionPath, as the way to get that information. Check out Section 8.4; supplying motion paths to Animate works exactly as it does for Animation.

The button animates x between 0 and 100 during the course of the effect by specifying both the from and to values for that property. y is animated to a value of 100 from whatever it was before the effect began; the valueFrom property is optional, as long as you want it to start from its current location. And width is animated from whatever it is now by 100 pixels, so the size effectively increases by 100 pixels during the effect. The difference between these last two ways of specifying the animation amount is that the one using valueBy always changes the value by the specified amount, whereas the valueTo version always changes it to the value of 100, regardless of the initial value.

This example also shows how to use transitions with Animate. As we saw earlier in Chapter 5, transitions make it easier to declare an effect that runs when states change, where the values being animated from and to are picked up automatically by the effect when the transition starts. In this case, we declare an Animate effect in a transition that animates the same properties as before, but without specifying the from/to values for the properties:

```
<s:Transition>
    <s:Animate target="{button1}">
```

188

```
    <s:SimpleMotionPath property="x"/>
    <s:SimpleMotionPath property="y"/>
    <s:SimpleMotionPath property="width"/>
  </s:Animate>
</s:Transition>
```

The object being animated, button1, is declared with state-dependent values for the properties that we want to change between states:

```
<s:Button id="button1" label="Transition Me"
    x="200" x.s2="300" y="0" y.s2="100" width.s2="150"
    click="currentState=(currentState=='s1') ? 's2' : 's1'"/>
```

button1 defines different state values for x, y, and width. These values are picked up by the transition when it runs to populate the from/to values of the transition effect. Clicking on the button toggles between the two states and plays the transition effect, resulting in an animation that is very similar to the effect that is manually played on the button object.

You can see the buttons after both the manually-played effect and the transition effect have run here:

Notice, in this example, that we are doing similar things with Animate to what we did in the earlier Animation examples in the previous chapter, but that the Animate effect handles the additional functionality of actually setting the animated properties on our buttons for us. Animate and Animation have similar functionality for animating properties between different values. However, in the case of Animate, we now have a simpler way of specifying the target object (button) and letting the Animate class handle the details of setting the animated values on our object. Also, in the case of the button animating between states using transition effects, the additional details of specifying the different values to animate from and to are handled for us by the state transitions mechanism.

As we noted earlier, the main purpose of `Animate` is as the superclass of the rest of the Flex effects. It provides the main capability that these effects rely on: associating an `Animation` with the target objects and properties being animated and setting the animated values on the object over time. Typically, you would not use `Animate` directly, but if you ever find yourself wanting an effect that does not exist in the current set of effects, then you may want to use `Animate`. You can achieve very custom effects just by using `Animate` to directly animate an objects properties.[2]

Now that we've seen how `Animate` works, let's look at some of the basic Flex effects that subclass from it.

9.2   The `Resize` effect

The `Resize` effect is responsible for animating the `width` and `height` of its target objects. It exposes from/to/by values through the properties named `widthFrom`, `heightFrom`, `widthTo`, `heightTo`, `widthBy`, and `heightBy`.

At its most basic level, the `Resize` effect is not much more than a simple wrapper around the from, to, and by properties of `SimpleMotionPath` objects for `width` and `height` properties of an `Animate` effect. In fact, that's essentially what's going on under the covers; Resize bundles up the information provided for its `width` and `height` from/to/by properties and creates the appropriate `SimpleMotionPath` objects internally to run the animation.

However, `Resize` also provides more capabilities that account for Flex layout constraints. This capability is not something that is apparent when manually playing an effect, but is very important when the constraints of an object change between states, as we will see in the following example.

Resize constraints

Layout constraints are styles or properties on objects that tell the Flex layout manager how to position those objects. For example, you may want a button to be positioned ten pixels away from the right border of its container, no

---

[2] Prior to Flex 4, it was sometimes necessary to create a custom effect class if you went past the built-in functionality of the existing Flex effects. And creating a custom effect class was not an obvious task. But with the flexible functionality of the `Animate` effect in Flex 4, creating custom effects should be as easy as declaring and playing an `Animate` effect that targets the appropriate object properties.

matter what size that container is. Instead of specifying the x property directly, and having to recalculate it whenever the container size changes, you simply specify a value for `right`:

```
<s:Button id="button" right="10"/>
```

In some cases, layout constraints specify not only the position of an object, but also its size. For example, if you specify both the `left` and `right` constraints of an object, the size of that object is dependent on its container's size. In this code, the button is always positioned ten pixels from the left of its container and has a width equal to its container's width minus twenty:

```
<s:Button id="button" left="10" right="10"/>
```

Let's look at an example, `ResizingConstraints`. Suppose we want to specify different values for the `left` and `right` constraints for the button in different states:

(File: ResizingConstraints.mxml)
```
<s:Button id="button" left="10" left.s2="50"
    right="10" right.s2="50"/>
```

In the first state, the button looks like this:

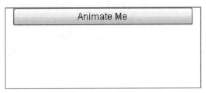

(Demo: ResizingConstraints)

In the next state, with different `left` and `right` values, the button looks less wide, like this:

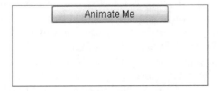

All we have to do to animate this change is to declare a `Resize` effect as the `Transition` for this state change:

191

```
<s:transitions>
    <s:Transition>
        <s:Resize target="{button}"/>
    </s:Transition>
</s:transitions>
```

Note that the effect doesn't specify any `width` or `height` information for the `Resize` effect; the effect is able to infer these values from the change in the layout constraints between the states.[3] This is the kind of extra logic that is built into the effects subclasses of `Animate`. On the surface, they are little more than utility wrappers around the named-property animating capabilities of the `Animate` class. But underneath, they each have extra logic which can help create very powerful effects with very little code, by using what they know about Flex GUI objects.

9.3   Transform effects

Three of the effects are grouped together, both logically and technically: the transform effects `Move`, `Rotate`, and `Scale`. These three effects act on their target object's *transform matrix*. The transform matrix of a Flex object is a data structure[4] that determines the placement and orientation of the

---

[3] In fact, you really should avoid specifying hard-coded animation properties when running effects within a transition. For one thing, the hard-coded values may be wrong in some situations, such as animating from a value that doesn't equal the current value of that property when the effect begins. But also, some of the extra logic built into effects only kicks in when no hard-coded overrides for these properties are supplied. The effects code assumes that if you supply specific values you must know what you're doing, and you'll lose the benefit from some of the automatic logic that might apply otherwise. So just follow this general rule: for effects that are run within transitions, set state-specific values on the object itself, not on the effect. Then the effect picks up the right values automatically.

[4] Specifically, this data structure is a matrix that holds information in its rows and columns about where the object is and how it should be rotated and scaled. Matrices are useful tools in computer graphics and are very commonly used for describing object placement and orientation. When I first took Linear Algebra in college, I thought that matrices were just some abstract notion in math meant to make me suffer an early and very dull death. But in my first computer graphics course later on, I realized they serve a very important purpose in graphics, as a handy and powerful utility for moving objects around ("transforming" them) between different spaces. For example, matrix math makes it possible to take an object defined in 3D coordinates and figure out where and how to draw it on the screen, by transforming the points of the object from its local coordinates into the screen's 2D coordinate

object; the object's (x, y) location, scale factors, and rotation are all handled through this matrix. So although you typically set these attributes of an object through these other properties (*e.g.*, object.rotation = 45 to rotate some object by forty five degrees), they affect the object's underlying transform matrix. Because the transform effects all act on that same underlying transform matrix, they coordinate their transform changes together. These transform effects are combined internally into one single transform effect, so that whenever the object is updated during an animation, all of the effects of movement, rotation, and scale are applied simultaneously in a single transform operation, thus ensuring that the effects work together to reposition the object instead of clobbering each others' efforts.

Because the effects combine internally, some nuances particular to transform effects exist that you should be aware of. Specifically, some effect properties are shared between transform effects that are running in parallel. The value of these shared properties is taken from the first of these effects to be declared. It is good practice to declare the same shared property with the same value on all effects running together, to make it obvious in reading the code what is happening at runtime. The shared properties include:

transform center The properties that affect the point around which the target object is transformed, autoCenterTransform, transformX, and transformY, are shared. You cannot specify that the transform center is shared for a Rotate effect and not shared for a Scale effect running at the same time; the single underlying transform effect uses the value that was declared first.

repetition Because these effects are combined and run together, the notion of repetition, as defined by the repeatCount and repeatBehavior properties, is not always workable. If a single transform effect is running, then everything should work as defined. But if multiple effects are combined, then repetition may not work as specified because of the way that the effects are combined internally. It is a best practice to hoist the repetition behavior up to a higher level, such as an owning Parallel or Sequence effect.

---

system. If you're interested in doing more with computer graphics and this is all new to you, I'd encourage you to learn more about matrices and matrix math. But you might pick up a graphics book on the subject and not try to learn it from my first Linear Algebra professor.

The transformation of transform effects in Flex 4

Prior to Flex 4, there were also transform effects: `Move`, `Rotate`, and `Zoom`. But in Flex 3, these effects operated independently. This resulted in some artifacts where multiple effects on the same object running in parallel would sometimes trample each other.

For example, a `Rotate` effect in Flex 3 automatically rotates the object about its center, but this means that the (`x, y`) position of the object changes as a side-effect (since that point is usually at the upper-left of the object, and that upper-left point changes as the object rotated). So if a `Move` effect is running at the same time on the same object, attempting to set the location of that upper-left point, the effects give conflicting instructions to the object. One effect tells the upper-left point to rotate about the object center and the other effect tells that same point to move to a new location. Similarly, a `Zoom` effect around the object's center changes both the scale factor of the object and its location, which might conflict with any other `Move` or `Rotate` effects running at the same time.

The transform effects in Flex 4 address this issue by combining the effects internally, making one overall effect that combines the instructions of movement, rotation, and scaling into a single transform operation that sets the target object at the right position and orientation at each update.

Along the way, there was also a rename: the new `Scale` effect takes the place of the old Zoom effect. Although "zoom" is a good name for a 3D effect that zooms an object out to or away from the viewer, "scale" seems to fit more with what's going on in this effect: changing the 2D scale factors of the object.

All of the transform effects subclass the `AnimateTransform` effect, which has all of the machinery for actually combining the different effects internally and calculating the transform operation for each frame. You do not call that effect directly, however; instead, you deal with the `Move`, `Rotate`, and `Scale` subclasses. These classes expose utility properties to gather the information they care about for each effect and feed that information into the superclass for the appropriate transform animation. Let's take a look at these effects now.

The Move **effect**

The Move effect moves a target object around the scene by changing its (x, y) location. The effect exposes from/to/by properties for the x and y properties of the target object in its xFrom, yFrom, xTo, yTo, xBy, and yBy properties.

 Animating objects to different locations is a good way to help the user stay connected to the changing state of the UI.

Besides this simple exposure of the utility properties for x and y, the Move effect, like the Resize effect we saw earlier, also handles situations with layout constraints. For example, in the MovingConstraints application, a button is positioned with a left constraint differently in two states:

(File: MovingConstraints.mxml)
```
<s:Button id="button" label="Animate Me"
    left="10" left.s2="50"/>
```

In the first state, the button looks like this:

(Demo: MovingConstraints)

When the application changes to state s2, the button changes location:

Just like the earlier ResizingConstraints example, all we have to do to animate this change between states is to declare a Move effect for the appropriate transition:

195

```
<s:Transition>
    <s:Move target="{button}"/>
</s:Transition>
```

The button slides smoothly from an x position of 10 to 50 when the state changes to state s2. Although the Move effect ostensibly deals only with the x and y properties of target objects, it also infers changes on these properties by looking at changes in constraint values.

> ## Disabling constraints
>
> In some situations, you actually want to ignore layout constraints during an effect, or even disable them completely while the effect is running. For example, if you want to move objects around in a container like HGroup that is trying to arrange the objects in a specific order and position, then you may need to tell the layout manager to stop doing that while the effect is running. Check out the disableLayout property on effects. It unsets layout constraints and tells the layout manager to avoid running layout on the effect's target's container for the duration of the effect. When the effect finishes, constraints are restored and layout is allowed to run on the target object again.

The Rotate effect

The Rotate effect exposes properties for a single parameter: the rotation angle of the target object. The angleFrom, angleTo, and angleBy properties tell the effect the rotation angle to rotate from, to, and (optionally) by. The rotation happens by default around the upper-left point of the object— its (x, y) point—but you can change this rotation center by setting the autoCenterTransform property to true to rotate about the center of the object or by setting transformX and transformY to rotate about a specific point instead.

The Scale effect

The Scale effect exposes properties to scale a target object in both x and y. Note this operation does not affect the width and height properties of the object; instead, we are changing the scale factor by which those properties

196

are multiplied to get the actual size of the object on the screen. By default, the scaleX and scaleY properties of Flex objects are both 1 (no scaling applied); this effect animates a change to those properties. The from, to, and by properties of Scale are exposed through its properties scaleXFrom, scaleYFrom, scaleXTo, scaleYTo, scaleXBy, and scaleYBy.

Transforming a button

Now that we've talked about the three transform effects, let's see them in action. Suppose we want to move, rotate, and scale an object around its center all at the same time. We collect the different effects inside a Parallel effect, which you will read more about in Chapter 11. For now, just think of it as an effect that plays a collection of child effects simultaneously ... because that's exactly what it does:

(File: TransformedButton.mxml)
```
<s:Parallel id="transformer" target="{button}">
    <s:Move xTo="300" yTo="100" autoCenterTransform="true"/>
    <s:Rotate angleBy="90" autoCenterTransform="true"/>
    <s:Scale scaleXTo="2" scaleYTo="2"
        autoCenterTransform="true"/>
</s:Parallel>
```

To play this effect, we set up the button to call its play() function:

```
<s:Button id="button" label="Transform Me" width="100"
        click="transformer.play()"/>
```

Initially, the button looks like this:

(Demo: TransformedButton)

197

After the effects run, the button looks like this:

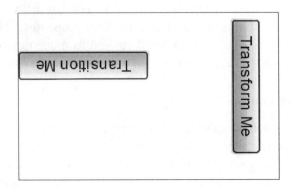

Similarly, we can set up a transform effect to run when a state transition takes place:

```
<s:Transition>
    <s:Parallel target="{button1}">
        <s:Move autoCenterTransform="true"/>
        <s:Rotate autoCenterTransform="true"/>
        <s:Scale autoCenterTransform="true"/>
    </s:Parallel>
</s:Transition>
```

Note here, as usual, less instructions to the effects are necessary because they pick up the appropriate from/to values from the state information on the target object:

```
<s:Button id="button1" label="Transition Me" width="100"
    x.s2="200" y="30" y.s2="100" rotation.s2="180"
    scaleX.s2="2" scaleY.s2="2"
    click="currentState = (currentState=='s1') ? 's2' : 's1'"/>
```

For both buttons, clicking causes the relevant effect to run, either manually or in a transition. A couple of important things are worth noting in the transform effect code in this example.

First of all, each effect has the same autoCenterTransform="true" statement, telling the overall transform effect that all of the operations happen about the center of the object. As we said before, it's important to set this property to the same value in all effects that are run in parallel to make it clear to anyone reading the code that all of the effects share this property value. In general, you probably want your rotating and scaling operations to happen about this center, rather than the default upper-left point, so your transform effects will probably use the same property/value setting. Only if you are running a Move operation by itself can you ignore this property. Whether that effect shifts the upper-left or middle point is irrelevant; either way it is just a shift in the (x, y) position of the object by some offset value. But in most cases of combining with rotation and scaling you should use autoCenterTransform="true" on all transform effects.

The other thing to notice is not as obvious from the code, and is related to our usage of autoCenterTransform="true": the x and y position of the object in each state, and therefore the values picked up implicitly by the transform effects, take into account the rotation center. For button1, as with most GUI objects, the default (x, y) position of an object in the window is the upper-left of that object. If we rotate or scale that object about its center, that (x, y) position changes because that upper-left point changes its location in the window. When we specify x and y for our object, we must take into account any relevant rotation and scale operations to position it appropriately. If we set these (x, y) values correctly in the states, any effects we run on the object do the right thing to animate from and to these values.

To get a better idea of how the transform center and the object position interacts, let's look at the RotationLocation example, seen here:

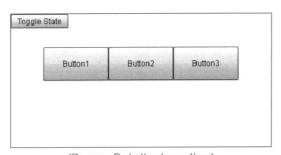

(Demo: RotationLocation)

First, we set up a button to rotate about it's (x, y) location, which is at its upper-left. In this case, we don't change its x and y positions between states, because we don't expect those values to change:

(File: RotationLocation.mxml)

```
<s:Button id="button1" label="Button1"
```

199

```
    width="100" height="50"
    x="50" y="50" rotation.s2="90"/>
```

For the transition effect on this button, we run a Move and a Rotate on this object. But we do not specify autoCenterTransform="true" because we simply want to rotate about the default transform center, which is the object's (x, y) location:

```
<s:Parallel target="{button1}">
    <s:Move/>
    <s:Rotate/>
</s:Parallel>
```

For the next button, we specify similar state information, where the object's (x, y) location does not change between states:

```
<s:Button id="button2" label="Button2"
    width="100" height="50"
    x="150" y="50" rotation.s2="90"/>
```

In this case, we want the object to rotate about the object's center, so we specify our effects appropriately (note that this effect targets two objects, since we use the same transition effect to operate on the third button, which we haven't seen yet):

```
<s:Parallel targets="{[button2,button3]}">
    <s:Move autoCenterTransform="true"/>
    <s:Rotate autoCenterTransform="true"/>
</s:Parallel>
```

Finally, we have a third button that we also want to rotate about its center, but we specify different (x, y) values for its rotated state:

```
<s:Button id="button3" label="Button3"
    width="100" height="50"
    x="250" x.s2="325" y="50" y.s2="25" rotation.s2="90"/>
```

The transition effect for this last button is the same as that for button2, since the Parallel effect that we saw earlier targets both objects.

Here are the results of running the transition to state s2:

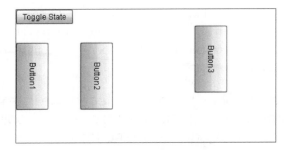

Button1 rotates correctly about its upper-left position and the rotated button is located at the same (x, y) position, pinned in place as it rotates into its orientation in state s2. Button2 looks very similar to Button1 in the s2 figure. But if you run the application, you see a difference when comparing the animation of Button2 to Button1. A conflict exists between the state information for the button, which does not specify a change in location, and the transition effect requested. On one hand, we told the button that it should not change x and y between states. But at the same time, we told the transition effect on that object that it should rotate the object about its center. The net effect is that the object attempts to follow both commands; the object tries to rotate about its center while keeping its (x, y) position at the same point, resulting in a rotation that is neither pinned at the upper-left nor operating around the object's center, but which ends up as if the object were pinned at the upper-left.

Button3 correctly handles both parts of a rotation-about-center transition; it specifies the correct x and y values for state s2 for an object of its dimensions that has rotated about its center. When the auto-centering effect runs on this button, it correctly rotates about the object's center during the entire effect and ends up where it should, with its (x, y) position rotated into a new location.

This dynamic of changing (x, y) locations between states due to rotation and scaling side-effects may not be common in your code; scaling and rotation are less common effects than moving objects, and you may not have to deal with the situation often. But if you do, the trick is to figure out the dimensions of the object before and after the operation and to set the (x, y) location of the object appropriately, given the transform center that you ask the effect to use.

9.4 The Fade effect

The Fade effect is used to fade objects in or out of the scene, by animating the object's alpha property over time. The controls for this effect are simple; you just set the alphaFrom and alphaTo properties to control the values that alpha animates between.

Fading objects is a useful technique in state transitions to smoothly add or remove objects that are coming into or leaving the UI.

To fade an object in, set the alphaFrom property to 0 and the alphaTo property to 1; this animates the object's alpha property from completely transparent (0) to completely opaque (1). Conversely, to fade an object out, set alphaFrom to 1 and alphaTo to 0. Leaving out the alphaFrom property fades to the specified alphaTo value from the object's current alpha value.

Let's take a look at an example. FadeButtons is an application showing various examples of fading buttons in and out, seen here:

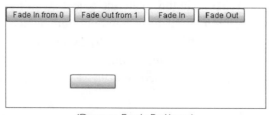

(Demo: FadeButtons)

Here is the code for FadeButtons:

(File: FadeButtons.mxml)

```
<fx:Declarations>
    <s:Fade id="fadeInFrom0" alphaFrom="0" alphaTo="1"
        target="{button}"/>
    <s:Fade id="fadeOutFrom1" alphaFrom="1" alphaTo="0"
        target="{button}"/>
    <s:Fade id="fadeIn" alphaTo="1" target="{button}"/>
    <s:Fade id="fadeOut" alphaTo="0" target="{button}"/>
</fx:Declarations>
```

```
<s:HGroup>
    <s:Button label="Fade In from 0"
        click="fadeInFrom0.play()"/>
    <s:Button label="Fade Out from 1"
        click="fadeOutFrom1.play()"/>
    <s:Button label="Fade In" click="fadeIn.play()"/>
    <s:Button label="Fade Out" click="fadeOut.play()"/>
</s:HGroup>
<s:Button id="button" x="100" y="100"/>
```

Note that we use different techniques of fading in and out between the pairs of Fade effects. The first two effects, triggered by the "Fade In from 0" and "Fade Out from 1" buttons, fully specify the from/to values for alpha. The other two, however, only specify the alphaTo property. By leaving out alphaFrom, these effects implicitly specify that the alphaFrom value should be determined dynamically when the effect starts. Whatever the button's alpha value is when the effect is played is the value that alpha animates from. Not only is it easier to specify effects without starting values, but it can make for smoother visual results as well, since starting from the object's current value may be better in general than starting from some value specified in the effect (which may not always be the same as the current value the object has, depending on what else is happening in the application).

For example, the "Fade In" button behaves exactly the same as the "Fade In from 0" button, as long as the target button is already invisible. But if the button is fully opaque already, then the "Fade In" button does nothing, because it is being told to animate alpha from and to the same value (1). This is probably the effect you want for fading operations; if you want to fade in objects, you probably only want to do it when the objects are invisible to begin with. The "Fade In from 0" button, on the other hand, always starts from alpha = 0. If the object is currently opaque, this causes it to blink out to invisible and then fade in.

Fade becomes more powerful when used in state transitions. It automatically picks up information about whether a target object is becoming visible or invisible and sets the alphaFrom and alphaTo properties automatically. For example, here's the code for the AutoFade demo:

(File: AutoFade.mxml)

```
<s:states>
    <s:State name="s1"/>
```

203

```
        <s:State name="s2"/>
    </s:states>

    <s:transitions>
        <s:Transition>
            <s:Fade targets="{[button0, button1, button2]}"/>
        </s:Transition>
    </s:transitions>

    <s:Button label="Toggle State"
        click="currentState = (currentState=='s1')?'s2':'s1'"/>

    <s:Button id="button0" label="Visible" x="100" y="0"
        visible="true" visible.s2="false"/>
    <s:Button id="button1" label="Alpha" x="100" y="50"
        alpha="0" alpha.s2="1"/>
    <s:Button id="button2" label="Existence" x="100" y="100"
        includeIn="s2"/>
```

This application has two states, s1 and s2. The three buttons behave differently as the application switches between the two states: the Visible button toggles its visible property, the Alpha button toggles its alpha property, and the Existence button toggles its existence in the application via the includeIn state syntax.

When the application first starts, as we can see in the following screenshot, only the Visible button is seen:

(Demo: AutoFade)

The Visible button is visible is because it is included in state s1 and has its visible and alpha properties set to make the object visible in that state. The Alpha button is not visible because its alpha value equals 0 in the start

204

state, which makes it completely transparent. The Existence button is also not visible at first because it is excluded from the container in state s1.

When the Toggle State button is clicked, the Visible button fades out and the other two buttons fade in:

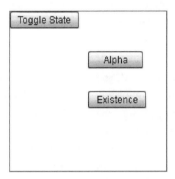

The Fade effect automatically does the right thing to all three buttons during a state transition. When an object changes its visible or alpha properties between states, or when it is coming or going from the GUI, Fade automatically chooses the appropriate alphaFrom and alphaTo values (either to 0 or 1, depending on whether it determines that the object is becoming visible or invisible).

Note that the logic of Fade to make objects appear and disappear at the right time during a transition may be dependent on the way that multiple effects are grouped. In general, a Fade effect running alongside other effects in a Parallel effect does the right thing, but when running in a Sequence effect (which we will see later), you may need to add an additional effect to add or remove the object at the right time. We will see more about choreographing this type of effect in Chapter 11.

9.5   The AnimateColor effect

The AnimateColor effect allows you to animate the color of a target object, like a SolidColor or GradientEntry.

Hue and cry: color animation done wrong

You might assume, given the flexibility of the Animate effect and its ability to target arbitrary objects, that you could just use the Animate effect directly on colors. And you could ... but you probably wouldn't get the result you were looking for.

By default, Flex 4 effects animate properties using simple numeric interpolation, deriving each animated value (v) with a parametric calculation based on the starting value (v0), the ending value (v1), and the elapsed fraction of the animation (f), like this: $v = v0 + f * (v1 - v0)$. Colors can be interpolated in this same numerical way since they are stored in unsigned integers. However, these integer color values are really more complex structures, consisting of separate red, green, and blue values that just happen to be stored in an integer for convenience. Interpolating between integer values is not the same as interpolating between the colors that they represent; the red, green, and blue components of the colors need to be treated separately.

As a simple example, here is a calculation of a color value half-way through an animation from red to blue. The starting value of red is written in hex as 0xff0000, which is an integer value of 16,711,680. The ending value of blue is written in hex as 0x0000ff, which is an integer value of 255. The mid-way point between these values is 8,355,967, or 0x7f807f. This result is a shade of green, with the green component (the 16 bits in the middle, 0x80) being higher than both the red and blue components. This is obviously not what we want—passing through a green value on the way from red to blue just doesn't look right. That hue has nothing to do with either the starting or the ending color values we were trying to animate between.

RGB interpolation: color animation done right

If, instead, we break apart the starting and ending colors in the previous example into their red, green, and blue channels and animate these values separately, we get something more reasonable. The red value animates from 255 (0xff) to 0, the green vaiue stays at 0 the whole time, and the blue value animates from 0 to 255 (0xff). The mid-way point for all of these components is red = 127.5 (0x7f), green = 0, and blue = 127.5 (0x7f). Given these separate color values, we reconstruct the complete color by putting the values in their proper places and get the value 0x7f007f, which is a magenta color. This color is a blend of red and blue hues, which is more what we would expect in this color animation.

The AnimateColor effect uses the RGBInterpolator class internally in order to get visually correct color interpolation. RGBInterpolator breaks the starting and ending colors into their component parts and animates each one separately, composing the results together at each frame to create the animated color. These colors can be specified by hex values (*e.g.*, 0xff0000 for red, 0x00ff00 for green, 0x0000ff for blue, and so on) or by common color names for specific colors (such as red, green, and blue).

You can see these two approaches, using Animate and AnimateColor in the AnimateButtonLabelColor example:

(File: AnimateButtonLabelColor.mxml)

```
<fx:Declarations>
    <s:Animate id="colorAnimBad" target="{button1}">
        <s:SimpleMotionPath property="color"
            valueFrom="0xff0000" valueTo="0x0000ff"/>
    </s:Animate>
    <s:AnimateColor id="colorAnim" target="{button}"
        colorFrom="red" colorTo="blue"/>
</fx:Declarations>
<s:Button id="button" label="Color My World"
    click="colorAnim.play()"/>
<s:Button id="button1" y="30" label="Color Me Poorly"
    click="colorAnimBad.play()"/>
```

Run the example and click on the buttons. You can see, when you click on the "Color Me Poorly" button, that the colorAnimBad animation, using Animate, animates the button label through several unrelated colors on the way to its final blue color. Then when you click on the other button, you can see how the AnimateColor animation changes that button's color smoothly from red through magenta to the blue color at the end.[5]

The arbitrary type system in Flex 4 allows you to do much more than just color animation, as we saw in Section 8.5, but color interpolation is a great example of why we need that capability in general. Users of this effect don't even need to know that such a capability exists, but it's worth noting because you may sometime want to take advantage of that capability for completely different reasons, such as animating non-numeric types, or complex data structures. Or you can just use the AnimateColor effect and appreciate what the Flex framework does for you.

---

[5] Note that you can get the Animate effect in this example to work exactly the same as the AnimateColor effect. You simply declare an RGBInterpolator object and set the interpolator property of the effect to that object. That's essentially what AnimateColor does under the hood. But as long as you have AnimateColor, why go to all that trouble?

207

Example: animating gradients

Another thing that is worth noting about the `AnimateColor` effect is that it also allows you to target arbitrary objects. We mentioned earlier the ability in Flex 4 to animate things that are not simply components, which was a limitation of Flex effects in earlier releases. For `AnimateColor`, this capability is essential, because often the `color` property (which may even be called something different than "color") is stored on a separate object altogether. For example, graphic objects like `Rect` and `Ellipse` are colored by the values in their stroke and fill objects. And these objects may be informed by `GradientEntry` objects, which are neither components nor graphic elements. They are simply data structures that hold color (and other) data. So the ability of Flex effects to target arbitrary objects is essential for effects like `AnimateColor` to do their job; they have to set that color value no matter where it's stored.

As an example of setting the properties of arbitrary objects, let's look at the `AnimatedGradient` demo application. In this application, an ellipse is given a gradient that is darker at the edge and lighter at the center, and the properties of that gradient are animated. You can see the initial view of the application here:

(Demo: AnimatedGradient)

I created the circle with a radial gradient to give it a 3D-like look. The circle is meant to serve as a button, and when it is pressed by the mouse I wanted to give it a kind of pushed-in appearance, so I needed to change the colors in the gradient to give it a darker dimple in the middle, as seen here:

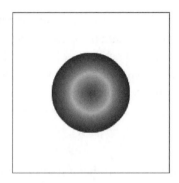

Here is the code for the gradient-filled ellipse:

```
<s:Group mouseDown="currentState='s2'"
         mouseUp="currentState='s1'">
   <s:Ellipse id="sphere" x="50" y="50"
              width="100" height="100">
      <s:fill>
         <s:RadialGradient id="gradient" >
            <s:GradientEntry id="center" color="0x80f080"
                    color.s2="0x408040" ratio="0"/>
            <s:GradientEntry id="middle" color="0x60a060"
                    color.s2="0x80f080" ratio=".5"/>
            <s:GradientEntry id="edge"
                    color="0x404040" ratio="1"/>
         </s:RadialGradient>
      </s:fill>
   </s:Ellipse>
</s:Group>
```

Rather than switching immediately to the depressed state, I want the button
to have a more tactile feeling of being pushed, so I added a transition effect
to animate the gradient between the two states:

```
<s:Transition>
    <s:Parallel duration="500">
        <s:AnimateColor targets="{[center,middle]}"/>
    </s:Parallel>
</s:Transition>
```

209

Here, the transition effect targets those elements that have `color` properties. Note that we don't bother animating the `edge` entry because its colors do not change between these states. There is no harm in doing so other than the wasted effort by the effects engine, since it would just create an animation that updates the property to the same value every frame.

Conclusion

In this chapter, we got our first introduction to Flex effects and saw some of the more fundamental effects in the system. The effects we covered here, in addition to the composite effects we will see in Chapter 11, probably constitute most of the effects that are commonly used in applications. The ability to move, resize, and fade objects, and choreograph them with other effects, are fundamental to creating rich applications. When combined with state transitions, this core set of effects provide a powerful toolbox of capabilities to make rich user experiences and applications that make for happier and more productive users.

In the next chapter, we will see some additional effects which take advantage of the new graphics capabilities introduced in Flash Player 10.

Chapter 10

Advanced Flex Effects

In the previous two chapters, I introduced Flex effects and discussed some of the most common effects that are used to provide great user experiences for applications. In this chapter, we'll see more advanced features of effects. Specifically, this chapter covers effects that build on recent[1] capabilities of the Flash player to provide advanced visual effects like pixel shaders and 3D.

10.1   The `AnimateFilter` effect

In Chapter 3, we discussed Flex filters and how they provide the ability to apply easy image processing effects to components and graphical objects: drop shadows, blurs, glows, and fully customizable Pixel Bender shader filters can be applied as filters to your objects to get great, rich effects. But these are all static effects; either an object has a drop shadow or it doesn't. Meanwhile, we have this powerful animation system that can target arbitrary objects in the system; why don't we animate the properties of the filters to get some dynamic image processing effects? That's exactly why the `AnimateFilter` class exists.

The `AnimateFilter` class animates any specified properties on a Flex filter, allowing you to get dynamic effects like a pulsating glow, or a deepening shadow, or very custom effects with Pixel Bender shaders. The effect takes two objects to act on: a target object to which the filter is applied and a `bitmapFilter` that is applied as a filter on the target object. It also takes a set of `MotionPath` objects, like the `Animate` effect discussed in Chapter 9, which specify the properties on the filter to be animated and the values they

---

[1] As of Flash Player 10, which is the latest player version as of the release of Flex 4.

animate between. When played, the effect applies the filter to the object, animates the properties on the filter, and removes the filter when it is done.[2]

Let's see how this works in an example. One useful technique for drawing a user's attention to something on the screen is a glow around the object. This can just be a static glow, to give the object a distinctive look. But to really draw the attention of the user, you could make the glow pulsate. This effect can be achieved by simply animating the translucency of the glow, which is controlled by the filter's alpha property. In this example, we animate a glow whenever the mouse is over the button, as seen here:

(Demo: GlowingFocus)

The animation is declared and played with this code in GlowingFocus:

(File: GlowingFocus.mxml)

```
<fx:Script>
    private function focusHandler(event:Event):void
    {
        glowAnim.end();
        glowAnim.play([event.currentTarget]);
    }
</fx:Script>
<fx:Declarations>
    <s:GlowFilter id="glow" color="0x00ffff"
        blurX="8" blurY="8"/>
    <s:AnimateFilter id="glowAnim" bitmapFilter="{glow}"
        repeatCount="0" repeatBehavior="reverse">
        <s:SimpleMotionPath property="alpha"
            valueFrom="0" valueTo="1"/>
    </s:AnimateFilter>
</fx:Declarations>
```

---

[2] This nuance of adding and removing the specified filter means that the AnimateFilter effect is appropriate for filter effects which are transient, not persistent. I'll talk more about this at the end of this section.

212

Meanwhile, we have a grid of buttons, each of which is declared like this:

```
<s:Button label="Button" focusIn="focusHandler(event)"/>
```

Whenever one of the buttons has the focus, instead of having the default focus object provided by the standard Flex button, the button pulsates with the glow we have defined. To make this work, we handle a `focusIn` event, end the current animation (in case the glow is already running on a previously focused object), and start the effect on the button that gained focus.

The effect is set up with a `GlowFilter` that has a cyan color and a blur radius that is double the normal size, to make it more obvious. The effect is set up to repeat indefinitely, reversing direction each time. It has a single `MotionPath`, which operates on the `alpha` property, animating it from 0 to 1 (the reversing repetition behavior animates it back to 0 every other time).

Note that the `alpha` property that we are animating is the one on the `bitmapFilter`, not the target object. This detail is distinct from the way that other effects work, where the properties animated are on the `target` object. Also note that we have not specified a `target` for the effect; this is because we play the effect on different objects, depending on which button receives the focus. Instead of using the `target` property on the effect, the effect uses the value passed into the `play()` function.

Since `AnimateFilter` can deal with any Flex filter object, we can just as easily point it at a `ShaderFilter` which uses a Pixel Bender shader. As in the previous glowing button example, `AnimateFilter` can animate the properties in a `ShaderFilter` and, therefore, in the underlying shader itself. Let's see how this works in an example:

(Demo: AnimatedCrossfade)

213

In the AnimatedCrossfade example, we have a simple image control that shows a picture. When we click it, we want to show a different picture:

But rather than simply pop the next picture into place, we would like to animate the change by cross-fading from the current picture to the next:

We accomplish the cross-fade effect by running an AnimateFilter effect on a Pixel Bender shader that calculates the blend between the two images.

First, let's see how the image control works. We load two sample images by embedding the images into the application. We also grab their BitmapData references for later use in our shader effect:

```
[Embed(source="images/GoldenGate.jpg")]
[Bindable]
```

```
private var GoldenGate:Class;
private var goldenGateBD:BitmapData;

[Embed(source="images/Harbor.jpg")]
[Bindable]
private var Harbor:Class;
private var harborBD:BitmapData;

private function creationComplete():void
{
    goldenGateBD = (new GoldenGate()).bitmapData;
    harborBD = (new Harbor()).bitmapData;
}
```

We then create an Image component and set its source:

```
<mx:Image id="img" source="{GoldenGate}"
    click="clickHandler()"/>
```

When the image control is clicked, the clickHandler() function is called, which starts the animation. But first, let's see what's going on with the effect. The effect we use loads a shader that was created in Pixel Bender, crossfade, which is similar to the example shader of the same name that ships with the Pixel Bender toolkit. Here is the code for this shader, which blends a start and end image in some calculated proportion:

```
(File: shaders/crossfade.pbk)
parameter float progress;
input image4 startImage;
input image4 endImage;
output pixel4 dst;

void evaluatePixel()
{
    float4 startPixel =
        sampleNearest(startImage, outCoord());
    float4 endPixel =
        sampleNearest(endImage, outCoord());
    dst = mix(startPixel, endPixel, progress);
}
```

In this shader, we first declare our input and output parameters. `progress` is the elapsed percentage of our animation, where 0 represents the start (at which we would see just the start image) and 1 represents the end (at which we would see only the end image). `startImage` and `endImage` are the starting and ending bitmaps that the shader blends together. `dst` is the output of this shader which is calculated in the `evaluatePixel()` function.

The functionality of the shader is very simple: it grabs the color value at the current pixel from both the start image and the end image and then calls the internal Pixel Bender function `mix()` which blends these two values according to the proportion given by the `progress` variable. We can animate the results of the shader by changing the value of `progress` over time via the `AnimateFilter` effect.

Since the `AnimateFilter` class takes a Flex filter, we need to create a filter from our shader class. We can do this by loading the Pixel Bender shader[3] into a `ShaderFilter` object, then using that filter in the `AnimateFilter` declaration:

(File: AnimatedCrossfade.mxml)
```
<s:ShaderFilter id="crossfadeFilter"
    shader="@Embed(source='shaders/crossfade.pbj')"/>
<s:AnimateFilter id="crossfader" target="{img}"
    bitmapFilter="{crossfadeFilter}"
    effectEnd="effectEndHandler()">
    <s:SimpleMotionPath property="progress"
        valueFrom="0" valueTo="1"/>
</s:AnimateFilter>
```

The `AnimateFilter` effect sets up an animation that changes the `progress` parameter in the shader gradually from 0 to 1, which gives us the cross-fade effect we want. But a couple of other details are necessary to make this effect work properly. First, we need to set up the image parameters appropriately when we run the effect. Next, we need to do some cleanup when the effect is done, which happens in the `effectEnd` event handler.

The effect starts when we click on the image, which causes a call into the `clickHandler()` function:

---

[3] Note that the shader we're loading is the .pbj file produced by the Pixel Bender Toolkit from the source code above. See Section 3.8 for more information on creating shaders.

```
private var newImageSource:Class;
private function clickHandler():void
{
    var bd0:BitmapData;
    var bd1:BitmapData;

    if (img.source == GoldenGate)
    {
        newImageSource = Harbor;
        bd0 = goldenGateBD;
        bd1 = harborBD;
    }
    else
    {
        newImageSource = GoldenGate;
        bd0 = harborBD;
        bd1 = goldenGateBD;
    }
    crossfadeFilter.shader.data.endImage.input = bd1;
    crossfader.play();
}
```

This function does a couple of things. First, it caches information about
the image that we're cross-fading to in newImageSource to be used later
when the effect finishes. Second, it supplies the endImage parameter to
the shader filter, so that the filter is all set up and ready to go. Note that
we are not supplying the startImage parameter; this is assumed by the
ShaderFilter to be the object that is being filtered. In our case, we leave
the image control (the filtered object) with its start image until the effect
finishes, so the image control itself supplies the startImage input that is
blended with the endImage value that we set up here. Finally, play() is
called on the crossfader effect we created, which animates progress on
the shader and performs the cross-fade.

When the effect starts, it applies the crossfadeFilter to the image
component, so that what we see on the screen is the filtered image, which
is the calculated result of our shader that is being animated. Underneath,
that image control still has the original source property that it had when it
was clicked, so it still thinks it is showing what we used as the startImage

parameter to the shader. We need to change that property when the effect ends and calls the `effectEndHandler()` function:

```
private function effectEndHandler():void
{
    img.source = newImageSource;
}
```

When this handler runs, our effect is finished. We change the `source` parameter of the image and the user sees the picture to which we cross-faded.

It's worth noting that `AnimateFilter` is specifically useful for transient filter effects—when you want to add a filter to an object at the start of an animation, animate the properties of that filter, and then remove the filter when the animation is done. For effects that simply want to animate the properties of a filter that is already on an object, and which should stay on the object when the effect is done, you should use the `Animate` effect discussed in Chapter 9. The `Animate` effect is written specifically to be able to animate properties on arbitrary objects, and it works like a charm on animating filter properties. For an example of this technique, look at the `PicturePerfekt` example in Chapter 3. The animation in that demo on the grayscaling shader filter uses `Animate` to do the job.

Although `AnimateFilter` can be used for bitmap-based shader transitions, a different effect exists that is especially designed for shader transitions: `AnimateTransitionShader`.

10.2 The `AnimateTransitionShader` effect

Like `AnimateFilter`, the `AnimateTransitionShader` effect is for animating filters. But some important distinctions exists between these effects: `AnimateFilter` is a general utility effect that animates any Flex filter, while the `AnimateTransitionShader` effect is specifically for use with Pixel Bender shaders and state transitions. This effect is usually used indirectly via its simpler subclasses `Wipe` and `CrossFade`, but it's worth understanding how this class works in case you want to create custom shader transitions.

This effect has four properties, some of which are supplied automatically when the effect is used in a transition:

shaderByteCode This is the pixel shader that the effect runs when it is played. You can embed the resource and instantiate it to get the required ByteArray, as shown here for some fictional shader Foo.pbj:

```
[Embed(source="Foo.pbj",
    mimeType="application/octet-stream")]
private static var FooShaderClass:Class;
private static var fooShaderCode:ByteArray =
    new FooShaderClass();
```

Any shader used by this class is expected to conform to a particular contract so that the class can use the shader generically. In general, the shader needs to have two image inputs in addition to the first one that is assumed by Flash (more on that later), a progress value that is the animated value, and width and height parameters that describe the dimensions of the input images. Here's a bit more detail about each of these:

progress This is a value between 0 and 1 that is animated by the effect. Your shader should use this property to determine the animated result, with 0 representing the start of the animation and 1 representing the end.

image parameters There must be three image inputs. The first of these is the input assumed by Flash as the object being filtered, and this image can have any name. The shaders used by the effect do not actually use this parameter,[4] but it is important to reference this input in your shader code to avoid having Pixel

---

[4] The reason for this is a bit beyond the scope of what we're talking about here and not something you need to understand beyond knowing that you have to supply this dummy variable, but here's the scoop. It is far easier and more correct to create a transition between two bitmaps using only those bitmaps, not including the current state of the filtered object. This is because the filtered object may change in other, unrelated ways in a state transition that we do not want factored into the result, so we take it out of the equation by simply using our input images for the shader result and ignoring the filtered object. But since Flash assumes that you always want to use that object as the first input image, you have to put it in your shader code and account for the fact that Pixel Bender tries to optimize-out any unused parameters. It's a bit of a hack, but the result is shaders that can be used interchangeably between different transition effects and transitions that can smoothly perform the required tasks without any oddities of the underlying object causing problems.

Bender optimize it out when it compiles the shader. For example, you can query the pixel value from the current location, outCoord(), from this input. The other image inputs must be named from and to. An important caveat about these images is that they must be the same size; shaders expect to work with inputs of the same size, so the AnimateTransitionShader effect has the same limitation.

width, height These parameters hold the dimensions of the input images (note again that both images must be of the same size). Although you may not need these parameters in your shader, the AnimateTransitionShader effect sets them when it is played, so your shader must declare the parameters. Note that, like with the unused first image input, you must reference these parameters in your shader in order to defeat Pixel Bender's optimization of compiling out unused parameters, so even if you do not need them you should reference them in your shader code.

If you want to see examples of how these parameters are declared and used, check out the source for the CrossFade.pbk shader used by the CrossFade effect in the Flex SDK.

shaderProperties This Object is a key/value map that holds any additional properties specific to your shader that should be set when the effect starts. The shader properties discussed in the preceding paragraphs are set automatically by the effect. But if you have any additional parameters in your shader that need to be set at runtime, this is how you set the values for those properties. You can set these properties in the typical ways of setting map values on an object. For example, if your shader has a direction parameter that you want to be equal to 1 when the effect starts, you set that value like this:

```
shaderEffect.shaderProperties = {direction : 1};
```

bitmapFrom, bitmapTo These bitmaps are created and supplied automatically when the effect is run in a transition (which is, as the effect's name implies, the typical use case). Usually, the effect is run on a target object in a transition. When the transition effect starts, the effect captures a bitmap snapshot of the target object in its start and end states. You can, optionally, run the effect outside of a transition, in which case you need to supply these bitmaps yourself. If you need to capture a bitmap of your object, you might want to use BitmapUtil.getSnapshot(), which is the function called internally by the effect to capture a bitmap of components. Note, as we discussed above, that these from/to bitmaps must be the same size, since the underlying shader expects to operate on bitmaps of the same size.

AnimateTransitionShader is available for you to use, supplying custom shaders to create great shader-based effects. But it also exists to handle the common functionality for two simple effects that you can easily use without writing any shader code: Wipe and CrossFade. Just like their superclass, AnimateTransitionShader, these effects are most commonly used in state transitions, but they can also be used outside of transitions by supplying bitmaps to the effects.

10.3   The Wipe effect

A common effect to run when changing the look of any object, like switching between pictures in an image component or between screens of an application, is a "wipe" effect. This effect gradually reveals the next version of the object you are changing to by dragging an invisible line across the object. On one side of the line is the old version and on the other side the new one.

A wipe effect is a useful technique when you want to gradually reveal a different version of a GUI object.

The Wipe effect takes a single direction parameter in addition to the from/to bitmaps that we discussed in the previous section. The direction takes one of four String constants defined in the WipeDirection class: LEFT, RIGHT, UP, or DOWN (which are simply constants for the strings "right," "left," "up," and "down," which may be easier to use from MXML code). This property defines the direction that the wipe moves to reveal the second object. For example, direction = WipeDirection.LEFT results in a wipe that starts at the right of the object and proceeds to the left.

10.4   The CrossFade effect

The CrossFade effect provides an easy way to get a cross-fading transition between different states of an object. In the AnimatedCrossfade example in Section 10.1, the AnimateFilter effect was used to animate the progress parameter of a cross-fading shader. But the Flex SDK comes with a built-in CrossFade effect that makes even that small amount of effort unnecessary.

 Cross-fading between two different states of a visual element is a powerful technique to keep the user engaged and informed of the changes between the two versions.

To use the effect, create a transition with it that targets the object that we want to cross-fade, and it takes care of capturing bitmap snapshots of the target before and after and animating the underlying cross-fade shader. As with the Wipe effect discussed earlier, it is not even apparent, or important, that this effect uses a Pixel Bender shader to do its job. You just have to declare it, give it a target, and put it in a transition and it handles all of the rest of the details.

Let's see an example of how this effect might be used. In Chapter 9, we saw in the AnimatedGradient application how we might animate the gradient of an ellipse to give it a 3D-like effect of being pushed in. In that case, the gradient was centered around the middle of the object:

(Demo: AnimatedGradient2)

To get the animated effect, we just needed to animate the color property of two of the gradient entries. Let's take another swipe at that application, in the AnimatedGradient2 demo.

In this version, the initial gradient is centered around a point in the upper-right portion of the ellipse:

This offset gradient center gives the impression that the light source is somewhere above and to the right of the viewer, which looks more realistic than the previous attempt where the virtual light source came from the direction of the viewer. We offset the gradient center by using the `rotation` and `focalPointRatio` properties of the `RadialGradient` fill for the ellipse:

(File: AnimatedGradient2.mxml)

```
<s:Ellipse id="sphere" x="50" y="50" width="100" height="100">
    <s:fill>
        <s:RadialGradient id="gradient" focalPointRatio=".5"
                rotation="-45" focalPointRatio.state2="0">
            <s:GradientEntry id="center" color="0x80f080"
                    color.state2="0x408040" ratio="0"/>
            <s:GradientEntry id="middle" color="0x60a060"
                    color.state2="0x80f080" ratio=".5"/>
            <s:GradientEntry id="edge" color="0x404040"
                    ratio="1"/>
        </s:RadialGradient>
    </s:fill>
</s:Ellipse>
```

Note that the gradient shifts to being centered around the middle again in state s2, because we want to give the impression that the button is being pushed in the middle:

Here is the transition effect that we used before, which animates the gradient entry colors:

```
<s:AnimateColor targets="{[center,middle]}"/>
```

If we run this effect now, we get an unpleasant snapping artifact as the gradient center jumps suddenly from the upper-right to the middle at the start of the transition. This abrupt change happens because the state change causes the gradient center to get its new state value immediately upon the state change occurring. The transition changes the gradient colors gradually, by running AnimateColor on those properties. But any properties not covered by those effects, including the gradient center, will immediately adopt their new state values. We can handle this situation by animating the focalPointRatio property as well:

```
<s:Parallel>
    <s:Animate target="{gradient}">
        <s:SimpleMotionPath property="focalPointRatio"/>
    </s:Animate>
    <s:AnimateColor targets="{[center,middle]}"/>
</s:Parallel>
```

This gives a smoother animation, moving the gradient center toward the middle at the same time as the gradient colors are changing. But I found that a simple cross-fade gave an even better effect, simply blending the visual results of the two states. And its even easier to code:

```
<s:CrossFade target="{sphere}"/>
```

In this version, we don't need to think about gradients, colors, color animation, focal point ratios, or anything else. We just use the CrossFade effect, which captures the before/after images and blends them together to get a nice cross-fading result instead.

As a final example of AnimateTransitionShader, let's put together a few of the techniques and effects described above to show how we might transition between different components in an application. This code is from the ShaderTransitions example, shown here:

(Demo: ShaderTransitions)

In this application, as in the earlier `AnimatedCrossfade` application, we have a simple `Image` control that holds a picture. The `source` property of that picture is declared through state syntax to have different values depending on the state of the application, and when we click on the image it toggles between the states:

(File: ShaderTransitions.mxml)

```
<mx:Image id="img" source="{GoldenGate}" source.state2="{Harbor}"
  click="currentState=(currentState=='state1') ? 'state2':'state1'"/>
```

A button in the GUI is also affected by the state change. The button is used to emphasize the fact that shader-based effects are not just for image objects:

```
<s:Button id="button" label="To Harbor"
  width="90" label.state2="To Bridge"
  click="currentState=(currentState=='state1') ? 'state2':'state1'"/>
```

When the application changes states, it animates the transition using different shader-based effects, selectable through the radio buttons at the top of the application.[5]

---

[5] Note that this isn't really the way you'd want to write a real application. Don't make the users of your applications choose their preferred user experience; just pick an appropriate transition instead of having them decide. Some freedom is a good thing, but too much can lead to anarchy, chaos, and a complete breakdown of a functioning society. You don't want to be responsible for that, do you? But for the purposes of this explanation, I wanted to have the user select the transition to see the result.

Three effects are used in the transition, with one of the effects (Wipe) having one of four variations depending on the user selection. These effects are declared in the Declarations block:

```
<s:CrossFade id="crossfader" targets="{[img,button]}"/>
<s:Wipe id="wiper" targets="{[img,button]}"/>
<s:AnimateTransitionShader id="blackDip"
    targets="{[img,button]}"
    shaderByteCode="{FadeThroughBlackShaderClass}"/>
```

The CrossFade and Wipe effects just reference the effect name, assign an id to be used elsewhere, and set the targets that they act on. The super-class effect, AnimateTransitionShader, must also set shaderByteCode, because it has no default shader (unlike the Wipe and CrossFade subclasses, which internally load and set the shaders that they use). In this case, the shader transitions its targets by fading them out to black and then back up into the final state. This shader was loaded in script code like this:

```
[Embed(source="shaders/FadeThroughBlack.pbj",
    mimeType="application/octet-stream")]
[Bindable]
private static var FadeThroughBlackShaderClass:Class;
```

The Pixel Bender code for that shader is in FadeThroughBlack.pbk. Its parameters are just like those for the built-in CrossFade shader and its evaluatePixel() function is quite similar, too:

```
(File: FadeThroughBlack.pbk)
void evaluatePixel()
{
    // Acquire the pixel values from both images
    // at the current location
    float2 coord = outCoord();
    float4 color0 = sampleNearest(src0, coord);
    float4 fromPixel = sampleNearest(from, coord);
    float4 toPixel = sampleNearest(to, coord);
    float4 blackPixel = float4(0, 0, 0, 1.0);
    float prog = progress;

    if (progress < .5)
```

226

```
    dst = mix(fromPixel, blackPixel,
            (progress / .5));
  else
    dst = mix(blackPixel, toPixel,
            ((progress - .5) / .5));
  // workaround for Flash filter bug that
  // replicates last column/row
  if (coord.x >= width || coord.y >= height)
    dst.a = 0.0;
}
```

The logic in this shader code works as follows: assign the pixel values for the from and to images to fromPixel and toPixel, create another pixel value to represent the color black (blackPixel), then calculate the final pixel value. If the animated progress parameter is less than .5, which is less than half-way through the animation, then fade to black by cross-fading between fromPixel and black. Otherwise, the animation is more than halfway complete, so cross-fade between black and toPixel. The other code in the shader is there mainly to keep Pixel Bender from optimizing-out the src0 and width/height parameters (as well as performing a boundary check on the dimensions).

A single Transition is declared for the application:

(File: ShaderTransitions.mxml)
```
<s:transitions>
    <s:Transition id="transition" effect="{crossfader}"/>
</s:transitions>
```

This transition uses the CrossFade effect by default, but selecting any of the radio buttons changes the effect used by the transition. When the state changes, the transition runs and the specified effect runs. For example, if the user chooses the "Black" radio button, the handler for that selection sets the transition effect accordingly:

```
transition.effect = blackDip;
```

To run the application, click on the desired transition effect radio button and then click on either the image itself or the button at the top right. Note that both objects, the image and the button, transition smoothly to the new state. Even though Pixel Bender is all about image processing, the objects it acts on don't need to be images. Flex captures images from the before/after states of those objects and runs the shader on those bitmaps, giving you smooth transition effects regardless of what the target object is. For example, here's a screenshot of the application during a transition using a `Wipe` effect that moves to the right. Note that both the button text and the image are being wiped to their new values:

I wouldn't necessarily choose the FadeThroughBlack shader for most of my button transitions (the other transitions are less jarring for objects that don't dramatically change between states), but you can choose the type of shader effect you need for your situation. And if you need something that is not provided in the default `CrossFade` and `Wipe` effects, then go ahead and write your own shader and work directly with `AnimateTransitionShader`.

10.5   3D: A new dimension to Flex effects

In Flash Player 10, the player's graphics capabilities added a whole new dimension. Literally: Flash added the ability to position and orient objects in the third dimension. Up until that point, Flash display objects (and therefore Flex components) could only be positioned in the x/y plane; you could put them anywhere you wanted to within the application window, but it was just a 2D surface. External libraries, like PaperVision, took on the work of figuring out the 3D math and rendering the final pixels into the 2D Flash world, but Flash itself only understood 2D.

But as of version 10, Flash display objects can be moved, rotated, and scaled in three dimensions. Now a display object not only has a x and y position, but also a z position. Setting z to a negative value makes it larger (because it is closer to the user than the x/y plane) and setting it to a positive value makes it smaller, further away from the user. When z is equal to 0, which is the default, objects reside in the x/y plane as they always did.

Similarly, you can now rotate in 3D as well. The old `rotation` property on objects is a rotation around the z axis (the axis going from the user into the screen, orthogonal to the x/y plane). Display objects now also have `rotationX` and `rotationY` properties, for rotating around the x axis (left to right, as seen by the user) and y axis (top to bottom, as seen by the user). I think of these rotations as the standard wave (`rotation`, or `rotationZ`), the toddler wave (`rotationX`), and the queen's wave (`rotationY`).

Finally, you can also scale in z with the new `scaleZ` property on display objects. Just like the old `scaleX` and `scaleY` properties scale an object in the x and y directions, `scaleZ` scales them in the new z direction, toward and away from the user.

Flash does not currently offer a complete 3D modeling engine. In particular, Flash has no "Z buffer," which means that if you draw 3D-positioned objects over one another, they are not properly depth-sorted and you end up with, well, interesting artifacts.[6] But you can still get some amazing effects with just the current capabilities.

With all of these new wonderful 3D graphics capabilities in Flash, it made sense for Flex to add new effects to enable 3D animations. That's why Flex 4 introduced the `Move3D`, `Rotate3D`, and `Scale3D` effects.

These 3D effects are similar to their 2D counterparts (`Move`, `Rotate`, and

---

[6] A Z buffer is used by 3D software and hardware to store the z value of each pixel that is drawn. This approach allows correct depth-sorting on a per-pixel level because any pixel that lies further away from the viewer than one already drawn into the Z buffer will not be drawn. Without a Z buffer, each object is simply drawn to the screen in the order in which is is rendered, with no regard to its 3D position relative to the other objects in the scene. This approach can result in artifacts because objects that are further away may appear in front of closer objects just because they were rendered after the closer objects. Working around this limitation involves careful sorting of objects so that they are rendered in the correct order, splitting some objects into multiple, smaller pieces to avoid rendering overlap issues, or simply avoiding the issues entirely by performing simpler 3D tasks that do not result in these kinds of artifacts. By the way, the Flash rendering approach is called the "painter's algorithm," presumably because it is like painting coats of colors onto a surface, where the last coat painted is the one that the viewer sees. Or maybe it's because whoever named it wasn't very good at painting and had rendering artifacts all over the walls of their house.

Scale); they work together to provide cooperative transform effects. In fact, they are all subclasses of the AnimateTransform class that we discussed in Section 9.3. The 3D effects are all subclasses of AnimateTransform3D, which is itself a subclass of AnimateTransform. This means that everything we said earlier about transform effects sharing properties and running together in a single transform effect instance holds true for 3D effects as well. In addition, some new 3D projection properties in AnimateTransform3D are similarly shared among these 3D effects.

Part of the 3D functionality provided by the Flash player for displaying 3D content provides a "perspective projection" calculation when drawing the objects onto the screen.[7] Projection is a standard process in 3D graphics rendering where the system takes information about an object's location in 3D space and calculates where the object's pixels should show up on the application window in order to look like they really are 3D objects. Of course, how that projection is calculated depends on several factors, including where the "eye" is positioned that you are projecting toward, the distance of the view plane from the eye, and the width of the view. All of these parameters define what's called the "view frustum." In order to perform the 3D calculations in the way that you want, Flex needs to know how you want that frustum set up for the effects, so it exposes a few properties that you can set appropriately. I'll skip most of them, like fieldOfView and depthOfField and leave them for readers that really want to explore 3D to a greater depth. But it is worth calling out a few that you may have to deal with in your applications:

applyLocalProjection This property tells Flex to set the projection properties specified on the effect prior to running the effect. If this property is false then the projection properties of the parent container (where projection properties are set) are left alone. The default value is true, so 3D effects always set projection properties by default. This is usually what you want for simple effects, because you probably also want the projection centered around the object, which is the purpose of the autoCenterProjection property.

---

[7] A full discussion of 3D graphics and perspective projection is way beyond the scope of this little Flex book. If you're interested in knowing more about the topic, I'd suggest you first check out the Flash API documentation on some of the new 3D graphics classes, like PerspectiveProjection. And if that's not enough, dive into great 3D graphics books like the classic *Computer Graphics: Principles and Practice* tome by Foley, van Dam, Feiner and Hughes. But you shouldn't need all of this background just to understand the discussion and examples covered here.

autoCenterProjection This property tells Flex to set up the projection
properties for the 3D effect to center the view around the target object. If you are rotating the object about its center, then the effect
usually looks best when the projection is centered around the object
as well. Without this setting, the projection may cause the object to
look oddly distorted, depending on where the object is relative to the
current projection center (which, by default, is at the center of the parent container). This property defaults to true since it is probably the
value you want for simple 3D effects like a flip rotation. Note that the
applyLocalProjection property must also be set to true for this
property to have any effect.

projectionX, projectionY If you do not want to center the projection
around an object, but want to set it to a particular location, use these
properties to set that point relative to the object itself.

removeLocalProjectionWhenComplete This property controls whether a
projection applied to the parent container, if applyLocalProjection
is true, is removed when the effect finishes. If not, the projection set
on the parent container persists after the effect ends. The default value
for this property is false, so the projection change persists by default.
This may seem counter-intuitive at first; you might expect any changes
made by an effect to be temporary. But depending on what the effect
does, you may want the projection to be persistent. For example, if
you rotate an object into the third dimension, say by forty five degrees
around the y axis, then removing the effect's projection settings when
it finishes will probably make the object visually jump as the default
projection is re-applied. If the object stays positioned or oriented in
3D when the effect finishes and you want the object to look the same
after the effect as it did during the effect, then you should make sure
the local projection stays set on the parent.

One side-effect of setting the local projection that is not immediately apparent until you hit it is that animating different 3D target objects inside the
same container will, by default, center the parent's projection around each
target object, causing the other objects that are currently being projected to
jump as their projection is changed. This is to some extent just a limitation
in the current 3D system that you need to work around; each container just
has one projection center, and all of the children of that container share it. A

231

couple of workarounds exist for this situation: put 3D objects in their own containers (or at least in containers that do not have other objects that will be transformed in 3D), or set the `applyLocalProjection` property to `false` for all of the 3D effects running on the container's objects so that they all use the default projection center of the container instead of setting their own projection when they run.

As with the transform effects that we discussed in Chapter 9, these projection properties are shared in the single underlying instance of the 3D transform effects. This means that when multiple 3D effects are running in parallel on the same target object, they share the projection properties set on the first such effect. So it is best to set the same values for these properties on all 3D effects to make it clear when reading the code what is actually happening at runtime.

Another important detail about the 3D effects is that they change the default value of a property in the `AnimateTransform` effect that we haven't talked about yet: `applyChangesPostLayout`. This property is `false` by default for the 2D transform effects because you typically want to transform objects in a layout-friendly way. For example, if you `Move` a button, you want the layout manager for the button's container to figure out how to place the button given its new location. But the situation is different for 3D: the Flex layout system does not understand 3D, so it doesn't know how to place items correctly given 3D positions and orientations. So instead of moving and rotating the objects in the transform that the layout manager uses, the objects are transformed post-layout. That is, all 2D transforms are applied to the object normally, then layout occurs, then the post-layout changes occur where the object may move further in 3D unbeknownst to the layout manager. This functionality happens through the use of the `postLayoutTransformOffsets` structure in Flex components and graphic elements. We don't need to go into more detail on this here, but it is worth mentioning that the 3D effects all affect this structure by default, and are therefore not affecting layout by default. So you may get different layout behavior by using `Move3D` to position an object in x and y than you get by using `Move` to do the same operation. The value of `applyChangesPostLayout` is the reason.

Now that we've seen what's happening for the `AnimateTransform3D` superclass and for 3D effects in general, let's take a look at the actual 3D effects that you might use in your code.

10.6 The Move3D effect

This effect moves an object in 3D, including the standard x and y, but also the z dimension. The properties controlling the effect are similar to those in the Move effect, but are extended to 3D:

xFrom, yFrom, zFrom These properties define the location that the effect starts from. If not specified, the current location of the object is used as the starting place.

xTo, yTo, zTo These properties define the location that the effect moves the object to. If not specified, the current location of the object is used as the end location (except in the case of state transitions, where the end location may come from the state information).

xBy, yBy, zBy These properties define the amount in x and y to move the object. Given a by value and either a from or to value, the effect calculates the missing value.

10.7 The Rotate3D effect

The Rotate3D effect is similar to the 2D Rotate effect, but extended into 3D to rotate the target object around any of the three axes. One important difference from the 2D effect is that no "by" property exists to specify an angle offset to rotate by; this was done to allow more flexibility in the API since this effect may allow rotation around an arbitrary axis in the future. Locking in the "by" property into the current 3D rotation API may have limited that functionality.

Properties are exposed for the rotation angle of the target object around each of the three axes. The angleXFrom, angleXTo, and similar properties for the y and z axes tell the effect the rotation angle and axis to rotate the object from and to. The rotation happens by default around the upper-left point of the object—its (x, y) point—but you can change this rotation center by setting autoCenterTransform to true to rotate about the center of the object or setting transformX, transformY, and transformZ to rotate about a specific point.

233

10.8   The `Scale3D` effect

The `Scale3D` effect is much like the 2D `Scale` effect, but also animates scaling in the z direction:

`scaleXFrom, scaleYFrom, scaleZFrom` These properties define the scale factors from which the effect starts. If not specified, the current scale factors of the object is used as the starting values.

`scaleXTo, scaleYTo, scaleZTo` These properties define the scale factor to which the effect animates. If not specified, the current scale values of the object are used as the end values (except in the case of state transitions, where the end values may come from the state information).

`scaleXBy, scaleYBy, scaleZBy` These properties define the amount in x, y, and z to scale the object. Given a by value and either a from or to value, the effect calculates the other value.

Note that an object that is only in a 2D plane (no point of the object is at a different z point than any other point of the object) is not affected by a scale in z, because no z dimension exists on the object that can be scaled. An example of an object that could be scaled in z (with visible effect) is a grouped object whose child objects have different z positions or orientations, like a 3D cube.

 3D animations can be used effectively for transient effects like flipping an object over to reveal information on the back, or moving a clicked button in and out to give it more life.

Unless you are writing an application that really uses 3D, where objects are really positioned and oriented in 3D (the "cover flow" interface in iTunes come to mind), you may find yourself using 3D animations more for transient UI effects, like flipping panels over to reveal something on their backside, or more subtle 3D effects that draw the user's attention. As an example of this kind of temporary effect, let's take a look at the `ThreeDButtons` example:

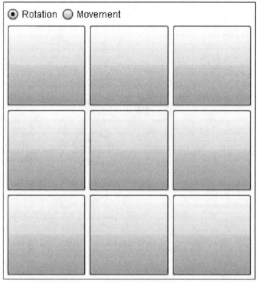

(Demo: ThreeDButtons)

This application shows a grid of 9 buttons, with radio controls at the top of the window. Hovering the mouse over any of the buttons causes the 3D effect selected by the radio button to run. The "Rotation" effect rotates the button 360 degrees around the y (vertical) axis:

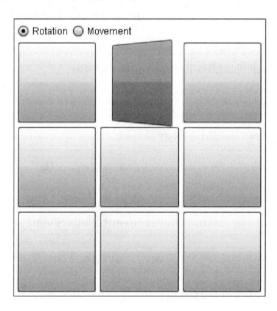

The "Movement" effect moves the button out toward the user and then back into place on the x/y plane:

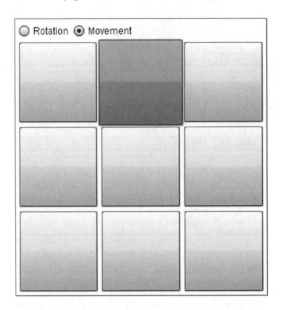

In both cases, the button runs the effect once and the button settles back into place in 2D. The object is only in 3D for the duration of the effect, demonstrating the kind of transient 3D effect that is typical with these 3D transform effects.

The hover effect works by handling the mouseOver event for each button, as we see in this declaration for one of the buttons:

```
(File: ThreeDButtons.mxml)
<s:Button width="100" height="100"
    mouseOver="animateHover(event)"/>
```

The animateHover() function is defined in script code:

```
private var animatingTargets:Object = new Object();

private function animateHover(event:MouseEvent):void
{
    if (animatingTargets[event.currentTarget] === undefined)
    {
        var effect:Effect;
```

```
    if (rotationButton.selected)
        effect = rotator;
    else
        effect = mover;
    effect.target = event.currentTarget;
    animatingTargets[event.currentTarget] = effect;
    effect.play();
    }
}
```

The logic with the `animatingTargets` object is a technique to ensure that we do not repeat an effect on the same button while an effect is already running. Otherwise, we might either constantly restart an effect or run multiple, conflicting effects on a button when the mouse moves out of and back over that button, causing another `mouseOver` event. To avoid this, we temporarily add our object as a key in the `animatingTargets` object map and avoid the effect-starting logic if the object is already in the map.

To start the effect, we first check which radio button is currently selected so that we know which effect to run. We then set the effect target to be the current event target (which is the button whose `mouseOver` event we are currently handling), add the target to the `animatingTargets` map, and play the effect.

The effects are declared like this:

```
<s:Rotate3D id="rotator" angleYFrom="0" angleYTo="360"
    autoCenterTransform="true"
    effectEnd="effectEndHandler(event)"/>
<s:Move3D id="mover" duration="200"
    zBy="-30" repeatCount="2"
    repeatBehavior="{RepeatBehavior.REVERSE}"
    effectEnd="effectEndHandler(event)"/>
```

The `Rotate3D` effect is set up to rotate the target object one full rotation (360 degrees) around the y axis. The effect sets the transform center at the center the object. By default, the object would rotate around its left edge, which is not the visual effect we are looking for here. Finally, we register a handler for the `effectEnd` event, where we remove the target object from the `animatingTargets` map to free it up for future animations:

```
private function effectEndHandler(event:EffectEvent):void
{
    delete animatingTargets[event.effectInstance.target];
}
```

The Move3D effect is slightly different because we need the effect to reverse and repeat. Where the Rotate3D effect rotates all the way around to its original orientation, the Move3D needs to reverse to get the object back to where it started. We put a smaller duration on this effect because with the reversing/repeating behavior we're running the effect twice, so the default duration of 500 milliseconds would make the overall effect too long. The movement is specified by the zBy property, which causes the effect to move its target object -30 in z (toward the viewer). Then the reverse animation takes the object back 30 units in z to put it back onto the x/y plane. Finally, we handle the effectEnd event, like we do with the Rotate3D effect, to remove the target object from the animatingTargets map. Note that we do not need to auto-center the transform like we do for the Rotate3D effect because we're simply moving the button; the center of transformation is irrelevant.

I wouldn't suggest making all, or even any, of the buttons in your applications have either of these behaviors when the mouse hovers over them. You don't want to annoy your users with a UI that's rotating all over the place as they move the mouse around in the window:

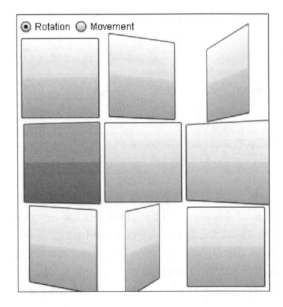

But similar techniques that flip or move objects in 3D can be effective and useful when applied appropriately.

Conclusion

In this chapter, we saw how to use some of the Flex 4 effects that take advantage of recent, powerful graphical capabilities of the Flash player. Since Flex 4 effects can target any kind of object and any type of property, your applications can now animate filters and 3D properties of your objects to get very rich, animated experiences.

In the next chapter, we will wrap up our discussion of Flex effects with composite and action effects, which are used when creating complex combinations of multiple effects playing together.

Chapter 11

Effect Choreography

Compelling animations often use a combination of effects playing together. This chapter is about the effects that are used to choreograph these sequences of effects to get much more complex and interesting results than you can get with just one effect at a time.

These choreographic effects come in two categories: composite effects, which allow you to sequence together multiple effects, and action effects, which perform atomic operations that are useful when used in combination with other effects.

11.1 Composite effects

When I hear the term "choreography," I think of dance, Bob Fosse, and a chorus line of rhinestone-clad performers stamping the floor in rhythm. Without choreography, it's just a mess of bodies and costumes. When using composite effects, there's a similar dynamic; lots of different, complicated things all running simultaneously. A little careful choreography helps make that UI dance (but without the rhinestones).

CompositeEffect, through its two subclasses Parallel and Sequence, exists to help developers play multiple effects in an organized fashion. Often, you want effects to play at the same time, or one after another, or in some combination of the two. For example, animating an item's insertion into a list may consist of first moving the other items out of the way and then fading the item in. Making a panel appear in a window may entail fading it in while also sliding it in from the side. Interesting menu effects may consist of first opening the menu background then fading in the items in the menu one by one. Many different possibilities exist to structure effects together, but a mechanism is needed to organize the effects to play both together and one after the other. That's why the `Parallel` and `Sequence` effects exist.

The `Parallel` and `Sequence` effects share common elements:

`childEffects` This array holds the list of effects that are played when the composite effect is played. The details of when they are played depends on whether the composite effect is a `Parallel` or `Sequence`. `childEffects` is the default property of the composite effects, so in MXML code you do not have to use this property explicitly. Composite effects are typically just declared with a set of effects inside of them, like this:

```
<s:Parallel>
    <s:Move/>
    <s:Resize/>
</s:Parallel>
```

`duration, targets` These properties act just like they do in other effects, except in this case they pass the values for these properties to each of the child effects of the composite effect. Each child effect can override these properties to substitute their own `duration` or `targets`, but otherwise they simply inherit these property values from the composite effect.

`play()` As with other effects, this function starts the composite effect. For composite effects, this means that the child effects start playing in the sequence appropriate for the type of composite effect that it is (`Parallel` or `Sequence`).

Now for a closer look at the composite effects: `Parallel` and `Sequence`.

11.2 The `Parallel` effect: keeping it together

The `Parallel` effect plays all of its child effects simultaneously (in parallel). When `play()` is called on the `Parallel` effect, all of the child effects are started at the same time. The effects may still start at different times (if they have startDelays) or end at different times (if they have different durations), but they will at least all play() at the same time.

> Some complex animations are effective when played simultaneously, such as fading and sliding in a component, or moving several objects together, or moving and resizing an object.

The Parallel effect is useful when you want to structure several effects to play together, such as fading and sliding in a component, or moving several objects together, or moving and resizing an object simultaneously. As an example of this effect, let's look at the PanelSlideFade application. When the button is clicked in this application, a Panel moves in from the left side of the application window. As the Panel moves, it also fades in.

Here is the code for the animation:

(File: PanelSlideFade.mxml)
```
<fx:Declarations>
    <s:Parallel id="slider" target="{panel}">
        <s:Move xTo="0"/>
        <s:Fade alphaFrom="0" alphaTo="1"/>
    </s:Parallel>
</fx:Declarations>
```

And here is the code for the controls:

```
<s:Button label="Send in the Panel" click="slider.play()"/>
<s:Panel id="panel" title="The Panel"
    width="300" height="200" x="-350" y="40"/>
```

In this application, the Move and the Fade effects target the panel object, they both run for the same duration (the default of 500 milliseconds), and they play at the same time.So the panel slides in as it fades in, becoming fully opaque as it settles into its final position.

The application initially looks like this:

243

(Demo: PanelSlideFade)

When the button is clicked, the panel slides and fades into place:

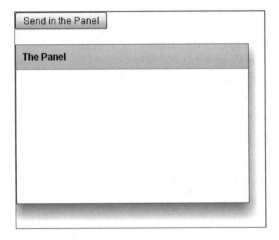

11.3 The Sequence effect: you follow me?

As its name implies, the Sequence effect runs its child effects in sequence, one after the other. The act of one child effect ending causes the Sequence effect to play the next child effect in the series, continuing until all child effects have played, at which point the Sequence itself ends.

Some complex animations are more effective when played one after the other, such as resizing or clearing an area first to make room for a new element that moves or fades in.

This effect is useful when you want to run effects in a series, or structure the effects in a dependent fashion, so that one effect starts when another ends. The technique is used for visual effects that are dependent, such as resizing an empty space to make room for an item before then fading it in, or moving components out of the way to make room for some other component.

As an example, suppose in our previous application that slid the panel in from the side that there were other components occupying that space. We still want those objects in the window, but located elsewhere in the UI. In this case, we need to make room for the panel by moving the objects out of the way. We could move them in parallel with the panel, but it might make more sense, and make a more visually clean experience, to perform these actions separately. That is, we want to move the objects out of the way in the first part of the action to make room for the panel, then slide the panel into place.

I find this two-part approach better in cases where the objects do not have the same exact motion. If the objects being shifted to make way for the panel move the same distance and in the same direction as the panel, then moving both sets of objects in parallel works. But in the code we're about to see, the buttons move one way and the panel moves another. It is less distracting and noisy to the user to run these actions separately. This ordering of animations is perfect for a Sequence effect.

When animations are performing very different tasks, it is less noisy and distracting to run them in an ordered sequence, rather than in parallel.

We can now see the power of using both `Parallel` *and* `Sequence` together as we structure some effects to run at the same time (the slide/fade of the panel) and some to run one after the other (moving the buttons out of the way first, then playing the parallel sliding effect). Here is some code from the `PanelSequenceParallelSlide` application, seen in the screenshots on page 246 and page 247:

245

(File: PanelSequenceParallelSlide.mxml)

```
<fx:Declarations>
    <s:Sequence id="shiftSlideSequence">
        <s:Move target="{buttonGroup}" yTo="260"/>
        <s:Parallel target="{panel}">
            <s:Move xTo="0"/>
            <s:Fade alphaFrom="0" alphaTo="1"/>
        </s:Parallel>
    </s:Sequence>
</fx:Declarations>
<s:Button label="Send in the Panel"
    click="shiftSlideSequence.play()"/>
<s:HGroup id="buttonGroup" y="40">
    <s:Button label="Some Button"/>
    <s:Button label="Some Other Button"/>
</s:HGroup>
<s:Panel id="panel" title="The Panel"
    width="300" height="200" x="-350" y="40"/>
```

Here is what the application initially looks like:

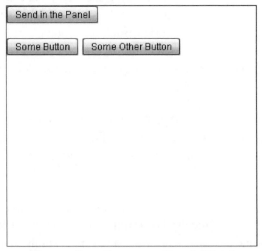

(Demo: PanelSequenceParallelSlide)

And here is what it looks like after the effect plays: the buttons are moved out of the way and the panel fades and slides into place.

246

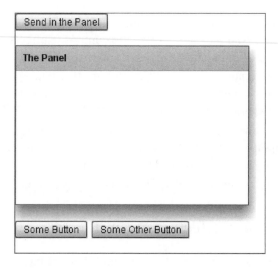

In this example, note how no targets are declared on the Sequence effect itself because its child effects act on different targets so it doesn't serve any purpose to provide default targets for the parent effect.

With composite effects, and the ability to nest them as seen in this example, we can create all kinds of complex and interesting effects and carefully control the timing of how and when certain effects are executed. Now let's see how to run other simple actions as part of these overall composite effects.

11.4 Action effects

Sometimes, in the middle of a complex animation enabled by the composite effects we just discussed, you want to perform single, atomic actions. For example, you might want to animate an object moving, then make it suddenly disappear, then perform some other effect. For this kind of single-shot action, we use *action effects*. Several action effects are available, but some that I find particularly useful are Pause, AddAction, RemoveAction, SetAction, and CallAction.

The Pause effect is about timing—waiting for a specified amount of time or until a particular event fires. The AddAction and RemoveAction effects handle adding and removing elements to and from their parent containers. The SetAction effect sets a property value. And the CallAction effect calls a function.

247

These action effects are not complex; they perform a simple task and then they're done. And they are not like the composite effects covered in the previous sections. Composite effects are about sequencing multiple effects to perform some complex action. The action effects are just child effects that run on target objects. But they are specifically intended to run within composite effects, not on their own. The kinds of actions they perform could easily be done without effects in normal procedural code. But they enable useful functionality to occur in the middle of effects sequences by performing their actions in the context of larger animations. They help composite effects do their job of enabling careful choreography of multiple animations.

11.5   The Pause effect: wait for it...

The Pause effect does exactly as you would think; it pauses for some duration or until some event occurs. By itself, the effect is useless—it is only interesting when combined with other effects in a Sequence.

First, let's see how the effect works. Pause has three main properties:

target   This property acts just like it does with other effects we have seen; it specifies the target that the effect acts on. However, unlike other effects, the Pause effect can run with no target. If the effect is simply waiting for its duration to expire, then it needs no target object. But if the effect is waiting for an event specified by eventName, then a target object is required (because the target object is responsible for dispatching that event).

duration   This property specifies how long the effect runs. If no eventName is specified, then the effect simply waits for this duration and then ends. If eventName is set, then the duration equals the maximum amount of time that the effect waits for that event, after which the effect ends, regardless of whether the event was received. So the duration acts as both a regular effect duration, specifying how long the effect runs, and as a timeout, specifying how long to spend waiting for the named event to be received.

eventName   This optional property specifies the name of an event for which the effect listens. If no eventName is supplied, the effect simply runs quietly in the background until the specified duration expires, at which time the effect ends.

248

If an `eventName` is specified, then the `target` of the effect must be able to dispatch events (it must implement the `IEventDispatcher` interface), because the effect internally adds itself as a listener of that event on the `target`. The effect ends when either the event is received or the specified `duration` elapses, whichever occurs first.

The only reason to ever use the `Pause` effect is if you want to wait in a sequence of other effects for either a set amount of time or for some event to occur. Then the effect provides a useful way to pause the execution of other effects pending this occurrence. You can usually achieve that same kind of time delay by adding a `startDelay` to the next effect, which causes a delay for the specified amount of time before starting. But sometimes a `startDelay` does not fit the purposes. For example, if you need to create the reverse of some sequence of effects, a `Pause` is sometimes necessary to take the place of the reverse of a `startDelay`.

As we discussed in Chapter 5, when using the `autoReverse` property on a transition it is critical to have the reversing transition effects be exact mirrors of each other, including the total duration.[1] If one of the effects begins with a `startDelay`, then a `Pause` in the reverse effect is the best way to mirror this delay.

As an example, let's look at the `ReversingPause` demo. This application has a very simple transition that moves it's target object between states. However, the effect has a `startDelay` on it, making it a bit trickier to reverse because of that asymmetric behavior. Here is the code for the transition:

(File: ReversingPause.mxml)
```
<s:Transition fromState="s1" toState="s2"
        autoReverse="true">
    <s:Move target="{button}" startDelay="250"/>
</s:Transition>
```

The application is seen here:

---

[1] Note, as I mentioned when discussing `autoReverse` in Chapter 5, that the reverse transition must actually exist; Flex does not automatically create a reverse transition for you. So if you have a transition from state s1 to s2 with `autoReverse="true"`, then it will only reverse on the fly if there is some transition that is declared that will run from state s2 to s1.

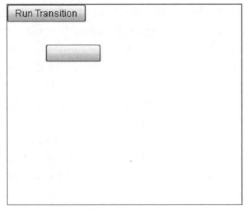

(Demo: ReversingPause)

The reverse transition is not simply a Move of the same 1000 milliseconds duration, nor one with a 1250 milliseconds duration that includes the startDelay amount, nor one with a startDelay itself. None of these mirrors the original effect of waiting for 250 milliseconds and then moving the target for 1000 milliseconds. Although some of these alternatives have the same total duration, the object is not in the exact opposite place during the effect, so reversing on the fly does not work correctly. Instead, we need a reverse effect that moves the target for 1000 milliseconds and then waits at the end. To get this result, we can use a Sequence and a Pause, in addition to the Move:

```
<s:Transition fromState="s2" toState="s1"
        autoReverse="true">
    <s:Sequence target="{button}">
        <s:Move duration="1000"/>
        <s:Pause duration="250"/>
    </s:Sequence>
</s:Transition>
```

We've shown using Pause for a simple delay in a composite effect. You can also use the event-waiting capability of the effect to choreograph complex actions that are dependent upon events in the system. For example, you could have one effect start when another effect ends, via the EFFECT_END event on the first effect. Choreographing effects is usually handled within the same composite effect, such as a Sequence effect which runs one effect after the other. But with the Pause effect, you could have completely separate effects that cause each other to run by waiting on events. Which approach you take depends on your situation. If you can easily structure your effects together in a single composite effect like Sequence, then that is probably the more straightforward way to go. But if you find yourself with separate effects that are dependent upon each other, you might instead use Pause and the EFFECT_END event to create that dependency.

11.6   AddAction and RemoveAction

The AddAction and RemoveAction effects coordinate adding and removing objects from a container. These effects are useful when choreographing a set of actions that includes objects coming into existence or going away during a transition. We saw in Chapter 9 that the Fade effect automatically handles adding and removing a target object in the process of fading it in and out. This is true when Fade is used in a transition either alone or as child of a Parallel effect. But when Fade is used in a Sequence effect, or when other effects are used to get an appearing/disappearing effect in a transition, then the effects need some help to tell them when to add or remove their target objects.

   Let's take a look at the AddRemoveTransition example. In this application, we have two states and two transitions to animate between them. In the first state, we see only a button on the screen:

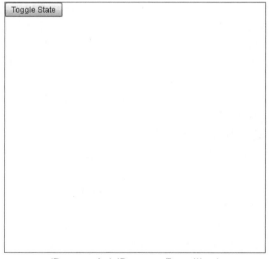

(Demo: AddRemoveTransition)

Clicking on this button toggles to the other state, in which we see the same button over toward the right, a panel on the left, and several buttons below the panel:

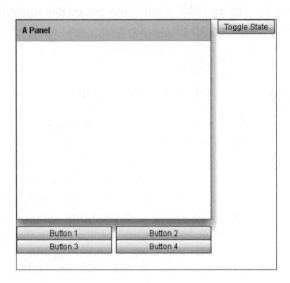

Here's the code for the components:

(File: AddRemoveTransition.mxml)
```
<s:Button id="button" label="Toggle State" x.s2="310"
    click="currentState = (currentState=='s1')?'s2':'s1'"/>
<s:Panel id="panel" title="A Panel"
    width="300" height="300" includeIn="s2"/>
<s:HGroup width="300" y="310" id="button12Group"
    includeIn="s2">
    <s:Button id="button1" label="Button 1"
        width="50%" includeIn="s2"/>
    <s:Button id="button2" label="Button 2"
        width="50%" includeIn="s2"/>
</s:HGroup>
<s:HGroup width="300" y="330" id="button34Group"
    includeIn="s2">
    <s:Button id="button3" label="Button 3" width="50%"/>
    <s:Button id="button4" label="Button 4" width="50%"/>
</s:HGroup>
```

252

Note, in this code, that we have separate `includeIn` values for `button1` and `button2` and their containing `HGroup`. This is because we handle the buttons separately in our transitions below, so we need to have them added to their respective containers at different times.

Now suppose that we want to transition to the second state in the following sequence:

1. Move the "Toggle State" button to its place on the right.

2. `Scale` the panel around its center from 0 to its normal size.

3. Move `button2`, then `button1` into their places.

4. Fade in `button3` and `button4` together.

The first attempt at this effect might be something like this, where we simply encode the above sequence of effects as described:

```
<s:Transition fromState="s1" toState="s2"
    autoReverse="true">
    <s:Sequence>
        <s:Move target="{button}"/>
        <s:Scale target="{panel}" scaleXFrom="0"
            scaleYFrom="0" autoCenterTransform="true"/>
        <s:Move target="{button2}" xFrom="-150"
            disableLayout="true"/>
        <s:Move target="{button1}" xFrom="-150"
            disableLayout="true"/>
        <s:Fade target="{button34Group}"/>
    </s:Sequence>
</s:Transition>
```

But if you run this transition (which you can do in the application code by deleting the various `AddAction` effects in the final version), you see that you don't get at all what you wanted. As soon as you click on the button, the panel and all of the buttons pop into their final places. When the first effect finishes moving the "Toggle State" button, the panel disappears and then scales in from its center. Then buttons 1 and 2 disappear and slide into place separately. Then buttons 3 and 4 blink out and fade in. Although you can see the correct animations occur, the overall effect of transitioning objects onto

253

the screen is completely ruined by the fact that everything in the second state simply pops into place at the start of the transition.

The reason that the components suddenly blink in is that the states engine automatically adds items that are in the next state prior to playing the transition.[2] If we do not want these components to appear at that time, then we need to supply extra information to the transition effect to prevent it from occurring, or to change when they appear. This is exactly the purpose of the AddAction effect.

AddAction performs two tasks in a sequence: it removes its target object from the parent (which the states mechanism has automatically added) when the overall transition begins[3] and then later, when the AddAction effect actually runs in the sequence, it adds that target object back in. This pair of actions essentially mutes the normal operation of states to add the object in when the state changes and delays that step until the AddAction effect runs.

To use AddAction, place the effect immediately before whatever other effect you use to make an object appear during the transition. For example, since we want our panel to scale into place, we place the AddAction immediately before the Scale effect. Similarly, we run an AddAction on button2 just prior to moving the button, and so on. The resulting sequence of effects looks like this:

```
<s:Transition fromState="s1" toState="s2"
    autoReverse="true">
    <s:Sequence>
        <s:Move target="{button}"/>
        <s:AddAction target="{panel}"/>
        <s:Scale target="{panel}"
            scaleXFrom="0" scaleYFrom="0"
            autoCenterTransform="true"/>
        <s:AddAction target="{button12Group}"/>
        <s:AddAction target="{button2}"/>
        <s:Move target="{button2}" xFrom="-150"
```

---

[2] In fact, the state change has already occurred when a transition begins. The process of starting the transition is one of the things that happens during the process of changing the state. The fact that some of the objects are in their prior state is due to the transition mechanism of restoring the values from the previous state so that they can be animated to the final state values.

[3] See the aside on single-threaded rendering on page 255; there's a trick here to being able to add and remove items without the user noticing.

> ## The magic of single-threaded rendering
>
> You might have noticed that the objects are still being added by the states mechanism before the transition begins. The AddAction effect immediately removes them, but won't the user notice if they are added and then quickly removed? Well, no—this is the advantage of Flex's single-threaded rendering system. These things happen all in the same sequence of instructions and are complete before control is turned back over to Flash to render the next screen update. So even though we may add a component to its container, thus making it displayable in the window, the component won't show up if we remove it before returning control back to Flash. This trick of doing and then undoing actions prior to returning control back to Flash is at the heart of how transitions work in general. The state mechanism sets the next state values on all of the objects, then transitions record these state values and roll back the properties to their pre-state-change values prior to playing the transition effect. Since all of this happens before returning from the state-setting function, Flash is none the wiser and it's as if nothing happened.

```
          disableLayout="true"/>
      <s:AddAction target="{button1}"/>
      <s:Move target="{button1}" xFrom="-150"
          disableLayout="true"/>
      <s:AddAction target="{button34Group}"/>
      <s:Fade target="{button34Group}"/>
    </s:Sequence>
  </s:Transition>
```

If you run this transition, the final code in the AddRemoveTransition example, you see that our sequence of effects occurs just as we outlined previously. An extra AddAction handles adding button12Group prior to adding and moving each of its buttons because we are handling the buttons separately from their group.

Now for the reverse transition. We would like to have the objects animate back out of this state in the opposite way that they animated into this state:

1. Fade out button3 and button4 together.

2. Move button1, then button2 off of the screen.

255

3. Scale the panel to 0 into its center to make it disappear.

4. Move the "Toggle State" button back to its original place on the left.

Our trivial attempt at this sequence might look like this:

```
<s:Transition fromState="s2" toState="s1"
        autoReverse="true">
    <s:Sequence target="{button}">
        <s:Fade target="{button34Group}"/>
        <s:Move target="{button1}" xTo="-150"
            disableLayout="true"/>
        <s:Move target="{button2}" xTo="-150"
            disableLayout="true"/>
        <s:Scale target="{panel}"
            scaleXTo="0" scaleYTo="0"
            autoCenterTransform="true"/>
        <s:Move target="{button}"/>
    </s:Sequence>
</s:Transition>
```

But if you run this transition code (which you can do by deleting the other effects in the final version of the code in AddRemoveTransition), you'll see that this is not what you get at all. In fact, you hardly get any animation. All of the controls on the left blink out immediately, and finally after a long delay the button on the right moves back to the left.

Once again, the normal states machinery has defeated our simple attempt to sequence our effects. Just as we saw in the original state transition, the states machinery sets up the visibility (or, rather, the existence) of all of the components of the next state prior to running the transition. In this case, that means that all of the objects that do not exist in the next state are automatically removed from the GUI. The fact that we want to Fade, Move, and Scale those objects out during the transition is irrelevant; they simply don't exist in the GUI when our transition begins.

This is where the RemoveAction effect comes in. Just like AddAction, which tells the transition when to add its target object in, the RemoveAction effect tells the transition when to remove its target object. At the beginning of the overall transition, a RemoveAction automatically adds its target object back to its parent container in that the states mechanism removed. Then, when the effect is played in the sequence, it removes the target object.

256

The typical use of RemoveAction is to place it *after* the effect which is meant to animate the object out of view. For example, a RemoveAction is placed after our Scale effect on the panel object so that it scales out of view and is then removed from the GUI. With the addition of several RemoveAction effects to keep our target objects around until we've had our way with them, the transition looks like this:

```
<s:Transition fromState="s2" toState="s1"
        autoReverse="true">
    <s:Sequence target="{button}">
        <s:Fade target="{button34Group}"/>
        <s:Move target="{button1}" xTo="-150"
            disableLayout="true"/>
        <s:RemoveAction target="{button1}"/>
        <s:Move target="{button2}" xTo="-150"
            disableLayout="true"/>
        <s:RemoveAction target="{button2}"/>
        <s:RemoveAction target="{button12Group}"/>
        <s:Scale target="{panel}"
            scaleXTo="0" scaleYTo="0"
            autoCenterTransform="true"/>
        <s:RemoveAction target="{panel}"/>
        <s:Move target="{button}"/>
    </s:Sequence>
</s:Transition>
```

Note, in this code, that there is no RemoveAction after the Fade effect; this is because auto-removal functionality is built into that effect (because Fade is commonly used for this exact purpose, to fade objects out of view). In the reverse transition, when objects are fading in, an AddAction effect is required in order to delay adding the object until it is faded in. But in this case, Fade automatically removes the object when it finishes.

If you run this reverse transition in the example, you see that it now works both ways, and we get exactly the behavior of our two transitions that we wanted ... *but* we're not quite done yet. If you run the forward transition again, you'll see that our panel does not reappear. What happened?

The way that the Scale effect is written in the transitions causes the target object to always scale in from 0 and out to 0. But if the current scale factor of our panel is 0, then scaling in from 0 simply leaves us with a 0-scale panel. Since our first scaling-out of the panel scales it to 0, then the next time we try to scale it in, it's just scaling from/to 0. We could rewrite the `Scale` effect to manually scale the panel from/to 0 and 1, thus guaranteeing that the panel always scales from 0 to 1 when it scales in. But another way to solve this is to reset the scaling factor values when we're done scaling it out, by using the `SetAction` effect, described in the next section.

11.7 The `SetAction` effect: assign of the times

The `SetAction` effect performs a very simple task: it sets a named `property` to a specified `value`.[4] As with the other action effects, this effect is intended for use in effect choreography, when you want to set some value during the middle of a larger sequence of effects. If you just need to set a value outside of an effect, you can do that much more simply than by running this action effect. (Why run an effect to set some `foo` object's x property to 5 when you can simply call `foo.x = 5`?) But such procedural code is not as easy when you are in the middle of an effects sequence, which is where `SetAction` comes in handy.

`SetAction` is particularly useful for setting properties to appropriate values based on what other effects have caused, or what they need. For example, you could set the `height` property of an object to zero at the beginning of a sequence so that a later `Resize` effect could resize from zero, or you could set the `visible` property of an object to `false`, so that it is then faded in by a later `Fade` effect. Or you can restore a value to something sensible after its value is changed as a side effect of some other operation, which we will see in the following example.

In the `AddRemoveTransition` example of the previous section, we saw how our transition ran correctly the first time, and ran in reverse correctly after that. But the second time we attempted the forward transition, the panel refused to show up because its `scaleX` and `scaleY` properties had been set to zero by the `Scale` effect in the reverse transition:

(File: AddRemoveTransition.mxml)

```
<s:Scale target="{panel}" scaleXTo="0" scaleYTo="0"
    autoCenterTransform="true"/>
```

---

[4] Note that `SetAction` works just as well with style names as property names. In Flex 3, there were separate `SetStyleAction` and `SetPropertyAction` effects. In Flex 4, the functionality of these two effects has been combined into the single `SetAction` effect.

When the forward transition runs, the Scale effect on the panel does nothing to counter that zero-scale, because it assumes that the target object has a reasonable default scale factor that it is scaling up into:

```
<s:Scale target="{panel}" scaleXFrom="0" scaleYFrom="0"
    autoCenterTransform="true"/>
```

We could fix by this writing this Scale effect to hard-code the scale factor, like this:

```
<s:Scale target="{panel}" scaleXFrom="0" scaleXTo="1"
    scaleYFrom="0" scaleYTo="1"
    autoCenterTransform="true"/>
```

This solution would certainly work for the current situation, where we know that our panel should be at a scale of 1 in x and y. But in some situations, and with other properties, hard-coding the from/to values in effects is not a "scalable" solution. It is better to let the object and the states mechanism determine the correct "to" value (and usually the "from" value as well, although here we are specifically trying to scale from a zero-dimension, so using the "from" values is okay for this example). A better approach would be to make sure that whatever causes the object to have the zero scale factor resets the values to something reasonable when it finishes. We can do this with a SetAction effect.

The SetAction effect takes the name of a property and some value and assigns that value to the property when the effect is run. For example, the following code is equivalent to foo.x = 5:

```
<s:SetAction target="{foo}" property="x" value="5"/>
```

Since the Scale effect in the reverse transition causes the problem with our panel's scale factors, we add SetAction effects to the sequence to reset our scaling factors back to reasonable values when that effect is done. Including the RemoveAction that we added after the Scale effect to remove the panel, the new scaling code now looks like this:

```
<s:Scale target="{panel}" scaleXTo="0" scaleYTo="0"
    autoCenterTransform="true"/>
<s:RemoveAction target="{panel}"/>
<s:SetAction target="{panel}" property="scaleX" value="1"/>
<s:SetAction target="{panel}" property="scaleY" value="1"/>
```

Now you can run the code, toggle the states three times and ... Argh! It's still not correct! Now we can at least see the panel scale in, but it happens in the wrong place. As you can see in the following screenshot, the panel is now positioned down and to the right of where it should be. In fact, you'll notice that the panel is located at the center of its original location. This is a clue to the problem:

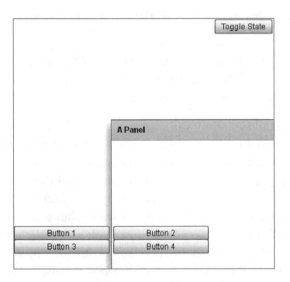

If you think about it, when we scale the panel out, we're not only setting the scale factor on the panel, but also its (x, y) location in the window. Since the panel scales down around its center, it changes not only its scaleX and scaleY properties, but also its x and y properties as a consequence. To fix the problem, we need to correct this side-effect of the Scale effect by restoring x and y to the upper left, via a couple more SetAction effects:

```
<s:SetAction target="{panel}" property="x" value="0"/>
<s:SetAction target="{panel}" property="y" value="0"/>
```

Now for the complete, correct code for the reverse transition:

```
<s:Transition fromState="s2" toState="s1"
        autoReverse="true">
    <s:Sequence target="{button}">
        <s:Fade target="{button34Group}"/>
        <s:Move target="{button1}" xTo="-150"
```

```
        disableLayout="true"/>
    <s:RemoveAction target="{button1}"/>
    <s:Move target="{button2}" xTo="-150"
        disableLayout="true"/>
    <s:RemoveAction target="{button2}"/>
    <s:RemoveAction target="{button12Group}"/>
    <s:Scale target="{panel}"
        scaleXTo="0" scaleYTo="0"
        autoCenterTransform="true"/>
    <s:RemoveAction target="{panel}"/>
    <s:SetAction target="{panel}"
        property="scaleX" value="1"/>
    <s:SetAction target="{panel}"
        property="scaleY" value="1"/>
    <s:SetAction target="{panel}"
        property="x" value="0"/>
    <s:SetAction target="{panel}"
        property="y" value="0"/>
    <s:Move target="{button}"/>
  </s:Sequence>
</s:Transition>
```

Now, if you run the transition backward and forward, it continues to perform as desired. The panel is properly restored after the reverse Scale operation by the timely addition of the four SetAction effects, which reset the scaleX, scaleY, x, and y properties appropriately.

11.8 CallAction: form versus function

The CallAction effect is a simple mechanism for calling a named function. You can obviously do this in your procedural code quite easily and don't need an effect to do it for you. But this effect is useful when you need to call a function in the middle of a sequence of effects. It is similar to the SetAction effect, except where SetAction simply sets the value of a property on a target object, CallAction calls any arbitrary function on its target object.

The effect takes a target (just like most other effects), a functionName string that specifies the function to be called on the target object, and an optional `args` array, which holds the arguments that should be passed into the function.

Conclusion

This chapter introduced the concept of effect choreography. While composite and action effects are simple to use and understand, they add powerful functionality to the overall set of Flex effects. They enable complex and interesting effects when you combine multiple effects on multiple targets for larger application transitions and animations.

The next chapter will discuss how various techniques covered throughout the book can be combined to create a rich application user experience.

Chapter 12

Picture Perfekt

To put together just a small sampling of the techniques that we've discussed in the book, this chapter will talk about the `PicturePerfekt` application. This application revisits topics in graphics, filters, and animation to end up with an image viewer that shows how these visual aspects of Flex 4 can be used to create a rich application experience:

(Demo: PicturePerfekt)

Several subtle effects are happening in the application in addition to the reflection, including drop shadows for the thumbnails, a glow around the currently-selected thumbnail, and an animated grayscale effect as the mouse hovers over and out of each thumbnail.

12.1 Reflection

The reflection effect is the same one that we developed in Section 3.9. In fact, this demo uses the same `ReflexionContainer` class to view the images:

```
(File: components/ReflexionContainer.mxml)
<s:BitmapImage id="image"
        source="{source}" smooth="true"
        width="{imageWidth}" height="{imageHeight}"/>
<s:BitmapImage id="reflection"
        source="{source}" smooth="true"
        width="{image.width}" height="{image.height}"
        maskType="alpha" scaleY="-1"  filters="{[blur]}">
    <s:mask>
        <s:Group>
            <s:Rect width="{image.width}">
                    height="{image.height}"
                <s:fill>
                    <s:LinearGradient rotation="-90">
                        <s:GradientEntry color="white"
                                alpha="1"/>
                        <s:GradientEntry color="white"
                                alpha="0" ratio=".4"/>
                    </s:LinearGradient>
                </s:fill>
            </s:Rect>
        </s:Group>
    </s:mask>
</s:BitmapImage>
```

The reflected image is produced by scaling a copy of the image negatively in y. A more realistic version is produced by a combination of blurring the reflection and using an alpha mask that makes the reflection gradually more transparent as it gets further from the reflected image. Take a look at

Section 3.9 for more information on the technique, and look at the code in the `ReflexionContainer.mxml` file in this chapter's project for the details.

12.2 Drop shadows

The thumbnails in the `PicturePerfekt` application stand out from the background with the use of drop shadows, which we discussed in Section 3.5. Rather than just using the same drop shadow filter for every thumbnail, I customized each shadow to project in a different direction. I figured if the main picture is reflecting straight toward the user, then the virtual light source must be straight overhead. To give the thumbnails a bit more unique look, I created a shadow for each one that is based on a local light source coming from the middle and above. Notice how the thumbnail on the far left casts a shadow down and to the left, whereas the one on the far right casts a shadow down and to the right, and the thumbnail shadows in the middle are somewhere in between, smoothly changing from left-cast shadows to right-cast shadows based on where each thumbnail is relative to the middle of the application window:

Shadows are added to the thumbnails in the function `addFilters()`:

(File: PicturePerfect.as)

```
private function addFilters():void
{
    for (var i:int = 0; i < thumbnails.numElements; ++i)
    {
        var img:Image =
            Image(thumbnails.getElementAt(i));
        var shadow:DropShadowFilter =
            new spark.filters.DropShadowFilter();
        shadow.blurX = 6;
        shadow.blurY = 6;
        shadow.quality = 2;
        shadow.color = 0x808080;
```

265

```
        shadow.distance = 5;
        shadow.angle = 45 +
            ((thumbnails.numElements - i) *
            90 / (thumbnails.numElements));
        var newShader:Shader =
            new Shader(new GrayscalerShaderClass());
        var grayFilter:ShaderFilter =
            new ShaderFilter(newShader);
        img.filters = [grayFilter, shadow];
    }
}
```

This code creates a DropShadowFilter and changes various properties from their defaults to get a shadow that is larger, lighter, smoother, and further away from the target object. Then the angle of the shadow is calculated to get a shadow direction that is based on the thumbnail's distance from the center of the window.

Finally, the shadow filter is set on the thumbnail, along with the grayscale filter, which we'll discuss later.

12.3   Selection glow

When the user selects one of the thumbnails, its picture becomes the one displayed by the large image in the window. It is helpful to the user to give them an indication of which thumbnail is selected (besides the obvious indication that the picture in the thumbnail matches that in the larger, reflected image).

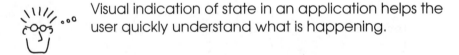

Visual indication of state in an application helps the user quickly understand what is happening.

I use a large colored glow around the selected thumbnail to indicate the current selection:

The glow is declared like this:

266

```
<s:GlowFilter id="glow" color="0xffaa00"
    blurX="20" blurY="20"/>
```

When the user clicks a thumbnail, two things happen: the large image shows the picture indicated by the thumbnail, and the thumbnail is given a glow. These changes are made by the changePicture() function, which is called when a thumbnail receives a click event:

```
private function changePicture(event:MouseEvent):void
{
    var image:Image = Image(event.currentTarget);
    picture.source = image.source;
     if (currentThumbnailIndex >= 0)
    {
        var oldSelectedThumbnail:Image =
            Image(thumbnails.getElementAt(
                currentThumbnailIndex));
        var glowIndex:int =
            oldSelectedThumbnail.filters.indexOf(glow);
        var oldFilters:Array =
            oldSelectedThumbnail.filters;
        oldFilters.splice(glowIndex, 1);
        oldSelectedThumbnail.filters = oldFilters;
    }
    var filters:Array = image.filters;
    filters.splice(1, 0, glow);
    image.filters = filters;
    currentThumbnailIndex =
        thumbnails.getElementIndex(image);
}
```

The large image gets its new content by setting its source property to be the same as that of the thumbnail. Then the glow filter is removed from the thumbnail that it is currently filtering. Finally, the glow is added to the list of filters on the clicked thumbnail, and we're done. Note that we're not setting the thumbnail's filters property to an array that just contains the glow filter; this would remove the shadow and grayscale filters that are also filtering each thumbnail. We have to add and remove the glow from each thumbnail dynamically while leaving the other filters in place.

12.4 Animated colorization

Finally, I wanted some indication of user interaction with the thumbnails. Whenever a UI event may occur due to some user action, it's good to indicate that possibility to the user. For example, when the mouse hovers over a button, the button should change slightly in appearance to indicate that pressing on the button will cause a click event.

Whenever a UI event may occur due to some user action, like when the mouse hovers over a button that may be clicked, it's helpful to visually indicate that possibility to the user.

In this case, I wanted each thumbnail to indicate that a mouse click would result in the action of replacing the content of the large image with the picture in the thumbnail. I achieved this effect by using the grayscale shader that we saw in Section 3.8. To make the application feel more dynamic and alive, I animated the effect.

Each of the thumbnails is grayscale by default; only the large, reflected image is in color. This grayscale effect is accomplished with the `grayscaler` Pixel Bender shader that we discussed in Section 3.8. We create a new filter for each thumbnail to allow each filter to act independently and add it to the `filters` of each thumbnail in `addFilters()`:

```
var newShader:Shader =
    new Shader(new GrayscalerShaderClass());
var grayFilter:ShaderFilter =
    new ShaderFilter(newShader);
img.filters = [grayFilter, shadow];
```

Meanwhile, each image is declared in the MXML to handle `mouseOver` and `mouseOut` events:

```
<mx:Image source="{GoldenGate}"
        click="changePicture(event)"
        mouseOver="mouseOverHandler(event)"
        mouseOut="mouseOutHandler(event)"/>
```

When the mouse enters or exits a thumbnail, the mouseOverHandler() or mouseOutHandler() function is called. These functions call, in turn, the runColorizingAnim() function. The handlers are the same except for the second parameter passed into runColorizingAnim(); this value determines whether the animation will make the thumbnail color (1) or gray (0):

```
private function mouseOverHandler(event:MouseEvent):void
{
    runColorizingAnim(Image(event.currentTarget), 1);
}

private function mouseOutHandler(event:MouseEvent):void
{
    runColorizingAnim(Image(event.currentTarget), 0);
}
```

The runColorizationAnim() function creates and plays an Animate effect to change the colorization property of the ShaderFilter:

```
private function runColorizingAnim(image:Image,
    endVal:Number):void
{
    var target:ShaderFilter =
        ShaderFilter(image.filters[0]);
    var runningAnim:Animate = currentAnims[target];
    if (runningAnim != null)
    {
        runningAnim.stop();
        delete currentAnims[target];
    }
    var anim:Animate = new Animate(target);
    anim.duration = 250;
    anim.motionPaths = new <MotionPath>[
        new SimpleMotionPath("colorization",
            null, endVal)];
    anim.play();
    anim.addEventListener(EffectEvent.EFFECT_END,
        effectEnd);
    currentAnims[target] = anim;
}
```

269

The runningAnim logic is to prevent running multiple animations on the same target simultaneously. We store each animation in a Dictionary object, currentAnims, with the target object as the key. If we detect an animation with that target already in currentAnims, then we stop that animation and remove it before playing the newly requested animation on the target. If the animation runs to completion, then a call to the effectEnd() function removes the entry automatically:

```
private function effectEnd(event:EffectEvent):void
{
    delete currentAnims[event.effectInstance.target];
}
```

After checking runningAnim, the code creates and plays a new Animate effect, which is what we use here to animate the colorization parameter on the shader filter. Rather than create a single Animate effect declaratively and play it here, we create a new one each time. This dynamic creation enables us to run and stop several different effects simultaneously, where a single Animate effect would stop all running instances when stop() is called due to the runningAnim logic above.

We create the effect to have a shorter duration than the default of 500 milliseconds; we want the colorization effect to be very quick. A single SimpleMotionPath object is set up to animate the colorization property on the shader filter, according to whether the thumbnail is being made color or gray. The null parameter indicates that it will start from whatever current value of that parameter is, and will animate to the endValue that was passed into the function.

This animation changes the colorization property just like the earlier Grayer example did in Section 3.8 with a slider. So as the user moves the mouse into the thumbnail, the picture changes smoothly from grayscale to color. And when the user moves the mouse out, the picture returns to grayscale. This animation provides a nice indication that the thumbnail being hovered over is the one that will provide the picture content if clicked.

Conclusion

This chapter put together a small handful of the techniques that we discussed elsewhere in the book, from graphic primitives to display the images, to reflection techniques using gradients and filters, to drop shadow filters for the thumbnails, to glow filters for thumbnail selection, to animating a grayscaling shader filter. Obviously, we covered much more in the book, and I would encourage you to experiment with this and other applications to see what else you can do. Add states to the application and transitions to animate between them. Use cross-fade effects to change between pictures. Animate moving the glow between thumbnails. Create custom component skins for the thumbnails. Have fun.

The next chapter gives some links to resources for more information.

Chapter 13

Go Have Fun

I hope you enjoyed this exploration of the graphics and animation side of Flex. More importantly, I hope that you learned enough to go create great user experiences, using some of the techniques and technologies in this book. Flex is a great platform for rich client applications, and the added facilities for graphics and animation in Flex 4 enable very rich client applications indeed (one might even say *filthy rich clients*[1]).

There are many things about Flex, Flex 4, and even the graphical and animation side of Flex that I didn't cover in this book, both because I wanted to focus on just the core elements that I found most critical to understand and because I wanted to finish the book in my lifetime. Fortunately, there are many resources readily available on the web for further Flexploration. Here are just a few of them:

My technical blog (`http://graphics-geek.blogspot.com`)

> On this blog, I've posted many articles, videos, demos, source code, and other fun content for graphics and animation development.

Flex devnet site (`http://www.adobe.com/devnet/flex/`)

> This site has lots of articles on Flex and links to other useful resources.

Flex team blog (`http://blogs.adobe.com/flex/`)

> This blog has announcements about various happenings in Flex.

---

[1] *Filthy Rich Clients* is my previous programming book, co-authored with Romain Guy, about graphics and animation development for the Java platform. But it's also a handy phrase meaning *very* rich GUI applications.

Flex.org (`http://flex.org/`)

This site aggregates content from the Flex world.

Tour de Flex (`http://www.adobe.com/devnet/flex/tourdeflex/`)

This awesome Flex application has tons of examples in Flex and lets you easily see how things work and copy the code for your own applications. It's a great way to see what you can do with Flex.

Flex open-source site (`http://opensource.adobe.com/flex`)

This site hosts the open-source Flex SDK. You can browse the source code and the documentation or even download the SDK source and build it. If you really want to know what's going on in Flex, there's no better way to find out than by poking through the SDK source code.

And if you like the writing in this book, but you wish it wasn't so darned technical, check out my humor blog at `http://chetchat.blogspot.com`. I can't promise it'll make you laugh, but I can promise it'll try.

Now go create great applications in Flex ... 4 Fun!

About the Author

Chet Haase is a graphics geek. During the Flex 4 release, he worked on the Flex SDK team at Adobe Systems, Inc., and was responsible for Flex effects, writing the new effects infrastructure and classes for the release. Prior to his work at Adobe, he worked at Sun Microsystems for several years, and co-authored the book *Filthy Rich Clients* about creating rich user experiences with the Java client platform. He currently works at Google, Inc., on the Android UI toolkit team. His entire career has been in graphics software, from the application level to APIs and libraries to drivers for graphics chips. As long as it puts pixels on the screen, he's interested. He earned a B.A. in Mathematics from Carleton College and an M.S. in Computer and Information Sciences from the University of Oregon.

Chet frequently posts articles and videos, including a veritable plethora of Flex graphics and animation tutorials, to his technical blog at `http://graphics-geek.blogspot.com`.

Chet also writes and performs comedy; you can see some his work in this completely unrelated field at `http://chetchat.blogspot.com`, and in his book *When I am King...*, which is available at Amazon.com.

Chet lives in Pleasanton, California, with his wife and three kids, with whom he needs to spend more time, now that this book is finished.

Index